Models of Adoption Support
What works and what doesn't

British Association for Adoption & Fostering
(**BAAF**)
Skyline House
200 Union Street
London SE1 0LX
www.baaf.org.uk

Charity registration 275689

British Library Cataloguing in Publication Data
A catalogue record for this book is available
from the British Library

ISBN 1 903699 25 8

Project management by Shaila Shah
Cover photographs (posed by models)
by Andrew Haig
Designed by Andrew Haig & Associates
Typeset by Avon DataSet, Bidford on Avon
Printed by Russell Press Ltd (TU), Nottingham

BAAF Adoption & Fostering is the leading
UK-wide membership organisation for all those
concerned with adoption, fostering and child
care issues.

Models of Adoption Support
What works and what doesn't

Edited by Hedi Argent

BAAF
ADOPTION
& FOSTERING

Acknowledgements

First of all I want to thank all the authors who have contributed to this book from many different disciplines and perspectives. They have worked cheerfully, through several drafts, to complete this collection; the book is theirs.

I am grateful to Shaila Shah, BAAF's Director of Publications for her unfailing support and guidance, to Jo Francis, her assistant, and to colleagues who took the trouble to read the manuscript and to make helpful comments.

Finally, collections like these could not be put together without the generous contribution of families and children who do the real work and share their experiences with us. We are indebted to all of them.

The cases quoted in this book are based on fact but names and situations have been changed to preserve anonymity.

Hedi Argent
Editor
March 2003

Hedi Argent is an independent adoption consultant, trainer and freelance writer. She is the author of *Find Me a Family* (Souvenir Press, 1984) and *Whatever Happened to Adam?* (BAAF, 1998), the co-author of *Taking Extra Care* (BAAF, 1997) and the editor of *Keeping the Doors Open* (BAAF, 1988), *See You Soon* (BAAF, 1995) and *Staying Connected* (BAAF, 2002).

Contents

Introduction   1
Hedi Argent

1. **The simplicity and complexity of support**
   Cas O'Neill   7

2. **A wish list**
   Helen Wilkins Oakwater   26

3. **Providing effective adoption support – a new model for
   a new Act?**
   Jeffrey Coleman   48

4. **Consultancy to set up a service**
   Marion Hundleby   73

5. **Understanding normality in adoptive family life:
   the role of peer group support**
   Kay Chamberlain and *Jane Horne*   87

6. **The Nottingham Drop In: providing mutual support for
   birth mothers**
   Jenny Jackson   100

7. **Youth work with adopted children and young people**
   Stephen Eccles   112

8. **"Am I alone in this grief?" User support for transracially
   adopted and fostered people**
   Perlita Harris   129

9. **Working with black adopted children and their families:
   the Post-Adoption Centre's experience**
   Monica Duck   147

10. **Support for intercountry adopters in the Jewish
    community**
    Jacky Gordon   160

11. **Adoption support for disabled children and their families**
    Hedi Argent   171

12. **Adoption panels and adoption support**
    Alan Johnstone   189

13. **An after adoption panel: reopening closed adoptions**
    Maureen Crank   202

14. **Therapeutic approaches in adoption**
    Stephen Scott and *Caroline Lindsey*   209

15. **A model of post-placement therapy and support for
    adoptive families**
    Alan Burnell and *Jay Vaughan*   241

16. **Health and adoption support**
    Mary Mather   253

17. **Adoption support from an education adviser**
    Michael Prior   268

18. **'Where next?' A perspective on post-adoption services in
    Scotland**
    Barbara J Hudson   279

19. **Adoption support services for adults**
    Julia Feast   292

20. **Online adoption support and advice**
    Lois Williams   307

21. **Ending in disruption**
    Hedi Argent   316

    Contributors   322

    Index   327

Introduction

Hedi Argent

We knew it wasn't going to be easy. He had so many problems when he came to us; he wasn't likely to change that much in a hurry. But the agency was behind us all the way – from the day he was placed right through the adoption itself and after. They never made us feel a failure, they were ready with ideas to try this and that and we worked out some of the answers together. We're still struggling years on but it just helps to know we're not on our own. (Adoptive parent of a boy placed at eight years old.)

All the contributors to this collection write about adoption support. Until very recently, there was a tendency to draw a line between preparation and placement, post-placement support and post-adoption services. But social work practice and policy change and the language changes accordingly. Adoption support now covers *all* the work with children, adopters and birth families that is necessary to make an adoption happen and to make it endure. When this book was first thought of, it was to be called *Models of post-adoption services*; it has turned out to be *Models of adoption support*.

Thirty years ago it was still thought that adoption was the start of a new life for all concerned and the less said about it the better. A post-adoption service might then have been considered intrusive and perhaps even undermining. But the demand for more comprehensive adoption services has grown in response to the way adoption has developed. It has become evident that most of the children needing new families today, who have usually had a hard time before they are placed for adoption and who are not easy to place, are certainly not going to be easy to bring up. And even children placed as infants, we have discovered, may have to deal with difficulties due to the adoption factor at some point during childhood or beyond.

The need for support after adoption was first acknowledged in the

1976 Adoption Act (England and Wales) and the Adoption (Scotland) Act 1978. Section 1 of the 1976 Act came into force in 1981; it placed a duty on all adoption agencies to offer a service to all parties affected by adoption but the result was disappointing. All except a handful of agencies confined themselves to dealing with individual requests on an ad hoc basis or by referring to the few independent post-adoption centres that were set up during the next decade. A number of pioneering voluntary agencies provided a post-adoption package as part of their service and there were various users' groups, which highlighted the value of mutual and peer group support. Further progress over the next twenty years was slow and patchy, but as the need became more apparent, innovative models of adoption support were established, and all adoption agencies today aim to continue to support families, directly or indirectly, after an adoption order is made.

During this autumn of 2002, the Adoption and Children Bill 2000 has made its way through both Houses of Parliament. The resulting Act reaffirms the need for continuing adoption support; the Adoption Standards for England (2001) and the attendant draft Guidance underline that need. The consultation paper on adoption support produced by the Department of Health stakeholders' group in August 2002 invited comments from both professionals and service users. So far there is much emphasis on assessment of needs but little about obligations to meet those needs. The third chapter in this book traces the development of policy and legislation, ending with a critical analysis of the consultation document, *Providing Effective Adoption Support*. Regulations are to follow soon, and another round of consultations in 2003 will precede more Regulations regarding wider adoption support. Will we eventually have a *New model for a new act?* It is interesting to compare a possible framework for the future with the many varied accounts in this book of work in progress.

There is some movement among the present activity and legislation to make us feel hopeful that funds will follow to maintain a new model, which should, of course, be widely available to everyone affected by adoption. Money is not only a matter of concern to the potential providers of adoption support but also to the receivers. Although much is said publicly about lack of funding for agencies, there is less discussion about the significance of financial support for adoptive families. Yet at a time when Government is pushing for more adoptions, it is surely appropriate to make a proper study of what people need in order to make room in their lives and in their homes for one – or perhaps two, three or even four – more children. Many kinship carers and long-term foster families would adopt if they were assured of sufficient financial support.

There is an uneasy legacy in adoption policy from the days when infertile couples, who had anyway planned to have children, adopted infants to build their family. Somehow it is still thought to be not quite acceptable to ask for money in return for having a child. And there is the view that the money would be better spent on birth parents to prevent family breakdown in the first place. Surely this is not a true choice for adoption practice, which, we have to presume, begins where family preservation must leave off.

People who have the capacity and the desire to become parents to older, troubled children, to disabled children and to sibling groups, may already have a family, may not have planned to have more children or simply cannot afford to do so. They may have to adjust their work, their leisure activities and their whole lifestyle. Not many people have space in their homes or in their cars for a sibling group, or for a wheelchair, without adequate financial help. Transport and housing are essential requirements but there are often other considerations: should the parents of twelve-year-old twins, who have managed to pay for holidays abroad every year, be penalised because they will not be able to afford to go if another child is placed with them? They didn't mean to have more children; but they like being parents and they can see that there are children out there who need them. Whatever financial support is offered in the way of adoption allowances, special grants and equipment, there is no danger that anyone will do it for the money but money may make it more possible for more children to be adopted.

Before any service is offered, there has to be a proper assessment of needs, which must include listening to what potential users say they want. "*A wish list*", compiled by an adoptive parent, is a pivotal contribution to this anthology; it tells us many things we ought to hear and makes us aware that we have to go on listening and hearing if we want to create a flexible service for changing needs.

Adoption services may be partially or wholly "contracted out" to specialist organisations; St Francis Children's Society, Nottingham, offers consultancy to agencies setting up a new adoption service or wishing to develop existing services; the opportunities and hurdles of "contracting out" for both the purchaser and the provider are thoroughly explored in *Consultation to set up a service.* In one area, where a voluntary agency operates the whole post-adoption service for a county council, the purchaser and provider could not agree on how to present their model for this collection; the advantages and disadvantages of splitting up pre and post-order support are still being evaluated.

Some local authorities, voluntary agencies and consortia run innovative projects for birth parents, adopters and adopted children. LINK in Essex, Nottingham After Adoption and WMPAS (West Midlands Post-Adoption Service) contribute examples of mutual support groups and events for the three main parties to adoption. Norwood Jewish Adoption Agency and a special project for black and dual heritage adopted children at the Post-Adoption Centre in London, describe programmes for minority ethnic groups. PACT (Parents and Children Together) has just launched an online advice and counselling service for everyone involved with adoption.

Adoption panels are not usually thought of as offering support to adopted children and their families but their deliberations and recommendations can, and should, as one Chair of several adoption panels writes in *Adoption panels and adoption support*, pave the way for practitioners to negotiate an adoption support plan in the very early stages. After Adoption, Manchester, as described in Chapter 13, has established an After Adoption Panel to deal specifically with contact, search and reunion problems that may arise after an Order is made.

Adult adopted people need services too. ATRAP works solely with transracially adopted adults and *Am I alone in my grief?* is a poignant alert about outcomes in transracial adoptions. Another contributor, in *Adoption support services for adults,* writes about the Children's Society's Post-Adoption and Care Project, which has led the way in counselling adults who have unresolved concerns about their adoption – concerns which may or may not lead to tracing birth relatives and reunions. A similar service for birth parents should result when the Adoption and Children Act is implemented.

Health and education are sometimes overlooked when after adoption support is considered; yet both are surely central, especially when older and disabled children are placed with new families. The Chair of the BAAF Medical Group, in *Health and adoption support*, urges that more attention should be paid to health matters throughout adoption work and that medical practitioners should have more training about adoption issues. It is, at least, a statutory requirement for every adoption agency to have a medical adviser, but only very recently has a voluntary agency appointed the first education adviser, who describes his role in *Adoption support from an education adviser*. The chapter on *Adoption support for disabled children and their families* gives some indication of their special needs, including those in health and education.

The use of therapy in adoption is sometimes decried as inappropriate and at other times hailed as the all-purpose panacea. It is neither, of course, but as several contributors testify, there is confusion about which therapy is suitable for which child. When the therapy embraces the adoption factor, a range of treatments can be enriching and supportive, as the two psychiatrists from the Tavistock Clinic and the Maudsley Hospital demonstrate in their joint chapter, *Therapeutic approaches in adoption*. Family Futures presents a specific *Model of therapeutic post-placement support* for work around attachment problems and early childhood trauma.

Scottish adoption support has developed along very similar lines to English and Welsh services. The Director of BAAF in Scotland shares her perspective of progress and problems and gives an overview of what is on offer north of the border and asks, *What next?*

Many common themes emerge in this book: scarce resources, staff shortages and frequent staff changes, much expertise, imagination and tremendous commitment. There is general concern about the lack of services for birth relatives and there is uncertainty about the purpose of contact after adoption. The diverse chapters do not present an overall view or a comprehensive review of current adoption support services, but they each give a snapshot of what is happening, they open up possibilities of what can happen and encourage thought about what should happen.

Finally, the real introduction to this book is the first chapter, which discusses and analyses the very nature of support. Unless we know what support is and what it is not, what it means to people who give it and to people who receive it, we are in danger of working without a supportive framework to guide us.

It is now the accepted wisdom that as adoptions become more complex, so adoption support becomes more necessary. But what exactly does that mean? When and how often do adopted persons, adopters and birth families need support? How much and what kind of support is available and how do they get it? Do social workers and families have different perceptions of what is helpful? Is peer group reassurance as important as professional expertise? How can support be measured and evaluated? If adoption support is high up on the new adoption agenda, then it is surely vital to understand what is intended, how it is provided and what is expected. *The simplicity and complexity of support* explores all aspects of what is perceived as supportive and what is not.

I don't really know what will help, but I'm hoping someone else does.
(Adoptive parent of five-year-old twins)

1 The simplicity and complexity of support

Cas O'Neill

I suppose basically you give yourself and your time. And you listen first of all, totally. You try to hear what they're saying – and then the second step is to really act on it. (Social worker)

It's being able to say the unspeakable without being judged. (Therapist)

Birth families and adoptive families have the same basic needs for support as other families. However, they may also need extra support, both practical and emotional, which is based on an understanding of the profound consequences for all concerned when a child moves from one family to another.

The everyday ordinariness of support, and our personal understanding of what we ourselves find supportive (and unsupportive), inevitably leads to a question – if support is so simple, why does it not happen routinely?

This chapter covers some of the theories which illustrate our understanding of support, a discussion of how support works (including some of the dilemmas for givers and receivers of support), supportive relationships (including what is valued in professional support) and non-support.

The theoretical material is illustrated with some of the findings of my longitudinal, action research project (undertaken in Victoria, Australia) on support within networks surrounding children who had been removed from their birth families by the child protection system. In this research, I talked with participants (birth parents and grandparents, children, permanent parents,[1] teachers, social workers and therapists) regularly over

---

[1] The term "permanent parents" covers adoptive parents, long-term foster parents and parents with a Permanent Care Order under the provisions of the Victorian Children and Young Persons Act 1989. A Permanent Care Order in Victoria, Australia, gives a child permanency without changing the legal relationship between child and birth family.

a period of three years about their experiences as givers and receivers of support.

Theories of support

Theories of what support is, and how it works, have arisen from various disciplines, including psychology, sociology and anthropology. Some of the key theories (Stewart, 1989) which give depth to our everyday understanding of support are summarised briefly here.

Attribution theory explains the way in which individuals formulate beliefs (attributions) to understand, predict and control their environment according to internal (person) factors and external (environment) factors. Attributions can be positive or negative. Support is seen as effective when responsibility for *causing* a problem can be attributed to the environment, while responsibility for *solving* a problem can be attributed to the individual. Support is also likely to be most effective when beliefs about causes and solutions by consumers, support network members and professionals are congruent.

Negative attributions arise because people may believe that individuals deserve what they get i.e. responsibility for causing the problem has been attributed to the individual, rather than to the environment.

Coping theory explains efforts to manage external or internal demands which threaten to overwhelm an individual. Coping is determined by the relationship between person and environment and is a transactional process with problem-focused and emotion-focused functions. Seeking support is itself a coping strategy.

Social exchange (or equity) theory covers reciprocity and the costs and benefits associated with giving and receiving support. Support is likely to be seen as unhelpful if it undermines self-esteem and people may be unwilling to seek or receive help if they feel unable to return the benefit. The extent to which people feel indebted depends on their perception of the rewards and costs for both parties, the donor's motives and impetus for action, and comparison with other situations.

It's sort of hard, because of this tremendous sense of independence I have . . . basically I hate asking. But I pick up their daughter on the way to school and so then I don't feel so bad if I have to ask them for a favour. (Permanent mother)

It is also useful to consider networks of communal reciprocity, in which people offer support simply because they themselves have been given support in the past.

Reference group theory (Merton, 1968) and *social comparison theory* (Stewart, 1989) inform our understanding of peer support. People who share similar complex situations are likely to compare themselves and their experiences with each other – either favourably or unfavourably. Those who are seen to be coping well are likely to be an inspiration and comfort to others, while those who are seen to be coping less well remind others that they may themselves be managing reasonably well in difficult circumstances.

Social network theory explores individual and group networks in terms of size, closeness, exchange/reciprocity and interactiveness (Milardo, 1988; Vaux, 1988). A large network with many links is likely to offer more possibilities for support than a smaller network, although the latter may allow for closer links.

Support is a network of people who you know you can call on . . . they are just there . . . even if you don't ever actually need them. (Permanent mother)

How support works

Support is essentially a communication process, in which each participant attaches meaning to events and activities. Both parties are givers and receivers 'caught up in a web that is ongoing and dynamic in character' (Albrecht and Adelman, 1987a, p 20), mutually influencing attitudes, beliefs, emotions and behaviours.

Clearly, support which is offered may not be perceived as supportive by the recipient. Indeed, research shows that providers of support tend to assume that they are giving more than receivers think they are being given (Sarason, Sarason and Pierce, 1990). Just as importantly, support is not static and givers' and receivers' understanding of support may change over time.

The functions of support are seen by Albrecht and Adelman (1987a) as:

- enhancing control, acceptance and social interaction; and
- reducing uncertainty i.e. ambiguity, complexity, lack of information and unpredictability.

Hupcey's (1998a, p 308–9) review of the literature in this area cites research which variously conceptualises support as a thing – *information, goods and services, resources*; a process – *interpersonal transactions, fulfilment of needs, nurturing relationships*; and/or an outcome – *the enhancement of well-being*. However, these different emphases don't acknowledge the dynamic interplay of relationship, the nature of the support itself and the meaning of what is given and received (for both givers and receivers).

Some of the themes which appear to be important to the process of support for recipients are:

- A sense of others simply "being there" – a belief that others are able and willing to provide support regardless of what is required. Support which is *perceived* to be available is more consistently related to outcomes than support actually received.

  My bedroom was all lit up like a Christmas tree . . . this breeze went straight past me and I was freezing cold . . . it was like the tip of a wing . . . it looked like an angel's wing – someone's watching over me, someone's beside me. (Birth mother)

- A sense of acceptance – the belief that others accept us as we are is strengthened when we see the support willingly given to us. Perceptions of having, and being worthy of, social support are seen as an extension of childhood attachment experiences.

- Feeling heard – being able to express frustration, without being judged, allows people to articulate uncertainties and problems in ways which help them to be more objective and effective.

  She [social worker] really listens and she really understands . . . I can really talk to her about anything and she doesn't criticise me or nothing. (Birth mother)

- Reliability
  It's good to be able to pick up the phone and know she'll ring back . . . she always does what she says she'll do . . . she never lets us down. (Permanent mother talking about her social worker)

- Renegotiation of support over time – support which is helpful at one point in time may not be at all helpful six months later.
  I wish she [social worker] had asked at different times what I needed from her. At the beginning I just needed encouragement, but later on I really needed help with his [child's] behaviour and I wanted to meet other parents . . . but I didn't want to be asking her for something new all the time – I wanted her to offer. (Permanent mother)

Giving and receiving support

The relationship between receivers and givers of support is complex, as there may be significant incongruity between what is expected (or hoped for) and what is offered. There tends therefore to be a range of in-built dilemmas for both givers and receivers of support:

1. For givers of support, there are dilemmas associated with the drainage of personal resources in offering support; the stress of taking on others' feelings of distress and insecurity; uncertainty about what to say or do; and concern that what they are offering is not being received as helpful.
2. For receivers of support, dilemmas may involve concerns about being judged or rejected; feeling increasingly helpless; being unable to provide reciprocal support; and balancing support in close relationships with support in other (including peer and professional) relationships.

In my research, participants' experiences of the tensions around giving and receiving support were generally similar to those reviewed in the literature, particularly the frequent lack of correlation between what was offered and what was needed.

Givers of support

The drainage of personal resources involved in care-giving was reported by not only the permanent mothers, but also by birth grandparents who had cared for, or were still caring for, grandchildren on a long-term basis. These people talked about the strain of being the primary caregiver for a troubled child, as well as their sense of being somehow "targeted" by the child's challenging behaviours.[2]

"Uncertainty over what to say or do" was also a theme in the research findings. Social workers and teachers were the groups most concerned about not causing conflict by saying the "wrong" thing – however, while this meant that open conflict was largely avoided, it also meant that potentially supportive words or actions by these professionals tended to be subsumed by a degree of silence on their part and/or the suspicion of the receiver that what was being said was not the total picture.

Givers of support also faced the dilemma of their help being undervalued, or not recognised, by recipients. This was true in varying ways for all research participants – for example, birth parents, birth grandparents and permanent parents talked about the frustrations of giving support to their children which was not recognised as such by either the children or by other people; and social workers, therapists and teachers talked about their concerns that the support they offered to birth families and permanent families was at times not recognised as such.

Receivers of support

Fear of judgement or rejection was an intrinsic part of the accounts of both the birth parents and the permanent parents. These dilemmas were related to situations of "avoiding saying too much", in which parents found themselves whenever there were difficulties with the child that they felt unable to manage – or when they were unsure of their relationship with professionals.

I felt naked, vulnerable, intimidated and very guarded ... I'm not going to open up now, because this woman [social worker] closed me up. (Permanent mother)

---

[2] One child told his permanent mother 'I behave badly, so I can make you angry – and I enjoy it, because it makes me feel better – it makes me glad that you shout at me'.

For many of the research participants, particularly the permanent parents, avoiding feelings of helplessness was therefore associated at times with the decision not to seek support.

Belief in the need for equity and reciprocity in relationships was a dilemma mainly for those permanent parents who had not parented their own biological children. This may well have had something to do with this group's relative lack of prior experience in the ebb and flow of exchanges which are almost inevitably part of life with children. Complicating this was also the issue of the children's behaviour – permanent parents sometimes felt that, because their children's behaviour was more difficult than that of other children, they could never repay a child-minding "debt" and therefore it was better not to ask for this kind of support.

Balancing support in close relationships with support in less close relationships tended not to be an issue for birth parents, as they had relatively weak family and friendship ties and compensatory networks of professional supporters.

In contrast, most of the permanent families had strong family and friendship ties. Many of them were actively wanting peer input from other permanent parents fairly early in the placements. However, there seemed to be little time and energy available, over and above what was needed to maintain existing family, friendship and work networks, for the establishment of new connections.

A further dilemma for receivers of support, highlighted by my research, and also reported elsewhere (Hupcey, 1998b), involves interactions in which the meaning of what is given is double-edged, i.e. it is not clearly negative, but neither is it completely positive.

There were many examples of this – for instance, when insufficient financial support was given, or when professional commitments to follow up on issues for birth and permanent parents were only partially fulfilled. In these situations, the meaning of the support for recipients was indeed murky, as on the one hand they had received something, but on the other hand they were left wondering why the support offered was limited and what their rights were in terms of asking for more.

Supportive relationships

Close personal relationships (with family and friends) are generally seen as the broadest source of support, both emotional and practical. However, as Millward (1994, p 13) writes, 'the disruption caused by difficult circumstances . . . could mean that the availability, or suitability, of help from various family members becomes a problem, necessitating more public than private support'.

As relinquishment of a child (voluntary or involuntary), or parenting a child with challenging behaviours, are both life situations involving "difficult circumstances", it may well be that birth parents and permanent parents need to look outside the family for support.

Research on friendship support indicates that, compared with family support, it is more likely to be voluntary, based on equality, concerned with assistance and activity sharing and providing confidentiality and emotional support. Emotional support from friends may therefore be more acceptable than from family in some circumstances.

When members of family and friendship networks act in a way which is perceived as unsupportive, then support may most easily be available from "weak tie" relationships (Adelman, Parks and Albrecht, 1987b), those which are separate from family and friends and which may include self-help groups, peers and professionals. Paradoxically, these "weak tie" relationships may offer accessibility, predictability and greater freedom to those seeking support, as well as a sense of community and the possibility of having "low-risk" discussions on "high-risk" topics (Giljohann, 1995).

The efficacy of self-help groups and peer support (which initially offer "weak tie" support) has been associated with:
- gaining (and maintaining) a sense of control;
- experiential knowledge – not only the wisdom and information gained from lived experience, but also belief in its validity and authority;
- the importance of shared stories, or "narratives"; and
- exposure to different interpretations of shared issues.

Professional support

Much of what is written about what is valued in professional support[3] comes from the psychotherapy and family therapy literature and implicit in all of it is the importance of relationship and a sense of partnership.

Marris (1991, p 89) sees the 'qualities of good social relationships and good experiences of attachment' as essentially the same – 'predictability, responsiveness, intelligibility, supportiveness and reciprocity of commitment'. Other professionals write about the importance of personal and professional qualities, development of the therapeutic relationship, focus on client empowerment, attending to the impact of self and applying therapeutic strategies appropriately (Coady and Wolgien, 1996).

Other important elements of professional support[4] which have been identified by service users are:

- affirmation – a sense of being seen as worthwhile;
- therapists sharing parts of their own lives with consumers and being "real" people;
- a sense of professional sincerity;
- a therapeutic bond – a feeling of being nurtured, which is not friendship, although it has some elements of it;
- a sense of comfort;
- therapists extending themselves beyond the job;
- being listened to;
- feeling understood;
- discovery of new ways to look at issues – a process which does not necessarily involve advice;
- congruence between the receiver's needs and what the giver is offering;
- clarifying meaning – "Is this what you mean?";
- being kept in mind between contacts.

---

[3] It is interesting to note that a recent study has shown that professional behaviours which parents find helpful correspond to behaviours that professionals themselves judge as ethical (Johnson, Cournoyer and Bond, 1995).

[4] For a summary of these elements, see Quinn (1996).

The elements of what tends to be valued in professional support (which Froland [1980] calls "formal care") – partnership, affirmation, predictability, responsiveness, mindfulness and listening – were validated by the participants in my research and they gave many examples of what this kind of relationship offered them:

> *I feel that she [social worker] and I work the same way . . . she listens to me, reassures me and makes suggestions in a low-key way e.g. she will say 'this other family I know, they tackled it this way'.* (Permanent mother)

> *Support means feeling cared for, being listened to, being able to have a bit of a grumble without being criticised.* (Permanent mother)

> *From day one we had continual support – not one of them [social workers] has failed to do what they said they would do.* (Birth grandfather)

Although there were differences between birth parents, birth grandparents and permanent parents in the kinds of support they wanted and/or received, in general they valued both professional support and peer support (as well as the support of their families and friends). While peer support was valued for the importance of shared stories and the empowering nature of experiential knowledge, professional support was seen as particularly helpful when it was offered by someone who had the characteristics of a "professional friend".

"Professional friends", who combined the warmth of a friend with the knowledge and authority of a professional, were experienced professionals who had few qualms about crossing the boundaries between their working and private lives. Many of these professionals gave support which was well beyond what their jobs required e.g. many gave their home phone numbers to permanent parents to use in case of emergency and some of the teachers tutored, or minded, the children in the school holidays. Their years of experience allowed them to cross the public–private boundary in a way which was appropriate and which did not seem to impose any burden of obligation on those they were supporting in this way.

Non-support – omission and commission

Curiously, the literature on support, per se, only alludes to non-support in passing e.g. 'if the action is intended to be positive, but the outcome is negative . . .' (Hupcey, 1998a, p 313) – and this does not cover the issues of omission and commission.

In contrast, the literature in the area of adoption and foster care, especially that relating to placement difficulties and disruption, covers non-support in some detail. For example, in an article written for mental health professionals, Nickman and Lewis (1994, p 753) state that 'adoptive parents often experience contact with professionals as more damaging than helpful'.

> It's like someone peeking over the fence all the time. (Permanent mother talking about social work involvement in her life)

The elements of non-support are often simply the opposites of elements of support – such as "lack of acknowledgement" as opposed to "acknowledgement". However, a simple dichotomy like this denies the power that non-support has in its own right, particularly for those who experience it.

In my research, there were two clear categories of non-support – the absence of support (omission), as well as behaviour which was experienced as actively negative (commission). Although both categories were mentioned far more by recipients than by givers of support, there were nevertheless some interesting instances in which givers talked about their perception of not being supportive. For example, a teacher talked about feelings of antagonism towards a child and therefore being unable to offer support to him; and professionals sometimes talked about a lessening of support towards permanent parents when the parents were not seen to be open enough with them.

Most birth parents in the research felt that they had been given few choices, that they were not listened to or believed, that decisions about their families were made on very selective evidence and that they were treated with a basic lack of courtesy:

> She [birth mother] felt so disempowered, because she's got an

intellectual disability, she's so used to adults telling her what to do and them always being right and her always being wrong, that of course when the doctor said to her 'you're not pregnant', she went home. So she actually delivered the baby at home . . . she didn't know what was happening. (Social worker)

His [birth father's] mother said to me in the hospital – 'you know you're going to get this one taken off you too and it'll be your fault . . . we told you that you should have had an abortion . . . you're going to be the worst Mum of all'. (Birth mother)

Non-support to permanent parents in this research tended to involve acts of omission, rather than commission. These included situations where the permanent parents felt that they were not treated as partners by social workers; that they had not been given all the available information about their child; that they were not given much-needed behaviour management strategies; that the seriousness of their situation was not believed; and that workers changed too frequently and were not available when needed:

She [social worker] is vague as anything, non-reactive and flat – like a cardiograph on a dead patient. (Permanent mother)

All I needed was to speak to her on the phone for five minutes – I rang for ten days, but she wouldn't even return my calls. (Permanent father)

A further important element of non-support involves gaps in shared meaning – differences (often profound) in the understanding of particular situations.

Gaps in shared meaning

The design of my research meant that I frequently heard different interpretations of the same events. While these were consistent within each person's individual context and also led to my own interpretation of what had happened, they nevertheless resulted in considerable misunderstanding and perceptions of non-support between research participants.

Some examples of this were:

- A child protection worker and some therapists talked very positively about the support that they had given to birth parents; however, the birth parents said that they had received no support at all.
- Teachers often felt that the best way to "protect" the child from the permanent parents' seemingly strict expectations was to avoid telling the parents of misdemeanours at school; the permanent parents would see this as teachers undermining their authority by colluding with the child.
- Social workers expressed disquiet about what they saw as negativity in the permanent parents' relationships with the children, allied with concerns around punishment; permanent parents, on the other hand, felt that not only were their needs as parents not being met, but also that outsiders could not possibly understand the stress involved in the child's challenging behaviours.
- Therapists expressed concern about a perceived lack of permanent parent commitment to therapy if both parents were unable to come to therapy or if there were too many missed appointments; permanent parents talked about therapists not understanding the competing needs of work and family.
- At times, therapists (and, to some extent, teachers) talked about the unsuitability of particular parents for particular children, or their belief that the placement agencies could have prepared the parents more appropriately; in contrast, social workers felt that they did the very best they could for both children and parents and that such criticism was unfair, given the relatively small "pool" of parents available and the pressing need to place the children in families.

An emphasis on clear communication seemed to be the most important ingredient in minimising gaps in shared meaning. This was most aptly described by permanent parents who talked about one of their social workers as always checking with them that he had understood what they were saying in the way they wanted to be understood:

What I just wrote down was this – let me read it to you and see if I got it right. Is that the way you meant it to sound?

So – what is support?

Researchers tend to conceptualise support as being made up of separate elements. Wan, Jaccard and Ramey (1996) are unusual in that they not only distinguish between emotional, informational, companionship and tangible support, but also suggest that different kinds of support are inter-correlated. The findings of my research, which confirm this, suggest that the separation of elements of support, even for the purpose of analysis, is overly simplistic.

In exploring how people experience support, the intrinsic connections between emotional and practical support, in particular, are inescapable. Receiving practical support is usually experienced as emotionally supportive, while receiving emotional support is likely to have practical benefits. Thus, while it may be useful to make distinctions between kinds of support, it needs to be recognised that these can be misleading.

The literature and research give us clear guidelines on what the experience of support, from a receiver's point of view, is based on:
- the overall importance of relationship, a sense of partnership and reciprocity;
- affirmation, acknowledgement and empathy;
- open communication, feeling listened to and believed; and
- commitment, responsiveness, reliability and a sense of "being there".

In contrast, non-support, from a receiver's point of view, is characterised by situations in which there is:
- lack of control and lack of information;
- lack of open communication, lack of honesty and experience of deception;
- judgemental attitudes and expectations;
- isolation and rejection; and
- feelings of anxiety and fear.

However, listing what is important for support does not quite describe its essence.

In her discussion of the need for "mindfulness", Layton (1995, p 28) talks about the importance of a therapist's way of being, "the spirit of how to be", in a therapeutic relationship. While none of the participants in my research talked about a way of being as such, it was in fact alluded to often by receivers of support, who struggled to find the words which might describe what true support felt like to them. They used phrases such as 'I'm not sure what it was about her, but I just felt very comfortable' and 'it felt like she was my friend' and 'she was so genuine' and 'he was very generous and open with us' to convey their sense of feeling safe, honoured, of having been profoundly nurtured, and of being able to trust absolutely that the other person had their best interests at heart.

While all the other elements of support (e.g. advocacy, reliability, practical support, etc.) were also very important, the crucial part seemed to be this way of being, which in turn influenced the relationship and the support which evolved from it.

The complexity of support can therefore be seen as involving a dynamic set of interactions which change over time and which encompass "way of being", relationship, exchange and meaning. The simplicity of support is what we all know it to be – communication and actions which involve feelings of safety, trust, understanding and reliability. It is worth offering this wholeheartedly.

> There was an immediate connection between her [worker] and me that hadn't been apparent with anyone else [from the agency] – she had the ability to zero in on exactly how I was feeling and to feel my pain with me. She showed by all her actions that she was really involved. People need to feel that they matter, that they are not just a number or a "caregiver". (Permanent mother)

References

In order to enhance the flow of the chapter, some of these references are not cited in the text. A copy of the fully-referenced chapter is available from the author by e-mail: cmoneill@bigpond.com.

Adelman, M, Parks, M and Albrecht, A (1987a) 'Supporting friends in need', in Albrecht, T and Adelman, M (eds) *Communicating Social Support*, California: Sage.

Adelman, M, Parks, M and Albrecht, A (1987b) 'Beyond close relationships: support in weak ties', in Albrecht, T and Adelman, M (eds) as above.

Albrecht, T and Adelman, M (1987a) 'Communicating social support: a theoretical perspective', in Albrecht, T and Adelman, M (eds) as above.

Albrecht, T and Adelman, M (1987b) 'Dilemmas of supportive communication', in Albrecht, T and Adelman, M (eds) as above.

Aldgate, J and Hawley, D (1986) *Recollections of Disruption*, London: National Foster Care Association.

Arntson, P and Droge, D (1987) 'Social support in self-help groups', in Albrecht, T and Adelman, M (eds) as above.

Bulmer, M (1987) *The Social Basis of Community Care*, London: Allen & Unwin.

Burbidge, A (1998) 'Changing patterns of social exchanges . . . issues in the literature', *Family Matters*, 50, pp 10–8.

Coady, N and Wolgien, C (1996) 'Good therapists' views of how they are helpful', *Clinical Social Work Journal*, 24:3, pp 311–22.

Delaney, R and Kunstal, F (1993) *Troubled Transplants: Unconventional strategies for helping disturbed foster and adopted children*, University of Southern Maine: National Child Welfare Resource Center for Management and Administration.

Duncan, B, Hubble, M and Miller, S (1997) 'Stepping off the throne', *Networker*, July/Aug, pp 22–33.

Eggert, L (1987) 'Support in family ties: stress, coping and adaptation', in Albrecht, T and Adelman, M (eds) as above.

Filer, J and Mahoney, G (1996) 'Collaboration between families and early intervention service providers', *Inf Young Children*, 9:2, pp 22–30.

Froland, C (1980) 'Formal and informal care: discontinuities in a continuum', *Social Service Review*, 54:4, pp 572–87.

Giljohann, B A (1995) *Helping Families After the Death of a Child from SIDS: The distinctive characteristics of the help of natural social networks and the help of other SIDS parents . . .* Unpublished MSW thesis, Melbourne: University of Melbourne.

Hatch, J (1997) *'Hearing their Stories' . . . Finding out about individuals' and families' experiences and perceptions of child protection intervention in their lives*, Melbourne: University of Melbourne.

Hupcey, J (1998a) 'Social support: assessing conceptual coherence', *Qualitative Health Research*, 8:3, pp 304–18.

Hupcey, J (1998b) 'Clarifying the social support theory–research linkage', *Journal of Advanced Nursing*, 27:6, pp 1231–41.

Irving, K (1998) 'Parents for children . . . building new families', *Children UK*, Summer, pp 4–5.

Johnson, H, Cournoyer, D and Bond, B (1995) 'Professional ethics and parents as consumers: How well are we doing?', *Families in Society*, 76:7, pp 408–20.

Kennedy, M, Humphreys, K and Borkman, T (1994) 'The naturalistic paradigm as an approach to research with mutual-help groups', in Powell T (ed.), *Understanding the Self-Help Organization*, California: Sage.

Krueger, M (1997) 'Using self, story, and intuition to understand child and youth care work', *Child and Youth Care Forum*, 26:3, pp 153–61.

Marris, P (1991) 'The social construction of uncertainty', in Parkes, C, Stevenson-Hinde, J and Marris, P (eds) *Attachment Across the Life Cycle*, London: Routledge.

Merton, R (1968) *Social Theory and Social Structure*, New York: Free Press.

Milardo, R (1988) 'Families and social networks: an overview of theory and methodology', in Milardo, R (ed.) *Families and Social Networks*, Newbury Park: Sage.

Millward, C (1994) 'Intergenerational family support . . . Help or hindrance?', *Family Matters*, 39, pp 10–3.

Nickman, S and Lewis, R (1994) 'Adoptive families and professionals: when the experts make things worse', *J Am Acad Child Adolesc Psychiatry*, 33:5, pp 753–5.

O'Neill, C (2001) 'Avoiding saying too much – the complexity of relationships between permanent parents and social workers', *Children Australia*, 26:2, pp 19–25.

O'Neill, C (1999a) *Support and Permanent Placements for Children*, PhD thesis, Melbourne: University of Melbourne.

O'Neill, C (1999b) ' "We weren't trained for this": teachers, foster care and permanent care', *Children Australia*, 24:4, pp 55–9.

O'Neill C (1993) ' "Do you mean, we're not the only ones?" Disruption – powerlessness and empowerment', *Children Australia*, 18:2, pp 13–7.

Pocock, D (1997) 'Feeling understood in family therapy', *Journal of Family Therapy*, 19, pp 283–302.

Quinn, W (1996) 'The client speaks out: three domains of meaning', *Journal of Family Psychotherapy*, 7:2, pp 71–93.

Rappaport, J (1994) 'Narrative studies, personal stories, and identity transformation in the mutual-help context', in Powell, T (ed.) *Understanding the Self-Help Organization*, California: Sage.

Ryburn, M (1994) 'Contested adoption – the perspective of birth parents', in Ryburn, M (ed.), *Contested Adoptions: Research, law, policy and practice*, Aldershot: Arena.

Sandmaier, M (1995) 'Friendship with a price tag?', *Networker*, July/Aug, p 35.

Sarason, I, Sarason, B and Pierce, G (1990) 'Social support: the search for theory', *Journal of Social and Clinical Psychology*, 9:1, pp 133–47.

Schilling, R (1987) 'Limitations of social support', *Social Service Review*, 61, pp 19–31.

Schmidt, D, Rosenthal, J and Bombeck, B (1988) 'Parents' views of adoption disruption', *Children and Youth Services Review*, 10:2, pp 119–30.

Schubert, M and Borkman, T (1994) 'Identifying the experiential knowledge developed within a self-help group', in Powell, T (ed.) *Understanding the Self-Help Organization*, California: Sage.

Sells, S, Smith, T and Moon, S (1996) 'An ethnographic study of client and therapist perceptions of therapy effectiveness in a university-based training clinic', *Journal of Marital and Family Therapy*, 22:3, pp 321–42.

Short, P (1996) 'Kinship, reciprocity and vulnerability: social relations in the informal economy', *Australian Journal of Social Issues*, 31:2, pp 127–45.

Stewart, M (1989) 'Social support: diverse theoretical perspectives', *Soc. Sci. Med.*, 28:12, pp 1275–82.

Valentine, D, Conway, P and Randolph, J (1988) 'Placement disruptions: perspectives of adoptive parents', *Journal of Social Work and Human Sexuality*, 6:1, pp 133–53.

Vaux, A (1988) *Social Support: Theory, research and intervention*, New York: Praeger.

Wan, C, Jaccard, J and Ramey, S (1996) 'The relationship between social support and life satisfaction as a function of family structure', *Journal of Marriage and the Family*, 58, May, pp 502–13.

2   A wish list

Helen Wilkins Oakwater

Introduction

Never criticize a man until you've walked a mile in his moccasins.
American Indian Proverb

I wish adoption didn't exist. Don't get me wrong. I am an adoptive parent and I love my children passionately; they have brought enormous joy and enlightenment into my life. Adopting them is the best thing I have ever done and I have no regrets.

But I wish they and others like them had never needed to be adopted. Why? Because my children, like many others, had a hard time in their first few years. Their birth parents also had a painful time and adoptive parents must expect to have a difficult time too.

Adoption is based on loss, pain and negative experiences. Children lose an entire blood family. Birth parents are bereaved of a child or children. Adopters often have issues of infertility or have lost children prior to their birth. From each participant's position in the adoption triangle come shattered hopes and dreams, fantasies, illusions and recurring grief. So let's not kid ourselves: adoption is tough for each person affected.

We need to acknowledge the extent of these tragic circumstances so that we can start from where an individual is – not where we would like them to be. Adoption support is often lacking where it is really needed. Why? Perhaps because often we don't want to shine a light into the dark sinister places where abuse, neglect and trauma live. We vainly hope that moving a child to a nice new family will solve the child's problems, undo all the early damage and they'll all live happily ever after. If an adoption breaks down, we sometimes hear the phrase, 'it was the wrong family'. We wonder that some birth mothers just keep producing children who are all subsequently adopted. We don't ask ourselves 'Why do they do that?'

We look at children, birth parents and adopters, passing judgement and opinion while looking through our own window on the world. Each of us is unique. We've each learned lessons in life through our own eyes, ears and minds. We digest information, experiences and traumas differently. We filter sounds, colours and feelings differently. Our view of reality is like a map and we each have our own unique map of the world.

Recognising that there are maps of the world that look very different to your own is the first step in making sense of experiences – yours or that of others. Until we acknowledge, honour and respect the reality of the birth parent, adopter and child, we are not in a position to understand them, help them, or to provide the appropriate resources for them.

We seldom offer adoption support in a form that is palatable to the recipients, because we don't stand in their shoes and see the world through their eyes. We try to plant our map on their world. We judge, we presume, we assume. We rarely listen wholeheartedly.

Children placed for adoption have often had horrendous experiences, many of which we don't know about, either as social work professionals, therapists or parents. But the child knows. Every experience is remembered and has moulded their view of the world. They will remember when their tummy ached with hunger, or being terrified in the dark, or the smell of stale beer, or the voice that knots their stomach, or the taste of curdled milk, or the throbbing in their head from the shouting, or the dry throat needing water or the sheer hell of being alone and unloved for days – but they will also remember the scent, smile or touch of their birth mother.

Sometimes the child's map is fragmented. A child living with a drug-abusing mother will have two mothers – a good one and a bad one, depending on her state. How does a very young child make sense of a woman who is sometimes very caring and loving and sometimes abusive and neglectful?

These children don't have the rose-tinted glasses we often wear when looking at them. They have wacky glasses that distort images and focus on the unexpected. Their survival strategies have resulted in a

27

hypersensitivity to other people's behavioural cues that are missed by the vast majority of us.

Birth parents who have also had dreadful experiences in their childhood, or who are substance abusers, may be unable to see or understand the damage they are inadvertently inflicting on their own children.

Adopters generally start with high expectations and hopes. As time flies by, the reality can arrive like a slap in the face, which knocks off the rose-tinted specs. Flexibility is essential – so that adopters can help their child make sense of their early life by recognising and respecting their child's view of the world.

The wish list

This chapter is intended to paint a picture and tell the story of the three sets of individuals who stand at each corner of the adoption triangle:
- birth parent;
- adoptive parent; and
- child.

We will try to look through their eyes into their world, hear their story and discover some of their feelings and wishes. We can't change the stories that have led to adoption but adoption support could go a long way to making those wishes come true.

The wish list contains three different types of wishes:
- One set is simply individual thoughts and wishes about particular aspects of adoption.
- Another set is based on a specific adoption issue or event where each participant's position is laid out, so the same scenario is seen from three different perspectives.
- The concluding set are hopes, wishes and dreams that would make a huge difference to all those involved in the adoption process.

Topics have been grouped together for ease of reading.

Some readers may find that the words become more real if read aloud or by changing the tone, accent or pitch of the voice. Try playing with these ideas – you might be surprised at what pops up.

If, while reading, you find yourself laughing or crying then congratulations; you have stepped into someone else's map of the world. Enjoy the view and the learning therein.

Until you walk a mile in another man's moccasins you can't imagine the smell. (Robert Byrne)

I just don't understand

Birth parent: I wish I still had Shamus. The social workers said I didn't look after him properly, that I didn't see to his needs. She didn't listen when I said I changed his nappy every day. I only left him alone for an hour. He was asleep. He was in a cot; if he'd woken he couldn't go anywhere. So what if he cried – it wouldn't harm him. All babies cry a lot, it doesn't hurt them.

She said the place was dirty and messy and the floor needed cleaning. So what; I didn't put my son on the floor, he stayed in the cot, that way he's always safe.

She said Shamus needed to interact more with me. We watched the TV together.

She said he needed other children to play with, but I told her he'd catch colds from them.

She said he needed more toys to play with. I don't see why, he had loads of teddies to play with.

She said I had to imagine how things looked, sounded and felt for Shamus.

She said Butch, the German Shepherd dog, was frightening Shamus. I told her his barking protected us from the local gangs who thump our door.

She said I couldn't look after him properly that 'in his best interest' he was being 'taken into care'. Why? I care for him just fine.

She said that, on balance, he needed adopting because I would never be able to care for him properly. That I couldn't put his needs before my own. I know that all he needed was me, his Mum.

I cared for him the best I could. I wanted Shamus so much. I loved him so much. I needed him to love me.

It tore me apart when they took him away forever. There is emptiness inside where his love for me should be.

It will be better next time. The baby growing inside me now will fill the gap that Shamus left. This time I'll keep my baby, because we both need each other.

* * * *

Child: I wish I wasn't frightened of big dogs. At 14 and six-foot tall it's pathetic.

* * * *

Adopter: I wish I knew why he lied. At lunch Benji told me I'd hit him at breakfast. I shouted at him when he dropped his bowl, but I've never laid a finger on him. I was on the opposite side of the room, but he believes I hit him. Why does he do that?

* * * *

Child: I wish I knew why I was scared of water and swimming.

* * * *

Child: I wish the smell of bleach didn't make me retch. It doesn't do that to anyone else I know. I wonder why that is.

* * * *

Birth parent: I wish I could see Louis. Why can't I see him after he's adopted? I saw him twice a week when he was fostered. After all, I am his Mum.

Birth parent: I wish I knew why the police smashed the door down and then ripped Frank out of my arms. I was so scared. Frank and I were both screaming and shaking.

Child: I wish I didn't jump so much at the sound of a loud bang. Other kids laugh at me and call me a saddo . Sometimes afterwards I shake. Sometimes I just scream. It's freaky and I hate it.

Adopter: I wish Frank was like the other boys in his class. I wish he'd just realise that hitting classmates is not a successful strategy for making friends. I've told him often enough. He just doesn't listen. He's now the class bully. I can't understand why he keeps doing it as it makes him unhappy too.

If I'd known then what I know now

Adopter: I wish I'd pumped the social workers for every fact and bit of information about his life. If we'd known the truth we would have done it differently. He'd still be my son and I'd have been a better parent because I would have understood him more.

* * * *

Child: I wish I'd understood why . . . Oh, I don't know what.

* * * *

Adopter: I wish I'd known about attachment disorder earlier. Looking back on it, Patrick had so many symptoms when he was six. He shaved the guinea pig. He lied about ridiculous things that didn't matter to anyone. He wanted to control everything and everyone. It was exhausting. We were told he was hyper-active. We were asked to manage his behaviour better – star charts were suggested frequently. One teacher, when he was six, wanted him suspended. Maybe if we'd received some support or some decent therapy or had an understanding ear, things would be different and he might still be at home.

* * * *

Child: I wish I'd been adopted sooner.

* * * *

Adopter: I wish I'd known about the long-term effect of abuse and neglect. I spent years believing it was my fault and I was a bad parent.

*   *   *   *

Birth parent: I wish I'd realised how much my drinking hurt them. I'd have given up the booze much sooner. They might be with me now if I'd stopped then.

*   *   *   *

Adopter: I wish I'd understood that my children were incapable of reciprocal love. I did everything I could – almost destroyed myself in the process, and yet they don't care about me at all, never have. I wiped their noses and their bottoms, always put their needs first. The marriage didn't survive; we were always at crisis point, never any time for ourselves. I have three children – one son in prison for GBH, one daughter who has two children of her own, both in care; and my youngest is a drug addict who I've not seen, or heard from, for 18 months. Their first few years were so awful – nobody could have parented them without huge amounts of therapy and help. We got none, however much we asked. They even made us pay for foster care when at 14, Amy refused to live at home or go to school. We were punished for someone else's crimes. What advice would I give to prospective adopters now? Be very, very careful and get support agreements in writing. Don't trust anything the authorities say.

Feelings and thoughts I wish I didn't have

Child: I think about her every day – I wonder if she thinks about me. Has she forgotten me?

Adopter: I think about her every day – I wonder if she thinks about us?

Birth parent: I think about her every day – I wonder if she thinks about me. Has she forgotten me?

*   *   *   *

Birth parent: My son was stolen from me by Social Services.

Child: My adoptive parents stole me from my real Mum and Dad.

Adopter: He steals from me the whole time. Sometimes I want to hurt my son the way he is hurting me. He has no reason to threaten me, hit me or steal my things. Some days I fear for my life . . . or my sanity.

* * * *

Birth parent: I wish I knew what my kids thought of me. I'm sure they hate me. Sometimes I hate me.

* * * *

Child: I was a bad baby. That's why she gave me away.

* * * *

Child: My Dad hated me, that's why he hit me so much. I wish I wasn't so horrible.

The rest of the world

Birth parent: I'm glad she went to a white family, she'll have a better life with them than a black family.

Child: I wish I looked like my Mum and Dad. Being adopted is bad enough, being a different colour makes it worse. On my fifth birthday when I blew out the candles I wished that my hair would be like Mummy's. My Mum does her best but my hair still doesn't look right.

Adopter: I wish I could braid her hair better. My hair is straight and mousy, so I don't have years of experience braiding afro hair. It takes all day, it hurts her and I hate that. I can't help her with make up and don't know which beauty products work best. Last week I bought a foundation, which being too dark made her look like Al Jolson and that upset me; fortunately she saw the funny side and made me wear it too. We danced round the kitchen, doing our best Black and White Minstrel impression and laughed like drains. It was funny, but it did hurt.

* * * *

Adopter: I wish I could tell the other Year 5 Mothers at school that, in his former life, my son survived repeated rapes, regular beatings and was in constant fear for his life. At Nursery he used to sit in the corner howling for hours, pull out his hair and flinch if you touched him. So what if he calls out in class and wanders around a bit. I am so proud of him, but I can't tell any one why. They just think he's the class nuisance.

* * * *

Child: I wish people knew how much I'd been through. I am now an average child. I'm getting OK grades at school – national average in my SATs. I'm patrol leader in Scouts, on the school football team; I have mates, argue (a bit) with my parents, hate broccoli, tuna and purple. But I didn't start off like this. I had a really bad start. My birth parents hurt me. I used to behave really badly and was scared of loads of things. I've done lots of therapy, which was really hard sometimes, but it has helped with the nightmares. But I can't tell my mates 'cause only weirdos do therapy and I'm not telling them about the abuse. They wouldn't understand and I'd die of shame if they knew. My Mum and Dad are the only ones who know how hard it's been for me and how far I've come. I'm quite proud of myself.

* * * *

Adopter: I wish I had a pound for every time someone told me that my son's behaviour is normal. It's not.

* * * *

Birth parent: I wish there was someone to share stuff with, who would understand. I can't tell anyone that my children were taken from me and adopted. I know that back then when I was a drunk I neglected them. But now I'm sober, in a different town, living an OK life and holding down a job. I've got a new set of friends who are great, but I could never tell them I'm a mother. I am so ashamed of having my two children adopted. Sometimes the pain, shame and self-hatred is all too much and I think about ending it forever. I cry for hours knowing I'm a terrible person.

* * * *

Adopter: I wish other parents at school would make some allowances for Darren. He doesn't get invited back for tea after school. I know he finds making friends difficult and he can get very over-excited, but we've had nearly all the boys in his class back here for tea at some point this term. The other parents just won't reciprocate. Some Mums often have coffee after drop off. They have never invited me. That really hurts. They know Darren is adopted and has been with us less than a year, yet not one has approached me. Yesterday one woman came to talk to me, but she only wanted to tell me that Darren had hit her daughter in the playground. I just wanted to cry.

Where are they now?

Child: I wish I was safe. I am terrified that one day the doorbell will ring and my birth father will have found me. I sometimes think I catch a fleeting glimpse of him from the car, or I hear a voice that sounds just like him. Yesterday on the way home from school I stood at the bus stop and I smelt him. I turned, it wasn't him, but it could have been. I started to shake and my mates laughed.

*   *   *   *

Child: I wonder if she had any more babies after me and my sister? I wish I knew.

*   *   *   *

Child: I wish I knew if my older brothers who went into foster care are OK. They should be taking their GCSEs now. I know they still see Mum, which is why I can't see them, but I really want to know if they are OK. Brendan was always so good to me; he used to pull funny faces and swing me to make me laugh. I wonder if he's going to college or got a job? At night I imagine he might be dead, then I pull the covers over my head and silently sob so no one hears me.

*   *   *   *

Birth parent: I wish I knew where she was. The telly and papers are full of the story about the girl who has disappeared and the police are searching for her. She is the same age as my Anna. They could have changed her name, it might be her. Every time there's a story about a girl who's been lost, taken or died, my heart pounds. Just for a second I think it's Anna, I catch my breath, look carefully and work out the age and check the hair colour. A moment of pure joy as I realise it's not her, then immediately I feel so guilty. How can I be so heartless? A family has lost a daughter, how could I feel happy about it? I know how much that hurts.

* * * *

Child: The annual letter arrived from my Mum today. Phew, that was a relief. It's a bit late this year. I thought she might be dead or have forgotten me. My stomach was churning before I read it. I'm never quite sure what she might say. She used to say stuff that really worried me. She says she's OK and trying to find a job. The paper felt really thin and her spelling is awful. It wasn't her fault she didn't go to school properly and has no qualifications. Mum and I talked about it, snuggled up on the sofa. She said (as always) how my birth Mum didn't really stand a chance of ever looking after me properly, that she was a little girl in a woman's body and probably always would be. We talked and cried about all the yucky stuff that happened to me when I was little, and how we both wished it had been different.

* * * *

Adopter: I wish that bloody woman could realise how much she hurts Charlotte by forgetting to send a birthday card. I put up with Charlotte's anger and disappointment for the next few weeks while she rips up books, scrawls over posters and says she doesn't care. Then at bedtime I hold her while she sobs and repairs her broken heart.

Direct contact

Adopter: I wish I could tell the self-satisfied mothers at the coffee morning that I'm edgy, uptight and anxious because tomorrow my children will be having a face-to-face meeting with their birth mother – the first time in seven years. She may not turn up, or turn up drunk, or sob throughout or be completely coherent and nice. I have no idea how anyone will react to any of this or to anything else. I am terrified. I just can't envisage how Carli and Desmond will respond on the day or afterwards. Will they want her, not me?

Birth parent: I wish I hadn't agreed to see them. I'm sure they'll hate me. After seven years they won't remember me. Why did I agree? . . . Because I miss them so much it hurts . . . every day it hurts . . . and I can't tell anyone. I just want to know they are OK, to smell them; to see the sunlight bounce off their hair the way it did in the hospital. I'm terrified that tomorrow I'll break down or bottle out.

Carli: I wish it were over. I can't really believe it: I'm seeing my birth mum tomorrow, first time since I was tiny. I keep thinking about her. What will she be wearing, what colour will her hair be, is it the same as mine? Will she like my new jeans? Will she mind Mum being there? Will she turn up? Will she like me?

Desmond: I'm not sure if I want to see her, I think I do and I think I don't. I don't know what I should think or feel.

Birth parent: I wish I could take them home afterwards and show them where I imagine them sleeping if they lived with me. They are still my babies.

*   *   *   *

Child: How could my birth mum lie to me like that? She said she'd stopped drinking – she reeked of alcohol, she was shaky and looked really old and ill. I wish she'd sort herself out.

*   *   *   *

Child: I can't concentrate on anything at school, I keep thinking back to last week when I had contact with my older brothers who are in foster care. Dad is out of prison and wants to see me. Darren told me when we went to the toilet together. It was supposed to be a secret; the social workers asked them not to tell me, but they did. I wish he was still locked up, so I'd be safe.

*   *   *   *

37

Adopter: Every time before I dread it. Afterwards there is just the relief. It's over for another six months. Noli and Kris are less upset each time we see birth mum. I think they realise she can't look after them and that's not likely to change. Noli actually said that she didn't behave like a Mum, she behaved like a child. Amazing that at ten he recognises it. Contact is such a reality check for the boys. They can see her with their own eyes, hear her words and feel their own emotional response to her. It may be tough, but I'm glad we do it. I just wish she had some more support. I'm sure she spends ages afterwards sobbing alone. She holds the boys so gently; I wish someone could hold her so tenderly.

Birth parent: I wish I could stop the pain in my belly that I have every time after I see Noli and Kris. They smell so good; I wish I could bottle it, like perfume and have a sniff every day. Every time I see them and they leave the room it's like them being taken from me the first time. I hate it. I don't know if I can do it again.

Dealing with the authorities – "them"

Adopter: I wish they could see it from my angle. They just think I'm an over-anxious, inadequate parent. I am sick of constantly battling and trying to get them to understand.

*   *   *   *

Child: I wish I could tell that teacher why this is so important to me.

*   *   *   *

Birth parent: They've taken my kids, dragged me through the courts, lied about me and now they want me to give them photos of my babies – the only thing I have left of them – so they can do a life story book (what ever that is) for Marcus and Ayesha. I wish those social workers would just leave me alone.

*   *   *   *

Child: I wish I had a safe place to run to when I start to lose it. That's why I run out of the gates – there is nowhere else to go.

*   *   *   *

Adopter: I am sick to death of explaining how this family is in a constant state of upheaval, anxiety and fear. AND IT'S NOT MY BLOODY FAULT. But will social services listen? Will they heck. They think it's our poor parenting; we can't control our children. They are right, we can't, which is why we need their help. They think we are to blame – the years our kids spent hungry in a chaotic, filthy, slum surrounded by drug-taking are blithely dismissed as irrelevant excuses. I wish I could make them listen. I feel so impotent.

* * * *

Birth parent: I wish they could, for just a moment, understand how I feel.

* * * *

Adopter: I wish I had taped that phone call. The woman in the Health Trust wanted to know what percentage of Alexi's problems were health related, what percentage were school or social services related. Don't they get it? This is a child, not a theoretical model that can be broken down into easily divisible parts. I'm sorry that my son does not fit neatly into an organisational structure that's convenient for them. How disagreeable of him. How outrageous that I should want my child dealt with as an individual who is greater than the sum of his parts. I don't know whether to laugh or cry. I'll probably do both.

* * * *

Adopter: I wish they would help. They all agree he can't live at home (not that he wants to), is struggling at school (when he's there), and his mental health is wobbly (the self-harming is increasing) and they agree he would benefit hugely from a place at a therapeutic boarding school. BUT they don't want to fund it and pass us round from one budget-holder to the next. We go round and round in circles. Meanwhile he becomes more disturbed, his behaviour gets harder and harder to live with. I wish there was one person in the local authority who would fight for us and help us through this administrative nightmare.

* * * *

Child: I wish Mr Thomas hadn't asked us to bring in a picture of ourselves as a baby. I haven't got one. I so wish I had. All the other kids clucked over each other's photos. Saying 'Oh you haven't changed', 'what a sweet dress' and other sick-making stuff. I said that all my baby photos, loads of them, were in my old house, which burned down. They didn't believe me. Not that I care. I was really angry – so I took sweets and money from people's pockets to make me feel better and them feel bad. It's not fair.

Adopter: I wish I could smack Mr Thomas from one side of the classroom to the other. I told him last month that sex education, birth and babyhood would bring up issues for Felicity. And yet he gives me no prior warning that baby photos are to be displayed. He had the brass neck to tell me 'It didn't matter if Felicity had no photo'. I stood in front of him with my mouth gaping like a landed fish – how could he be so stupid and insensitive. It may not have mattered to him, but it is such a source of pain and sadness for her. As usual, the school just ignores what I say. They just think I'm an over-anxious parent.

Dream time – wishes for adoption support

This section integrates the wishes of each corner of the adoption triangle into realistic, practical, specific adoption support. These are SMART wishes: Specific, Measurable, Achievable, Relevant and Timely. Each bullet point listed could be implemented within five years, some in five months, and others within five days.

This list could take up the whole book. It might appear to some that more adoption support will give an unfair share of resources and provisions to adopted children and those who care for them. Please remember that adoption support is about trying to neutralise the damage the child has experienced. It's levelling the playing field. It's about helping them to change their map of the world and repairing their core distortion. Unresolved damage festering inside a child will eventually explode outwards and harm all those in the blast zone. Adoption support is a necessity, not a luxury.

Money and strategy

- Adequate funds;
- Some new funding for new provisions – more than just the same old money re-presented again and again and again as seems to happen with Quality Protects funding;
- Strategic planning by the government and local authorities for a generation, not for half a decade please – adoption is a life-long issue;
- A real commitment to support adoptive families (the only family made by the state!) from placement through to 25 (not 18 or 21, because often adopted children are immature and reach real adulthood later than their peers).

The child's life

- A life story book for life, not a frill for placement. A life story book that has more than a couple of photos, dates and fluffy prose. That has the real reasons children were adopted. Hard facts. The brutal truth. Dates, addresses, times. Photos that will help the child make sense of their experiences, validate their memories and by doing so allow the child to come to terms with their past and be comfortable in their own skin.
  - Photos that show the grubby things, the dirt, the squalor, the poverty, the lack of furniture, the soiled bed, the reality of a child's circumstances.
  - Photos that show the good times, the playground, the parties, the paddling pool, the birthday cake, the friends, the holidays, the sunshine and the laughter.
  - Photos that show the painful things, the police photos of bruises or broken bones, the hospital reports.
  - Photos of all the people who have been involved with the child; relatives, friends, culprits, perpetrators, teachers, victims, social workers, nurses.
- All the schoolbooks, record cards, pictures drawn, certificates and stories written.
- A time line showing all significant events, including the day the child:
  - took first step;
  - spoke first word – what was it and to whom was it said?;

- fell in a puddle;
- was stung by a bee;
- rode a bike without stabilisers . . . into the pond in the park;
- had goodbye visit with Mum;
- went to the fair and was sick after too much candy floss;
- bought first wellies;
- lost first welly;
- visited a farm with the school and was bitten by a billy goat;
- lost first tooth;
- first heard about new adoptive parents;
- pushed a towel down the toilet flooding the bathroom floor;
- had vaccinations;
- last visited Grandpa before he died;
- had first paddle in sea;
- learned to write own name;
- had first speaking part in a school assembly;
- for the first time swam a width, a length or 100m, or 400m, or 1km.

Information for the child

- Full audit trail of decisions, actions (or lack of them) made by authorities. The reasons should be stated clearly.
- Full details of birth family – medical, social, psychological, education, thoughts, hopes, beliefs, skills, quirks.
- Information must be accurate, neat, legible, understandable, correctly spelt, free from subjective opinion and evidenced. We all know the pressure social workers are under, but for a child to return to their records, say 15 years after placement, to find errors in their date of birth, their name spelt incorrectly and a sibling missing from their Form E is just unacceptable. Equally, hearsay should be clearly indicated. The phrase 'it is thought . . .' should never appear. Who thinks it and why? The evidence must be there. A child, when reading these records and reports, should be allowed to form their own view of their history, from facts and evidenced opinion, not filtered through a social worker's belief that 'he won't need to know this'. That information belongs to the child and no one has the right to tamper with it, deliberately or inadvertently.

- Access to all records from pre-birth to adoption. This information must be accessible when the child needs and wants it. Restricting access until legal adulthood prevents the child fitting fragments of their life together. Rather like a jigsaw, the fragments, memories and context need reprocessing to make sense of them. Delaying the facts simply causes confusion for the child. It's often not new data; their mind and body already knows. The information allows them to reframe events and understand themselves better.
- Adult adoptees and their birth families need to know how to access this information and where to find support for searching and possible reunions with members of their birth families.

Holistic assessment of the child

- The assessment should not just be a single superficial snapshot. Drawing an analogy with a car, we need a full MOT at a garage with shiny state-of-the-art equipment operated by a team of intelligent, motivated, highly-skilled mechanics, who provide a full written assessment of the existing problems, indicate possible future concerns, note that the spark plugs need adjusting, which of the many noises are alarm signals, when to return for a service and then estimate the repair costs. Sometimes cars are assessed by a bloke we met in the pub, who works in a dingy garage with no inspection pit, hasn't bought new tools in a decade, can't find his glasses and ignores the rust pockets. Aaahhh . . . but, he is cheaper. Allowing our children to be assessed by Slack Harry is disgraceful. Let's not kid ourselves: Slack Harry currently walks the corridors in some social service, NHS and education departments, rusty spanner in hand.
- A common misdiagnosis is that of ADHD (Attention Deficient Hyperactivity Disorder). The "symptoms" or behaviours associated with ADHD are similar to those associated with attachment disorders. However, there are significant differences – an ADHD child won't sit for half an hour reading a book, a child with attachment disorder will (provided they feel safe). Yet a significant number of adopted (or long-term fostered) children are put on Ritalin for years through misdiagnosis. This is outrageous.
- The assessment will often need to be multi-faceted. Some children will

need to see specialist paediatricians and/or therapists and/or child psychiatrists and/or educational psychologists. Some children will need even more.

Treatments

- Access to the following and, where payment is required, funded by the authorities not the parents:
  - Within the National Health Service adopted children should be given the same priority as "children looked after". Their needs do not change on the granting of an adoption order.
  - Osteopathy and chiropractic treatment – many birth parents take their children to cranial osteopaths or chiropractors for manipulation soon after birth. No one ever does that for a child in foster care. (Remember that many adopted children have been hit in infancy which can distort the skeleton.)
  - Applied kineseology – a non-invasive diagnostic tool using muscle testing as a way of evaluating health and disease such as allergy, intolerances, nutritional and chemical deficiencies or abnormalities. (Remember, prior to birth adopted children may have had no prenatal care, may have suffered substance abuse, may have been flooded with stress hormones, mother's diet may have been poor. All this will affect the growth, development and formation of the foetus.)
  - Proven alternative treatments including homeopathy, reflexology, flower essences, reiki, massage . . . and whatever works for that child.
  - Extra educational support – tutors, after school and holiday activities and clubs.

Therapy and counselling

- Appropriate and effective therapy available to all when needed funded by the authorities. Please remember, therapy is tough for both child and parents. No one undertakes therapy unless they have to. It is not an easy option – it's often the last resort but can be hugely effective.
- Therapy that helps children understand and make sense of their early experiences. Talking therapy is often less effective for children if the

damage occurred when the child was pre-verbal. Therapist training needs to reflect this accordingly.

- Therapy that gets to the heart of the issue – a person's sense of self, their values and beliefs not just behaviour modification. Sometimes people need help in understanding and accepting that their view of themselves and their map of the world is skewed. (This applies to all corners of the triangle.)There is a desperate need for therapists trained specifically to work with adopted and long-term fostered children with attachment problems. A centre of excellence (virtual not necessarily bricks and mortar) should be established. The expertise exists – it simply needs disseminating.
- Counselling services for birth parents (whose children have been removed from their care) should be completely separate from social services, at a neutral venue provided by staff who are totally unconnected with the removal of their child.
- Counselling services for birth parents should be ongoing, non-judgemental and supportive. Birth parents may need long-term support to understand the circumstances of their child's adoption and to deal with the heavy grief and sadness they carry. One session (currently, often all that's offered) is just not enough.
- Therapeutic support available on demand – at 3pm on a Sunday if that's when it's most effective – telephone support will do.

Train, educate and enlighten

Facilitating learning for all those involved with adopted children, their birth family or adoptive parents, is arguably the most important of all interventions. The more knowledge an individual has, the more choices they have, the more empowered they become, the more positive the outcome.

- Social workers who deal with children should have specific knowledge and understanding of:
  - different family systems and structures;
  - importance of ethnicity, religion and culture, in relation to a child's identity, within a community, and within society;
  - child development (normal and abnormal), attachment patterns, loss and separation;

- effects of early traumatic experiences on a child;
- long-term impact of abuse, domestic violence and neglect;
- significance of continuity, connection and contact;
- criteria for removing child from a damaging home;
• Social workers should be informed of research, good practice developments and initiatives.
• Social workers need help to reframe the permanent removal of some children from their birth family as a positive outcome for the child, not as their failure in keeping a family together.

Adopters often travel along a very tortuous road while raising their children. They can't see what is round the next bend, so don't know what skills, tools, understanding or knowledge they will need in the future. They must be empowered and encouraged to access the learning they need throughout their child's life.

• Being an adoptive parent changes an individual in many ways. Embracing those changes is so much easier when you know why they are happening. Conferences, books, articles, videos, audio tapes and any other way of learning can help adopters to understand their experiences and may provide signposts for the future.

• Adopters need to meet other adopters who are at both similar and different stages of the process. Metaphorically, most adopters wear the same-size shoes because they often share experiences and feelings. Such interactions uniquely reduce the sense of isolation and guilt adopters can feel. I have read many books and attended many conferences, but my greatest insight has come through fellow adopters. I am a stronger and wiser person, and a far better mother for that learning. I am deeply grateful to them all.

• Teachers with responsibility for Children in Need and Learning Mentors in secondary schools should be the first to receive training about the impact of adoption on a child. This should include the forms and effects of infant trauma, adaptive behaviours, possible triggers and strategies for the management of the child. This module should be incorporated into teacher training immediately and should be used as an INSET Day (In Service Training) in all schools; local authority Education Officers should be included. They are often involved at crisis point; earlier involvement and knowledge will open up a wider range of options. A school-age child may need extra time at home to regress and attach to his or her adoptive parents. A flexible approach to school attendance would be beneficial.

• Many therapists within the Child and Adolescent Mental Health departments (and beyond) need some serious retraining. The new understanding of attachment, attunement and an infant's brain development has bypassed them. Excluding adoptive parents and refusing to share the content of a therapy session is ineffective, wrong and punitive. It leaves the parents ill-equipped to cope with the inevitable post-therapy fall out.

Adopters need recognition by all professionals that they are part of the solution; not part of the problem. We did not inflict the damage on our children; we simply live with the resultant behaviour while providing running repairs.

Fairy Godmother please grant these three wishes:
• Let children be born to adults who can fulfil their needs, keep them safe and be good enough parents.
• If birth parents are unable to nurture a child long term, let that child be removed quickly and placed with adopters without drifting in the care system.
• Let adoption support respect the recipient and start from where they are, not where anyone wants them to be; by standing in their shoes, seeing what they see, hearing what they hear and feeling what they feel; by honouring *their* map of the world, let adoption support be what's needed and wanted at that time, in that place, by that person. I wish.

You see things, and you say, 'Why?' But I dream things that never were; and I say, 'Why not?'

George Bernard Shaw

3 Providing effective adoption support – a new model for a new Act?

Jeffrey Coleman

The social worker wanted introductions to start and finish within a week. My husband broke his arm three days before the proposed start of the placement. When this, and other practical problems (need to obtain equipment; proximity of Christmas) were raised with the social worker, she said, 'Don't you want him then?'

Our child moved from fostering to adoption with us – we felt the lack of post adoption support was unbelievable and negligent, compared to fostering.

*[The home study] . . . was thorough, relevant and sensitively handled by the social worker . . . but did not really prepare us for the huge array of **practical** issues we were confronted with after placement, e.g. choosing child-friendly meals, finding suitable schools, deciding what time the children should go to bed, settling disputes between the siblings, etc. etc. "Normal" parents are able to grow into the job as their babies grow into children. For us the very steep learning curve was something for which we were largely unprepared.*

(Adopters' comments, taken from responses to a
BAAF Southern Region Survey)

Legislative background

In her foreword to *Providing Effective Adoption Support*, published by the Department of Health (DH) in June 2002, the Minister envisaged this consultation document as a key stage in taking forward the proposals made in the White Paper *Adoption: A new approach* (Department of Health, 2000b). The White Paper, having declared that the current legal duties on local authorities for adoption support were framed in very general terms, that provision was patchy, and that adopters reported that post-adoption support was the least satisfactory part of the adoption process, went on to make some ambitious commitments:

- to place a clear duty on local authority social services departments to provide post-adoption support, including financial support, planned jointly with local education authorities and the NHS, and available from the time a placement is made, for as long as it is needed;
- to start to identify best practice, and develop a new framework for post-adoption support services which will meet needs, which are not met in any other way;
- to set out a legal framework to ensure consistent provision of post-placement and post-adoption support;
- to ensure children and their new families have easy access to post-adoption support (as opposed to being routed through a general social services duty system focused on child protection) particularly where a child has been placed with a new family who live outside the council's area;
- to give all families adopting children, especially those who have been looked after, a new right to an assessment by their council for post-placement support which can be requested at any stage after the placement has been identified.

Government statements have continually raised expectations about what these measures can and should achieve. Jacqui Smith, the Minister of State, said on 20 May 2002 that 'better adoption services will be a key means of ensuring the stability of adoptive placements, and of encouraging more families to come forward to adopt . . . if people know that they can gain access to those services it can have a positive effect on their willingness to come forward to undertake adoption'. The Chairman of the Select Committee saw the need for 'a sea change in attitudes and a recognition that the local authority has a continuing role'.

Ministers have made clear these are priority changes to the adoption service to be implemented in advance of the Act as a whole. Therefore, it was the Government's intention to introduce improved adoption support for new adoptive families from April 2003. To meet this timetable, *Providing Effective Adoption Support* was followed by rapid public consultation on the draft Regulations (for adopted children and their adoptive families, including prospective adopted children and their prospective families) due for implementation as Phase 1 in April 2003.[1] At the time of going to press, the Government has announced that implementation will now be in October 2003. A similar process will ensue for the further Regulations promised for 2004 as Phase 2 (for adoption support for the wider network of all those affected by adoption).

The Adoption and Children Act received Royal Assent on 7 November 2002. The question of exactly how to enshrine into law the White Paper's commitments on adoption support proved highly controversial during the Act's final stages.

Clause 2(6) gave a basic definition of adoption support services, and Clause 4 set out the new duty on local authorities to respond to requests for assessment for these services. Much was to be left to Regulations, but BAAF played a leading role, in alliance with many organisations critical of these clauses of the Bill, in arguing that assessment alone was insufficient – there needed to be a statutory duty on local authorities to provide and fund such services, and this duty should have extended to health and education providers also.

When the first version of the Bill was introduced in 2001, Adoption UK (a network of adoptive parents) said in evidence that the new duty to provide an assessment was flawed 'when this duty is accompanied by the provider's right to decide whether or not to provide the services it has decided are needed'. Adopted children and families 'need access to the actual provision of support post-placement and post-adoption, not simply an assessment to determine the nature of that support'. After Adoption (a voluntary agency based in Manchester) held similar views: 'in order not to pathologise parties touched by adoption, support services need to be there as a matter of right, and not only if conferred by assessment'. The lack of obligation on health and education services to contribute to adoption support plans was taken up by MPs: 'Although the local authority is obliged to notify the health authority or local education authority of those needs, again the Bill seems to contain no provision to assign a duty of care to the local authority, to ensure that children receive the best possible services. I have been greatly concerned about that issue since I first read the Bill.'[2]

---

[1] David Hinchcliffe (Wakefield) HC, 20 May 2002.
[2] Sandra Gidley (Romsey) HC, 26 March 2001.

The continuing absence of this duty when the Bill was re-introduced after the 2001 general election was subject to widespread criticism in the House of Lords in the summer of 2002:

- 'Unless local authorities have a duty to provide support services and are resourced accordingly, many simply will not provide them'.[3]
- 'The language there [in the White Paper] is quite plain. I read that as a commitment to provide post-adoption support, and to impose a clear duty to provide that support. The White Paper did not say that local authorities would be given a duty to decide whether or not to provide post-adoption support . . . The reality is that when the budgetary climate is tough, local authorities will concentrate their resources on their statutory duties and cut down on the functions which they do not legally have to provide'.[4]
- 'I ask the Minister this: how will local authorities make assessments for something which may never exist? Part of an assessment process has to consider whether a person will get benefit from a post-adoption service. If that post-adoption service never exists, how do you build up an assessment on it? There is something illogical in this'.[5]

Underlying this dispute is a difficult issue – should the needs of adopted children receive a level of social services' resources that cannot be assured for other categories of children in need? Is it reasonable to 'put a duty to provide adoption support services at a higher level than applies to many other duties placed on local authorities'[6] as one speaker asked? In the debate this provoked the response: what about the needs of children statemented under the Education Acts? What about ensuring that the mental health needs of young people in adolescent units are properly met? What about a guaranteed level of preventive provision 'to ensure that people can keep their children, when they want to do so'?[7] Unfortunately it is all too easy to add to this list other categories of highly needy children lacking consistent and timely services – what about

---

[3] Earl Howe HL, 10 June 2002.
[4] Earl Howe HL, 27 June 2002.
[5] Baroness Barker HL, 27 June 2002.
[6] Baroness Barker HL, 27 June 2002.
[7] Baroness Howarth of Breckland HL, 27 June 2002.

services for children who have been sexually abused? What about services for refugee and asylum-seeking young people, pursued by war, poverty, racism, and 'the unravelling of nations'. Baroness Howarth concluded:

> If we ring-fence this duty in some way, my real concern is that we shall have one gold-plated group of children. My great desire is to ensure that this level of service is there for every child in this country who faces need.[8]

These are questions of fundamental importance. As yet, the goal of consistent and coherent provision of a range of family support and therapeutic services for children in need required by the Children Act 1989 is, on the Government's own evidence, still far from realisation.

- In April 2000 the Department of Health admitted that 'there is wide agreement, within and between central and local government, that there are too many plans for children and that, despite considerable effort at local level, there is insufficient coherence between them' (Department of Health, 2000c).

- *The Children Act Now* studies (Department of Health, 2001) acknowledged that 'social workers lacked the skills or training to undertake direct work with children and young people as a form of support', and that 'the variability in gaining access to appropriate services raises many questions about the purpose and processes of the assessment of children and the accurate identification of children who are "in need" of services'.

- On the available evidence, from findings by the SSI, the latest Chief Inspector's Report (Department of Health, 2002b) was obliged to reiterate this concern: 'evidence of a striking variability in the quality of service provided by local councils was found'.

Until the Adoption and Children Bill reached its final form, and the requirements of primary legislation regarding adoption support were clarified, these concerns could not be resolved. No doubt this partly explains why there was some uncertainty at the heart of the consultation document, *Providing Effective Adoption Support*, regarding the policies

---

[8] Baroness Howarth of Breckland HL, 27 June 2002.

and mechanisms for guaranteeing delivery of the White Paper promises. As a framework, it also suffered from the Government's intention to reserve much policy detail for the forthcoming Regulations. Nonetheless, one is left with an impression of a document based on a number of un-argued assumptions (e.g. on the role to be played by mainstream services) that is stronger on diagnosis than on the "effective" remedies promised by its title. Similarly, some of its suggested solutions to major current service dilemmas (e.g. on responsibility for cross-border placements) are just that: tentative suggestions unsubstantiated by argument.

Finally, perhaps because it was limited by the scope of the first tranche of Regulations due in April 2003, *Providing Effective Adoption Support* was almost exclusively concerned with support for adoptive families and children, and hardly mentioned birth families. The result is a truncated picture of the realities of adoption, and of the contexts in which services are to be provided. The effect of these omissions is to depict adopted children in a curiously abstract light, more "policy objects" than participants, let alone subjects in a complex and dynamic process. If adoption support should never lose sight of the value of 'helping children to find resolution to the connections with their biological families while simultaneously strengthening ties to their adoptive families' (Barth and Miller, 2000) these omissions carry a positively unhelpful message.

How far does *Providing Effective Adoption Support* provide a coherent and appropriate vision for the future of adoption support services in England? Does it bring the key issues sharply into focus? Does it maintain the momentum towards comprehensive adoption-sensitive and adoption-specific support packages apparently promised in the White Paper, or does its language shift the emphasis to the function of (and what amounts to an expression of faith in the availability of) *mainstream services* as the central resource, albeit in conjunction with adoption-specific services; in effect a rationalisation and retention of existing approaches to service delivery with a penumbra of adoption-specific measures? Is this shift of emphasis consistent with research messages that the challenges of being adoptive parents are substantially different from those of being biological parents?

An overview of the consultation document

Chapter 1 uses the term *adoption support services* to include services needed before and after (and this may be 'weeks, months and years' after) the adoption order is made and explains that the aim of the exercise is to identify:

- the range of services local authorities should put in place to deliver a comprehensive adoption support service;
- how adoption support services should be organised so that they are responsive and accessible to those who need them, at the time that they need them;
- how best to help those affected by adoption to access and navigate these services;
- the role of financial support in the overall provision of adoption support services.

Chapter 2, using 1998/9 Department of Health statistics and a forthcoming study by Selwyn *et al* (in press), profiles the characteristics of children adopted from care as 'a distinct subset of looked after children' with more challenging needs and a pattern of more frequent moves in care than the general looked after population, leading to a recognition that 'promoting more adoption will involve finding more families for increasingly vulnerable children'.

Chapter 3 is essentially a résumé of findings from the Prime Minister's Review (Performance and Innovation Unit, 2000) in relation to four practice areas – financial support, the record of social work, education and health as adoption support services, access to birth records, and contact with birth families – with critical comments on the shortcomings in current services.

Chapter 4, "The policy context", gives an update on the progress of the Adoption and Children Bill, and asserts the specific (and limited) commitment made in the Bill that councils will provide adoption support services 'based on need and on resources available'. Adoptive families can request an assessment at any time, i.e. after being matched, when the child is placed, as well as after an adoption order is made. Assessments will be based on the domains and dimensions of the *Framework for*

Assessment of Children in Need and their Families (Department of Health, 1999). Although the importance of "joined-up planning and provision" with education and health is stressed, little is said of the mechanisms to achieve this beyond the statement that when an assessment points to a need for specific health or education services, 'councils will be under a duty to notify the appropriate health body (including Primary Care Trusts) or local education authority of this need'.

Chapter 5 outlines existing responsibilities towards children in need under Part III of the Children Act 1989, and suggests that many of the services typically provided by social services 'will be of real interest and assistance to adoptive families'. In addition, the Integrated Children's System is expected to improve the quality of information available to adopters, 'both to support the matching process and to inform decisions about services required by the child and their adopters'.

Chapter 6, entitled "Research and evidence", is another résumé section, and one which belies its title. It highlights headline themes from some significant studies but is otherwise incomplete and inadequate as a research review.

The main sources are the SSI's *Adopting Changes* overview report from November 2000, Lowe and Murch *et al*'s study *Supporting Adoption: Reframing the approach* (1999), and also included is a table from a substantial US research report by Sedlak and Broadhurst (1993). This study, based on the case records of 2,200 children adopted between 1983 and 1987, shows how, for children with various "special needs", adoption support significantly reduced the time spent waiting for adoption. It perhaps needs to be made clear that by "adoption support" the American researchers were referring to monthly "adoption assistance" financial payments, set in at least half the cases in their sample at the same level as the previous fostering payments. The authors concluded that this level of financial payment acted as an effective "equaliser" for children who had various characteristics – being older, having a disability, needing ongoing treatment, having siblings, previous problems including placement disruption – that may have made it more difficult to find adoptive families for them.

The role that adoption allowances can play in encouraging carers to adopt (in the US) and in preventing disruption is coupled with criticisms of the current UK system as all too variable, discretionary and often redolent of charity rather than entitlement.

Chapter 7 provides a summary of adoption support services, Annex A is a glossary of terms, while Annex B argues that there are very few services only applicable to adoption (this is all too true), and that adoptive children and their families should receive assistance in accessing mainstream services. Key elements from a variety of these services are summarised.

The state of adoption support services: recent developments

Recognition of the need for comprehensive adoption support and post-adoption services was a gradual process, though by the mid-1980s many in the UK adoption world had become clear in their advocacy. A BAAF anthology (Argent (ed.), 1988) emphasised how we were beginning to learn from adopted children, adopters and birth families what services might be required, and were therefore less inclined to see adoption as a solution in itself for the problems of children experiencing significant trauma in early life.

Despite the pioneering work of many agencies, particularly in the voluntary sector, an authoritative text in 1997 (Triseliotis *et al*) could only describe the overall picture of adoption support services as "fragmented and variable", hemmed in by funding restrictions, the low priority accorded post-adoption provision, and the absence of policy and procedural guidance and of a strong legislative framework. Lowe and Murch *et al*'s major national study (1999) of adoption support in England and Wales, conducted between 1994 and 1998, while finding that 43 per cent of the sample children being adopted had special needs, found that the availability of relevant services was "something of a lottery" and that a number of placements seemed to succeed in spite of the system rather than because of it.

Limitations of research

Providing Effective Adoption Support would have been strengthened by a wider-ranging review of research, and ideally by having been preceded by a programme of evaluation studies. The recent literature review and

UK survey by Alan Rushton and Cherilyn Dance (2002) fills an important gap in the meantime, though their literature review is restricted specifically to services for non-relative adoptive parents and their adopted children in placements made from local authority care and within that mainly on adoptive families experiencing difficulties.

Rushton and Dance comment on the dearth of independent evaluations of the effectiveness of adoption support interventions, justifying wariness of over-confident claims from practitioners and therapists.

A particular gap in knowledge concerns the needs of black and Asian and other minority ethnic adoptive families. One study of black and minority ethnic children placed between 1979 and 1986 (Thoburn *et al*, 2000) tells us that 'some of the black parents told of their struggle to make some white workers understand their point of view and their attitudes towards parenting' but we need to know much more about the experiences and support needs of minority ethnic adopters, and the diverse perspectives their communities hold on adoption, to ensure future services are appropriately tailored to their needs and to guide recruitment activity.

Estimating and costing future need

The central message from the Department of Health overview of adoption studies, *Adoption Now: Messages from Research* (Parker, 1999), was that problems and difficulties do not disappear because a child is adopted into a committed and caring family. Although acknowledging in general terms that 'the Government should ensure that policy is framed in a way that reflects the needs of current and future looked after children', it is surprising that *Providing Effective Adoption Support* does not give more attention to estimating and costing likely levels of adoption support need. This gap in the document's coverage was also subject to comment in the House of Lords debates in June 2002:

> It is a very strange consultation document, with very few figures in it – a fact which puzzles me ... There is much in its description and analysis which is extremely useful, but it is deficient in two very crucial areas: evidence and funding.[9]

---

[9] Baroness Barker, HL, 27 June 2002.

Adoption support and post-adoption work is by its nature indefinite and inconclusive; it has to be there for service users as and when they need it. But for this flexibility and availability of response to be assured, an adequate infrastructure will need to be in place, and planning for this, in turn, needs to be grounded in good management information. Rushton and Dance's recent survey (2002) found that 'the most telling point concerning post-order work was that respondents did not know what the demand was likely to be. They did not want to raise people's expectations and then not be able to deliver'.

The Government's Public Service Agreement target of increasing by 2004–05 the number of looked after children adopted by 40 per cent and, if possible, 50 per cent, means that over 3,800 children should be adopted out of council care in the year ending 31 March 2005. The following table, from the Children Act Report 2001(Department of Health, 2002d), illustrates progress to date:

Figure 1.4

Looked after children adopted during the years ending 31 March 1997 to 2001

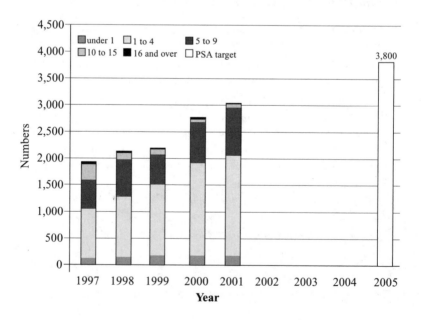

Children Act Report 2001

While the trend towards earlier decision making, enabling children to move to permanent alternative care if prospects for successful rehabilitation with their birth family are assessed as unlikely, is generally good news for younger children, the *Children Act Report 2001*'s analysis of current trends indicates that local authorities 'need to increase their efforts to make adoption available to the 5–9 age group'.

Any increase in the numbers of "late-placed" children will add to the demands on adoption support services. Rushton and Dance's snapshot telephone survey (2002) did not include questions about children waiting, or what the thoughts of their respondents would be on the support implications if more children from this older age range were to be placed for adoption. It was already clear, however, when respondents considered the challenging backgrounds – substance misuse, mental health problems, abusive or neglectful parenting – of the younger children now being placed, that they felt uncertainty about how these children might develop and what their support needs in the future might be. They anticipated that the areas of greatest need in the post-order period were likely to be for help with contact arrangements with birth family members, help with searching, and help for behavioural or relationship difficulties from psychological services.

Mainstreaming

Although recognising in general terms the vulnerability of children adopted from care, *Providing Effective Adoption Support* does not extend its inquiries to build a more detailed picture of their needs. Instead, it rests its hopes on mainstream services as the normal recourse for these children and families, with more adoption-specific services only being required to 'fill gaps in existing provision'.

We must take a step back to ask strategic questions:

1) Do adopted children have unusual needs by virtue of the amount or type of experiences they have had?
2) Can these needs be met by existing approaches to service delivery?
3) How special are the needs of adoptive families and children?

Barth and Miller's review of US findings (2000) reveal a clear pattern. Surveys of non-clinical community populations composed of adopted and non-adopted young people find adopted young people either in or near the clinical range for behavioural disorders at rates beyond those of non-adopted contemporaries. Researchers from the Colorado Adoption Project detected that adopted boys were significantly more at risk for conduct problems than a non-adopted cohort. Another study cited by Barth found that adopted children had parent-rated levels of disturbances that were substantially greater than the base rates reported in epidemiological studies, a significant finding even when allowing for over-vigilance in the adopters' reporting.

In *Joining New Families* (Quinton *et al*, 1998), 27 per cent of a sample of 61 children placed between ages of 5 and 9, had not developed mutually rewarding relationships with their new parents by the end of the first year, half the children had difficulties in at least one of their relationships with new parents, new siblings or peers, and serious new problems arose during the course of the year for over half the sample.

Updated research (Rushton and Dance, in preparation) when the children were on average 14½ years, i.e. 5–6 years after placement, found problem levels substantially elevated compared with matched community controls, both on total scores and all individual domains, especially over-activity, conduct and peer problems. Psychological problems had persisted for the group well into placement and 40 per cent scored in the abnormal range versus 6 per cent for the controls. While 71 per cent of the placements were still intact, a third of these placements remained highly problematic and had produced sometimes enormous strain on carers despite their high level of commitment.

These are surely outcomes which throw much light on the likely extent and type of future adoption support need. How well prepared are existing mainstream services for responding to these problems?

Using Barth's typology (2000), adoption support services can be divided into three basic categories: 1) educational and informational, 2) clinical, 3) material (adoption allowances and other financial support).

Educational and informational

How significant are the problems which emerge for adopted children in the school setting, and how responsive are school services?

School environments are of course very significant for children who have endured early adversities. Depending on the training, awareness, and policies and practices within a school, the educational experience may either ameliorate undesirable developmental outcomes or enhance later difficulties. In favourable circumstances they may enable maltreated children, who often have a poor concept of self, to develop self-confidence and empathy for others (Veltman and Browne, 2001).

In *Supporting Adoption: Reframing the approach* (Lowe and Murch *et al*, 1999), part of the culture of adoption placement practice was to leave schooling arrangements to adopters, and schools appeared generally helpful in that study. However, much other research suggests schooling is a problematic issue for adopted children. A third of the children in Thomas and Beckford's sample (1999) said they had been bullied although they did not necessarily attribute this to their adoptive status. The majority of children described changing schools in negative terms as "scary and strange" – not knowing anyone, having to make new friends, unfamiliar school systems and environments. In *Joining New Families* (Quinton *et al*, 1998), children in adoptive placements showed substantially more problems than their controls, with no marked changes in school behaviour over the year. Adopters said that information about their children's education had been misleading and educational needs had not been adequately assessed. Earlier research by the same team had recorded how adoptive parents had to adjust to slow educational progress and to respond to the school's reports of difficult behaviour, poor relationships with peers and teachers, and communication and concentration problems.

Other often reported problems include how adopted children, with varying knowledge of their personal histories, can be embarrassed by standard school exercises on genealogy and family trees, and how maintaining packages of educational support when adopted children move across administrative boundaries can prove difficult unless problems magnify and local referral procedures for children in need are triggered.

In sum there are strong messages for school environments to be much more adoption-sensitive than at present. Without such changes, there may continue to be a tendency to attribute school adjustment problems exclusively to the strengths and difficulties of the adopted child at the individual level. For example, the following vignette, drawn from a recent Adoption Panel report, of one child's early months, post placement, in a new school, is representative of many such accounts:

> *Samantha's school career got off to a rocky start. She found it difficult to stay on task and to cope with school routines and expectations – Samantha's way of dealing with this was to demand lots of attention from the teacher and to disrupt the other children.*[10]

Adopters may feel the White Paper's comment (2000b) that 'not all adoptive parents are familiar with the current education system' might just as truthfully have been reversed, and instead read: 'not all education professionals appear to be familiar with adoption'.

Clinical

In their telephone survey of staff from 120 local authorities and 23 voluntary adoption agencies, Rushton and Dance's (2002) respondents generally expressed disappointment in Child and Adolescent Mental Health Services (CAMHS) for placed and adopted children, finding them:

- over-stretched;
- under-resourced;
- struggling with difficulties in recruitment and retention of staff.

These factors led not only to long waiting lists (eight months in some areas), but also to dismay at the lack of priority given to adopted children and the lack of understanding of their specific needs. Most respondents in the survey felt that adopted children ought to rank as a priority for therapeutic services, mainly because of their histories and the risk of disruption if help could not be obtained, and that there persisted, in many CAMHS units, a culture of anticipating a "dysfunctional family". Around three-quarters felt that there were difficulties with the needs of adoptive families meeting CAMHS' criteria – services were usually focused on tightly defined populations of looked after children, with adopted children outside their remit. Apart from

---

[10] Information from BAAF. The child's name has been changed.

these delays and eligibility problems, there was sometimes concern at the inappropriateness of the approach taken by CAMHS personnel.

The recent Department of Health publication, *Safeguarding Children: A Joint Chief Inspectors' Report on arrangements to safeguard children* (Department of Health, 2002c), drawing on a wide range of inspection activity and recent fieldwork in eight local authority areas, can only echo these frustrations. Serious concern is expressed in almost all areas about CAMHS resources. Again the story is of long waiting lists, difficulty in accessing services either for advice for social workers or for referrals of children and their families for assessment, with the CAMHS agencies facing recruitment problems and shortages.

More studies convey disquieting messages. Researchers in Scotland (Minnis and Del Priori, 2001) found CAMHS services to be used by looked after children considerably less than would be expected from the levels of difficulty presented by the children in their samples. Responding to children with severe attachment difficulties was a particular challenge. These were disorders easy to miss in clinical settings, and even optimal use of the Looking After Children materials as a screening tool is likely to fail to identify some children with significant problems, despite these children being at grave risk. The researchers concluded that services should not be 'amorphous and generalised', but more specifically focused and supported by comprehensive psychological assessment.

Despite the poor state of knowledge of the mental health needs of children and adolescents, it is clear that children being placed from care are likely to have a potentially higher level of emotional ill-health. The National Service Framework for Children is due to publish standards for a wide range of health and social care services in April 2003. In the meantime, the combination of increasing need, and piecemeal and fragmented improvements in provision has recently prompted *Community Care* magazine to launch a national campaign, "Changing Minds", to press for urgent improvements via a national strategy, ring-fenced resources for CAMHS, and new and rapid service developments for this age group and its carers.

Again the adequacy of *Providing Effective Adoption Support*'s reliance on mainstream clinical services seems questionable.

Material services (adoption allowances and other financial support)

The starting point is the White Paper, which promised a "fair and flexible" financial framework. As there are no data collected centrally on the number of adopters who receive adoption allowances, the level of payment or the reason for the payment, it would have been helpful if *Providing Effective Adoption Support* had been accompanied by some updated survey information. However, key points from existing survey information are highlighted:

- the SSI's *Adopting Changes* report in November 2000 which found the percentage of placements attracting adoption allowances varied from 17 per cent to 68 per cent in the councils inspected;
- the earlier LAC98(20) survey recording gross inconsistencies, with some councils paying no adoption allowances at all, and others paying allowances in all of their placements;
- 28 per cent of those replying to an SSI questionnaire said they had not been given information about adoption allowances.

The White Paper encouraged adoption by foster carers where appropriate and the SSI is only too aware that 'the impact on foster carers considering adoption or on adopters on low income of belonging to councils which paid few or no allowances was crucial, and likely to be off-putting'.

The *Prime Minister's Review of Adoption* (Performance and Innovation Unit, 2000) acknowledged that the social security rules for the treatment of foster care and adoption allowances in the context of income support are complex. Unfortunately this is a complexity that adopters and their advisers will perhaps still need to master as *Providing Effective Adoption Support* says that 'financial support following adoption should not be used to replace available benefits but rather to fund expenditure which is beyond the scope of the benefits system', but fails to discuss solutions to the continuing benefit tangles. Nowhere is it suggested that an adoption allowance would be disregarded by the Benefits Agency in assessing entitlement to other benefits.

We are reminded that adoption allowances were 'intended as a contribution towards the additional cost of caring for a child'. If this is to remain the case, and allowances continue also to be subject to a means test, how is this going to enable adopters to feel that they are "entitled" to this support? In *Supporting Adoption: Reframing the approach* (Lowe and Murch *et al*, 1999) many of the children had special needs or were part of a sibling group and this meant that the cost of caring for them was higher than for a single child or one without special needs. The authors suggested:

> *At the very least, these children should be entitled to the same level of financial support as if they continued to be fostered . . . We recommend that a national standardised system of eligibility and levels of financial support be introduced, possibly by means of a state allowance rather than one paid by the adoption agency, removing financial questions from the question of adoption so decisions can be based entirely on the welfare of the child . . .*

After rehearsing the array of difficulties currently associated with the adoption allowance scheme, *Providing Effective Adoption Support* eschews detailed comment on what the shape of a the new allowance scheme will look like.

The feedback from the Rushton and Dance survey (2002) is that it is absolutely essential that solutions are found. The disparity between authorities and areas lead to considerable difficulties. Most of the professionals responding to the survey feel that families should not be means tested, that there should be a national formula which takes account of the likely needs of individual children, and that the way it is worked out is transparent. Some have suggested that it should be paid like child benefit.

It is frustrating that *Providing Effective Adoption Support* was so short on details and commitments in this quite crucial area of financial support.

Other key issues

"Cross border" placement

Providing Effective Adoption Support suggests that 'before the placement is made, a full and frank discussion needs to take place between the prospective adopters and the agency anticipating the kinds and sources of support the adoptive family and child may need and how they can be resourced', and that 'as a general starting point we consider that it would be sensible for the placing council to assess the child's needs and provide adoption support services until the adoption order is made. At this point, as a general rule, we consider it would be reasonable for this responsibility to transfer to the receiving authority, if the adoptive family lives elsewhere.' *Providing Effective Adoption Support* notes that the lack of consistent support across the country is a disincentive to councils placing beyond their borders. This contributes to delay and drift within the adoption process. Many social workers recounted difficulties they had experienced in supporting damaged children and struggling families that other agencies have placed without any reciprocal arrangements.

As Rushton and Dance(2002) commented:

The delays that can be caused while arguments ensue between various departments of the same authority (education, health and social services) or between different local authorities can be disastrous. Although some managers expressed one preference or the other, the impression is that most managers just want a rapid resolution to the problems.

Applicability of the 'Assessment Framework'

Providing Effective Adoption Support says that 'the adopters who live with the child on a day-to-day basis will know better than anyone else the problems the child is presenting and the help they need if they are to cope'. Is this insight reflected in its comments about assessment?

The approach taken is to promise a careful adaptation for adoptive families and children of the *Framework for the Assessment of Children in Need and their Families* (Department of Health, 1999).

We must hope that firmer information, including how this will be adapted for "children in transition" and families forming new relationships, will emerge with the consultation on the forthcoming Regulations. However, it is a cause for concern that *Safeguarding Children* (Department of Health, 2002c) has recently reported considerable difficulties around the effective use of the Assessment Framework in mainstream children and families work:

- almost all social services were struggling with the completion of the core assessments at all, let alone within 35 days;

- staff from other agencies often had minimal training in or understanding of the Assessment Framework;
- few agencies (other than social services) understood how they should participate in the Assessment Framework.

The help the Assessment Framework can provide in enabling staff trained in its use to link analysis of needs with an analysis of safety and risk has been welcomed by many in the wake of recent child care tragedies. However, many have also queried whether the Assessment Framework can work well for children in transition or in new families, or for adopters struggling to find ways to honour a child's past alongside their commitment to his or her future – contexts significantly different from the Framework's original remit. Important challenges lie ahead if we are to ensure that a structured and holistic approach to assessment is not achieved at the expense of easy service accessibility, promptness of help in emergencies, and respect for adopters' and adopted children's own perspectives on their needs and on the kinds of interventions they would find most useful.

Conclusion

Providing Effective Adoption Support is in the nature of an extended list of some of the key elements of adoption support, and is notably short on substantive and detailed policy proposals. The comments in this chapter have focused on a number of key concerns that will have to be addressed if the current investment in adoption is to achieve the child-centred outcomes the Government desires:

- ensuring that the new statutory right to assessment for adoption support needs is backed up (in subsequent regulations and guidance) by Standards, and levels of professional training and accountability that guarantee consistent, reliable and well-resourced support services;
- recognising the value to placed children and their adoptive families of having available a range of services *specific* to their needs;
- honestly acknowledging that many mainstream services are not currently equipped to provide a useful adoption support function, and that much will need to be done in terms of development, training and resourcing to remedy these deficiencies;

- addressing the fundamental issue of financial support for adoptive families in a way that realises the White Paper's commitment to a 'fair and flexible' system;
- providing a problem-solving approach to cross-border placements that enhances good adoption support planning and minimises discontinuities for adopted children and their families;
- ensuring an adoption sensitive approach to the assessment of support needs.

Postscript

Department of Health (2003) *Adoption: The draft adoption support services* **(local authorities) (transitory and transitional provisions) (England) regulations 2003 and draft accompanying guidance, London: Department of Health.**

These draft regulations take forward Phase 1 of the adoption support programme as pre-figured in *Providing Effective Adoption Support*, i.e. they are intended only to partially implement the Adoption and Children Act 2002's duties regarding adoption support, by providing "a minimum floor" of services, with full implementation of the Act currently scheduled for 2004. The details of BAAF's own response to the draft regulations, together with a response from a group of 22 organisations covering a wide spectrum within the adoption field, can be found at www.baaf.org. uk. The finalised regulations, to be laid before Parliament in March, for implementation in October 2003, are not therefore available for consideration at the time of going to press (February 2003).

A good many of the concerns raised in this chapter about *Providing Effective Adoption Support* would also apply to the approach taken in the draft regulations. Key points to highlight are:

- *Financial support*
  In October 2002 Jacqui Smith announced an extra £70 million to be ring-fenced for adoption support over three years from April 2003, as part of the 2002 Spending Review Settlement increases announced in April by the Chancellor of the Exchequer. This was a very welcome announcement, though in the absence of detailed projections on needs

and costs it is difficult to assess the difference this funding will make.

The detailed draft regulations on the financial support arrangements intended to replace adoption allowances have already been subject to much comment (see BAAF website). It is to be hoped that the "Costs and Outcomes" study referred to in *Providing Effective Adoption Support*, when published, will provide evidence lacking in that earlier document to guide decision makers on the longer terms costs of adoption, particularly as the draft guidance advises local authorities to "project forward" and anticipate the evolving needs of the child and his or her adoptive family.

- *The needs of birth parents*
  It is increasingly clear that postponing inclusion of the adoption support needs of birth parents within the regulations until final implementation of the Act has been an unhelpful approach. Apart from threatening to create confusion about the existing responsibilities of local authorities stemming from the Adoption Act 1976 and the National Adoption Standards towards birth parents, such a postponement may result in adoption support plans based on incomplete assessment information, particularly regarding contact plans. The Government's adoption programme has not always treated birth parents with the compassionate objectivity that is their due. For many birth parents, recovering effective social functioning after the involuntary relinquishment of a child for adoption through court intervention can be a bleak struggle indeed, but the availability of focused help in achieving this is essential if they are to be effective participants in the long-term planning needed for a child adopted from care. Further attention needs to be paid to these concerns in the regulations.

- *The role of education and health services*
  There is a requirement for local authorities to *consult* with local education authorities and Primary Care Trusts in the preparation of an adoption support plan and to send them a copy of the plan if they have "a role or responsibility" in its implementation. Despite the restricted scope of the Act, one hopes the part to be played by these key contributors to adoption support will be more robustly defined in the final regulations, especially when disagreements arise.

- *Assessment procedures*
  No further guidance, beyond general comments, is given in the draft regulations on how to develop assessment procedures that are both adoption-sensitive and compatible with existing approaches to children in need, though the commitment to work with local authorities to achieve progress in this area is undoubtedly to be welcomed.

- *Cross-border placements*
  The draft regulations will need to be modified to ensure that there can be smooth and well-co-ordinated arrangements, together with rapid dispute resolution when necessary, between authorities in cross-border placements, regarding the provision and funding of both adoption support and financial services.

As ever, the bare bones of any new regulations and guidance can only be brought to life through the commitment and skills of individual practitioners and managers, and it will be important to retain existing experienced staff as well as to recruit additional resources. This will be made easier if with the new duties and accountabilities comes an enhanced recognition by councils of the importance of this field of practice. Nonetheless we have a new Act; we can now use this opportunity to develop enlightened regulations, guidance and standards, and have a new model of adoption support which adopted children and adults, adopters and birth families need and want.

References

Argent, H (ed) (1988) *Keeping the Doors Open: A review of post-adoption services*, London: BAAF.

Barth, R P and Miller, J M (2000) 'Building effective post-adoption services: what is the empirical foundation?' *Family Relations*, pp 447–455.

Barth, R P *et al* (2001) *Assessing the Field of Post-Adoption Service: Family needs, program models, and evaluation issues – literature review*, http://aspe.hhs.gov/hsp/PASS/lit-rev-01.htm.

Department of Health (1999) *Framework for the Assessment of Children in Need and their Families*, London: Department of Health.

Department of Health (2000a) *Adopting Changes: Survey and inspection of local councils' adoption services*, London: Department of Health.

Department of Health (2000b) *Adoption: A new approach*, London: Department of Health.

Department of Health (2000c) *Children's Services Planning Consultation*, London: Department of Health.

Department of Health (2001) *The Children Act Now: Messages from research*, London: Department of Health.

Department of Health (2002a) *Providing Effective Adoption Support: issued for consultation*, London: Department of Health.

Department of Health (2002b) *Modern Social Services: A commitment to reform, The 11th Annual Report of the Chief Inspector of Social Services 2001–2002*, London: Department of Health.

Department of Health (2002c) *Safeguarding Children: A Joint Chief Inspectors' Report on arrangements to safeguard children*, London: Department of Health.

Department of Health (2002d) *Children Act Report 2001*, London: Department of Health.

Department of Health (2003) *Adoption: The draft adoption support services (local authorities) (transitory and transitional provisions) (England) regulations 2003 and draft accompanying guidance*, London: Department of Health.

Lowe, N, Murch, M, Borkowski, M, Weaver, A, Beckford, V and Thomas, C (1999) *Supporting Adoption: Reframing the approach*, London: BAAF.

Minnis, H and Del Priori, C, 'Mental health services for looked after children', *Adoption & Fostering*, 25:4.

Parker, R (1999) *Adoption Now: Messages from Research*, Chichester: Wiley & Sons

Performance and Innovation Unit (2000) *Prime Minister's Review of Adoption*, London: Cabinet Office.

Quinton, D, Rushton, A, Dance, C and Mayes, D (1998) *Joining New families: A study of adoption and fostering in middle childhood*, Chichester: Wiley & Sons.

Rushton, R and Dance, C (2002) *Adoption Support Services for Families in Difficulty: A literature review and UK survey*, London: BAAF.

Rushton, R and Dance, C (in preparation) *Predictors of Outcome of Late Placed Adoption: A longitudinal study.*

71

Rushton, R and Dance, C (forthcoming) *The Outcomes of Late Placed Adoptions: The adolescent years.*

Sedlak, A J and Broadhurst, D D (1993) *Study of Adoption Assistance Impact and Outcomes,* Rockville MD: Westat, Inc.

Selwyn, J, Sturgess, W, Baxter, K and Quinton, D (in press) *The Costs and Outcomes of Non-Infant Adoptions.*

Thoburn, J, Norford, L and Rashid, S (2000) *Permanent Family Placement for Children of Minority Ethnic Origin*, London: Jessica Kingsley Publishers.

Thomas, C and Beckford, V with Lowe, N and Murch, M (1999) *Adopted Children Speaking*, London: BAAF.

Triseliotis, J, Shireman, J and Hundleby, M (1997) *Adoption: Theory, policy and practice*, London and New York: Cassell.

Veltman, M W M and Browne, K D (July, 2001) 'Three decades of child maltreatment research: implications for the school years', *Trauma, Violence & Abuse*, Vol. 2, No. 3, pp 215–239.

4 Consultancy to set up a service

Marion Hundleby

What support should be available for those whose lives have been affected by adoption? How can services best be organised? And by whom? These are just some of the challenges that will face the statutory sector as it responds to requirements enshrined in a new wave of adoption legislation, regulation and guidance. This chapter examines the different ways in which two local authorities used external consultancy to review and develop their adoption support services.

The local suthorities in question are both London boroughs and, for the purposes of this chapter, will be referred to as London West and London East. Their similarities are few. Whereas London West is characterised by prosperity, its counterpart, London East, has significant areas of poverty and deprivation. Here, social services struggle to meet the needs of a population heavily dependent on the public sector for education, health and social care. The authority has high levels of adoption activity, and an immediate concern was to develop services that would support London East children placed from the care system. It was also recognised that quality post-adoption services could aid recruitment if enquirers compared the merits of various boroughs. This could be an important consideration at a time when competition for appropriate placements is fierce and authorities are not only driven by the needs of children waiting for families but also by government targets and timescales.

London East

The brief from London East was to assist the authority with the design and specification of a post-adoption service which was customised to the needs of the borough. The Nottingham Catholic Children's Society was contracted to provide consultancy for this stage in the process and, as lead consultant, I worked with the authority to define a service which would then be put out to tender. It was a condition of the contract that the agency involved in the design and specification would not be eligible to provide the actual service. Working within a generous budget, it was necessary to define the parameters of a service which would include the needs of the many children placed outside the borough. It was also vitally important to acknowledge the diversity characteristic of this part of London and to ensure that issues of ethnicity, culture and religion were adequately addressed. Once a service specification was drawn up and expressions of interest invited, all potential providers were offered the opportunity to enter into preliminary discussion and meet with the contract manager of the authority, together with the consultant. It was agreed that feedback would be provided for the agencies regarding their potential suitability at a later date. The service specification was further informed by the views of family placement staff, and efforts were also made to engage service users in dialogue with the consultant, both by questionnaire and by phone. It was envisaged that those agencies that remained interested in providing the service would tender formally according to departmental protocol.

Before our involvement with London East began, the department had already given careful consideration to the extent of current and future need. However, it became obvious that the preliminary thinking had not fully taken into account the various parties to an adoption, or the whole range of service requests that a local authority might face. While it is commendable to ensure that agency placements are well supported, the population serviced by any statutory agency will include adoption-related situations in which the authority has played no part. Families with adopted children will move into the borough, as will adopted adults. The Adoption Standards for England (Department of Health, 2001) require certain services to be available to birth parents, and in some circumstances other family members too. Furthermore, adoption takes many forms: it can be by foster carers, by family members, and may involve children from overseas. Although the commissioning authority was first of all focusing on a particular type of adoption, the service design needed to be much broader than this if it was to be meaningful in the longer term.

A three-part service model

Following a period of approximately four weeks, which allowed for familiarisation with demographic and departmental data, consultation with senior managers and an assessment of the core services to which the authority needed to give priority, a three-part service model was devised. This accommodated the important issues of diversity and distance, as well as having the potential to expand to include all parties to adoption.

Level 1 was designed to be available to all and included a number of ways in which the department could retain a link with the children they had placed and with their adoptive families. Support of a more general nature would be provided through events and newsletters, and details of these would be mailed as well as posted on the borough's website. There was also the opportunity to translate the information for those who did not have English as a first language, and to link adopters with each other for support and advice.

Level 2 provided services which were case-specific and easily accessible; in other words, individual queries would be addressed by phone or email, and would often include information about other services and a degree of "brokerage" on behalf of families to ensure their needs were met.

Level 3 was reserved for those crisis situations where a speedy response and direct work were often essential. Obviously the boundaries between these levels were not rigid, but by devising such a framework, it was possible to begin to cost the service for the borough's own placements according to projected levels of usage.

In some ways Level 1 was the easiest to cost as the number of children placed could be aggregated over a given period of time and calculations based on largely predictable expenditure, such as postage, organising and providing training events and producing written information. Staff time is clearly the largest component of any projected costing of this type, and it was emphasised throughout that a quality service could only be achieved if administrative and social work staff with the necessary skills and experience were available to the users of the service. Levels 2 and 3 were more problematic to cost. We examined records of expenditure which might inform the calculation, as in the absence of a defined service, it had been necessary for the borough to "spot-purchase" packages of support for individual placements and also to subscribe to an agency specialising in post-adoption work. However, it was very difficult to gauge the possible increase in demand for costly services which might arise, either due to the increasing challenges posed by children placed, or because the availability of a new service increases new demands. We therefore agreed to cost on the basis of a 50 per cent take-up per annum for Level 2, and a ten per cent take-up per annum for Level 3. Given that the management information supplied by the provider on a regular and frequent basis would detail services requested and offered, an analysis of these data would, in due course, give the clearest indication of usage and, therefore, of cost. This would also be the only way in which the "hidden" demand for services would emerge, in other words, from people living in the borough but whose adoption arrangements had no previous link with London East.

In-house or contracted out?

Since this consultancy was first commissioned, there has been cause for London East to reflect further on the solution which best meets their needs. Initially, they were firmly committed to using an external provider, and felt they had progressed beyond any debate about the advantages and disadvantages of such a strategy. However, as is so often the case, financial constraints led to a review of basic principles, and for a while it seemed impossible for the authority to fund the service to which it had first aspired. At the time of writing, a final decision is awaited, and although the commitment to provide a service of excellence remains as strong as ever, the intervening months allowed time for further deliberation. Other options, such as partial contracting out and the type of "complementary contract approach" agreed between the Post-Adoption Centre in London and East Sussex Social Services (Burnell and Briggs, 1995), were considered. Of course, it is not unknown for the consultant's brief to change over time. Margerison makes this point when writing about the factors that influence failure and success in consultancy: 'Keep close to the client as you proceed, in case their definition of the requirement changes' (Margerison, 1988, p 89).

We welcomed the opportunity to remain involved and during this time undertook some additional tasks, such as writing a paper on the implications of the Adoption Standards for adoption support, as well as assisting the borough to think through alternative approaches to service provision. We could appreciate why contracting the service out was attractive, especially when difficulties in recruiting staff and heavy demands on family placement workers make it extremely difficult to envisage adequate provision being developed in-house. Yet contracting out brings challenges too. The commissioning authority has to satisfy itself not only that the quality of service will be of the required level, but also that sufficient management information will be available to monitor the work, comply with standards of service delivery and satisfy the rigours of "best value". There are resource implications for the commissioning authority, as statistical information and consumer feedback can only be effective if scrutinised by staff who allocate time to comprehend its significance and use it as a catalyst for improvement. Furthermore, for contracting out to work well, there needs to be a long-term financial commitment of some magnitude. In common with many major initiatives, it is the "start up" costs which are likely to be the heaviest as it is at this stage that systems have to be put into place and made operational. But the cost is not only financial; it reflects badly on the authority if users of its services are advised that a certain level of service is available, and then find that it has been reduced.

As well as the interface between managers and the service provider when an authority decides to contract out the post-adoption work, there is also another very important interface between practitioners. This operates at two levels. At a practice level there is the need for systems to have records of work on individual cases so that files can be kept up to date and any relevant aspects of the service, which may be retained in-house (e.g. letterbox and the payment of adoption allowances), appropriately co-ordinated with external provision. On a more general level is the whole question of how the "learning loop" can be most effectively deployed when areas of work, which offer most insight into outcome, are delivered by an external provider. In a recent UK survey of adoption support, the authors warn of a 'lost opportunity for staff to learn from experience' (Rushton and Dance, 2002). It will be said, and with justification, that the manner in which a service is organised should first and foremost be of benefit to those who use it. An accessible, responsive and high-quality adoption support service is for the benefit of users, not staff. Yet in order to be really effective, ways have to be found to inform the present and future with the lessons from the past. Arrangements to second staff to the service provider, or for the outside organisation to offer a training programme or mentoring opportunities for local authority social workers, are just some of the ways in which knowledge and experience can be shared. However, whether services are provided in-house or contracted out, the local authority continues to hold a raft of responsibilities and will incur significant cost.

London West

Whereas the consultancy commissioned by London East was essentially task-based, our involvement with London West was of a different kind. Here we were being consulted about how well the proposed structure would work rather than being asked to make decisions about the structure itself. This required the consultant to assist people in the organisation to think and talk through what needed to be done about a particular task and then leave it to the organisation to complete that task. This is usually referred to as process consultancy or facilitation (Association of Management Consultants and Trainers, 2000).

The request for our input arose through a Department of Health funded project entitled *Adoption: A quality option*. Central to the project was the opportunity for three local authorities to work with Catholic Children's Society Nottingham to explore ways in which this specialist voluntary agency could work in partnership with the statutory sector. We tested how such a relationship could be established and developed over an 18-month period, and then reported our findings to the Department of Health in accordance with the conditions of the funding. Each participating local authority was invited to specify areas of particular concern, and together we decided the ways in which our input could be of greatest value. London West immediately highlighted post-adoption work, and requested that we give consideration to how the specialist staff in family placement could work more closely with their colleagues in area offices, so that systems could be unified and owned across the department.

There was no plan in this authority to contract out the post-adoption work, although there was recognition at both manager and practitioner level of the need for an analysis of the current demand for services, and a projection of the likely rate at which this would increase. To spearhead the work, London West had appointed an experienced family placement worker, with substantial knowledge of the authority, to a newly created specialist post. Her brief included leading on key tasks such as group work, the writing of procedures and ascertaining users' views about the nature and organisation of services. While the level of placement activity was not as great in London West as in London East, the member of staff in question faced a daunting task.

As consultants, we found we were working with the opposite strategy to the one favoured by London East, but once again we were working with a service design which had inherent areas of vulnerability. While the "in-house approach" avoided some of the dilemmas associated with contracting out, it was immediately obvious that expecting one member of staff to take on developmental as well as operational responsibilities in such a rapidly expanding area would quickly become unworkable, even if there was some sharing of the task with colleagues. It was therefore important that the consultancy concentrated on ways to organise and rationalise the work, and this approach underpinned all of our involvement with London West.

The areas of priority were as follows: firstly, systems needed to be devised to assist London West to quantify and describe the requests they received for adoption support services. As matters stood, there was no discrete referral system for this type of enquiry. Instead, it just got added on to someone's caseload in a manner that was expedient at the time. While there may have been a good reason for this, for example, that the worker was already known to members of the family, staff quickly became overburdened and found they were struggling to fulfil mainstream duties. It was essential also from the management information perspective that work could be categorised and trends monitored so that the service needs of all parties could be considered. This was particularly important in the light of research with birth families, which draws attention to an apparent preference for a service independent of the placing authority (Charlton *et al*, 1998).

While the straightforward objective was the design and implementation of a referral form, this in itself highlighted practice variation within the department. It was realised that different systems were in place depending on the route a referral took, and in particular whether it came via the family placement section or an area team. This had implications not only for statistical accuracy, but also for cross-referencing pieces of work. Thus even a relatively simple exercise such as the referral form was quick to uncover a further, although very necessary, area of work.

The second main task for us, as consultants, was to enable the authority to undertake an audit of its current post-adoption work, and to make a projection of future need. The audit tool we designed specified areas of work in relation to each party, for example, birth parents or adopted adults. It was further broken down into tasks such as letterbox or direct work with adopted children. In conjunction with the consultant, staff then completed three columns for each element of the service: who managed and provided the service, whether it worked satisfactorily and if there were outstanding issues that needed to be addressed. Such a framework could be adapted to suit the needs of any local authority, and in the case of London West it was particularly helpful to include intercountry adoption as this was an area of work which was increasing rapidly.

Services to birth parents (sample audit page)

a) Letterbox:

Managed/provided by:	Does it work?	Issues to be addressed:
F. P. Team	Yes, but only because numbers are small. Is likely to become unmanageable in the medium to long term.	Procedures need to be finalised.
Usually the worker involved in the placement provides the ongoing service. Locality teams also have a crucial role due to their direct work with birth family members and the need to understand and "own" procedures together with the F. P. Team.		Procedures also need extending to consider, e.g. sibling exchanges, what happens when young person reaches 18 years, dealing with participants who do not contribute.
		A database is needed for administrative and statistical purposes. Consideration will need to be given to the cost of such a system to the Department.
		A leaflet about the scheme, devised with service users could be helpful to adopters, birth family members and social services staff.
		Review the structure and principles that govern the present system of letterbox exchange.

b) Contact post-placement/post-adoption

Managed/provided by:	Does it work?	Issues to be addressed:
F. P. Team	Only possible because as yet numbers are small. Places a heavy burden on staff. Even if they do not have to be present, they are likely to have to deal with issues and ensure contact is recorded. May need to be part of the review of arrangements.	This task needs to be reflected in people's caseloads. Should form part of procedure/practice guidance. Should be monitored, reviewed and costed and form part of routine management information. Criteria for decisions in respect of face-to-face contact requiring personal supervision by F.P. Team.

c) Contact generally – post adoption: adults

Managed/provided by:	Does it work?	Issues to be addressed:
F. P. Team	Birth parents of adults receive a satisfactory service, and are dealt with promptly.	The service needs to be "visible" both in terms of numbers of people coming forward, the procedures for under-taking the work, and the policy that governs it. This is especially important in respect of birth parent initiated contact. Identification and agreement re: use of other local services of post-adoption support or post-adoption service, e.g. the Post-Adoption Centre.

Once the audit exercise was completed it provided a position statement as well as a focus for discussion with senior management about the growth and direction of the service. It also highlighted the number and diversity of staff who need to have an understanding of the possible post-adoption dimension in their work: professionals working with adults, with drug users, in mental health, schools, hospitals and in disability teams are just some of those who may benefit from inclusion in training.

The third request London West made to the consultant was for assistance with the writing of procedures. The audit tool gave us a helpful starting point as it acknowledged where existing procedures were absent or deficient, and where priorities should lie. But as anyone who has written this kind of document will know, it is a long and painstaking task. Our work with the department was time limited, but nevertheless it proved possible to be involved in some of the drafting process. We were also able to advise in the light of the very detailed procedures which were operational in our own agency. These were made available to London West as part of the consultancy agreement.

Conclusion

By way of conclusion it is necessary to reflect on the role of the consultant. Is it of real value or is it an unnecessary expense? If it is positive, why is this? While it would be unwise to generalise, our experience of working with both London boroughs showed us the benefit of involving someone from outside the organisation when change and development are necessary. Hope (1992), in his book entitled *Making the Best Use of Consultants*, says that one of the main benefits of using consultants is that they create momentum for change and ensure change takes place. This is in no way a criticism of the staff, who in both authorities were very able and suitably experienced. Rather, it is about the overview and distance that someone from the outside brings. They are not part of the organisational politics, or of entrenched dynamics that can so often run counter to effective and supportive working relationships. In the case of post-adoption development, such distance and overview are essential. It is an area of work which involves service users of all ages and in a multiplicity of circumstances. To address their needs appropriately requires a mindset which is strong on long-term strategy, creative in the use of resources and with the capacity for lateral thinking. It is often far easier for someone from outside to establish inter and intra-departmental initiatives than it is for employees. For example, we were particularly impressed by the richness of the dialogue when specialist and area staff shared their perspectives and worked together to devise procedures and practice guidance.

Another important function for us was to empower those charged with various tasks, and if requested, act as a mentor and source of information. As a voluntary adoption agency, our routine work involves liaison with local authorities all over England and Wales. This gives us a vast amount of comparative experience and usually means that if we don't know something or do not provide a particular type of service ourselves, we know someone who does. Because a consultant can probably direct matters more quickly and effectively, the commissioning authority can be saved time and money. This in turn helps to offset the expenditure, which is so often given as the main reason for not appointing a consultant.

While it is too soon to consider outcome in relation to our work with London East, the contract has been significantly extended from the five days originally negotiated, and the total number of days is likely to be nearer 20. In contrast, our work with London West was completed over a year ago, although certain informal links between our agencies continue to thrive. It has to be remembered that successful consultancy depends on both parties: the commissioning organisation as well as the consultant. Hope (1992) emphasises the importance of the organisation being ready and able to use the consultant in a beneficial way. Not only does he make reference to the need to fund consultancy, but he stresses the need for agreement at management level to use a consultant, availability of staff time, allowing the consultant access to information, and a general willingness to be subjected to scrutiny and to introduce change.

Summary

This chapter considers the consultancy needs of two London boroughs in relation to the design and development of their post-adoption services.

The boroughs had different needs. For London East, the key issue was service provision, and in particular whether this should be contracted to an external provider. The consultancy offered the opportunity to consider the advantages and disadvantages of this strategy.

London West was committed to developing their services in-house. Here the consultancy role was more to do with defining and quantifying post-adoption activity, and ensuring that procedures were the same and were owned throughout the borough.

The chapter concludes with some reflections on the task of the consultant, and considers whether consultancy can be of value in situations where there is a requirement to develop post-adoption services. A comment from London West gives one view:

> *The format you used meant that we were able to break down the enormous task of developing a post-adoption service into bite size chunks identifying the particular needs of the service users and how these could be met. The fact that you were not only consultants, but also fieldworkers with adoption support experience, had a positive effect. Our work with you helped to raise the profile of post-adoption work in the department. Until then the work was taking place in the adoption team but was invisible and did not show in the stats. The workshops we organised with you encouraged inter-agency and inter-departmental work. We have identified post-adoption work in the children and families teams and have looked at how assessment formats could be used to include adoption support needs at the initial stages of referral.*
>
> *This has also helped to identify the "Children in Need" criteria and led on to clarifying who should provide this service. All in all, the work we undertook with you has provided us with the foundations to build and develop a comprehensive post-adoption service that reflects the needs of all the individuals involved.*

References

Association of Management Consultants and Trainers, *Getting the Most from Management Consultants*, Updated 4th December 2000; http://www.act-assn. dircon.co.uk/GettingtheBestfromManagementConsultants.htm, 25 August 2002.

Burnell, A and Briggs, A (1995) 'The next generation of post-placement and post-adoption services: a complementary approach', *Adoption & Fostering*, 19:3, pp 6–10.

Charlton, L, Kansara, K and Oliver, C (1998) *Still Screaming: Birth parents compulsorily separated from their children*, Manchester: After Adoption.

Department of Health, *National Adoption Standards for England* (2001) London: Department of Health.

Hope, P (1992) *Making the Best Use of Consultants*, Harlow: Longman.

Margerison, C (1988) *Managerial Consulting Skills*, Aldershot: Gower.

Rushton, A and Dance, C (2002) *Adoption Support Services for Families in Difficulty*, London: BAAF.

5 Understanding normality in adoptive family life: the role of peer group support

Kay Chamberlain and Jane Horne

We do not know of any other family who feels the same way as we do. Is it us?

Adoptive parent, 2001

Introduction

In the absence of any other frame of reference, adoptive families may inevitably compare themselves to other families they know, but is this a helpful comparison for them to be making and can peer support groups provide a more useful understanding of "normality" in adoptive family life? In Post Adoption LINK we believe it can and does, and that this in itself can alleviate areas of stress in families.

Post Adoption LINK is a regional post-adoption service funded by eight adoption agencies (seven local authorities and one voluntary agency). It opened in the Eastern Region in October 1999. Since then staff on the Helpdesk advice line have taken calls from a growing number of adoptive parents who express a sense of being abnormal as a family. Many feel that they are not coping as well as they thought they would as adoptive parents. They want information on how to cope better or they feel that their adoption placement is in danger of disrupting. The sense of failing, of being abnormal, was typified by one family who felt that they had run out of ideas, strength and willpower, 'We do not know of any other family who feels the same way as we do' they said. They questioned whether they were lacking in some way as parents, asking 'is it us?'

It is generally agreed that peer support has an inherent value. Being able to identify and share with others in a similar situation has been demonstrated as a helpful coping strategy. In Post Adoption LINK we see this in terms of reinforcing for adoptive children, and their families, that their adoptive family experience is normal but different from that of other families. Unless families know this, they can fall into the trap of measuring their success as a family against parenting and family life that is not necessarily relevant to their status and situation as an adoptive family (Hughes, 1997).

Adoptive parents' concerns

In contacting the Helpdesk, adoptive parents expressed a number of common concerns which reflected the experiences of other adoptive parents (Howe, 1995; Lowe *et al*, 1999):
- feeling isolated;
- needing to share experiences;
- the apparent inability of friends and family to understand;
- their children's behaviour, poor concentration and memory;
- attachment issues;
- identity and contact with birth family members – what to do; and
- information giving – telling the hard facts.

Adopters contacting the LINK Helpdesk who had chosen not to return to their placing agency for support gave similar reasons for not doing so:
- they "had told the agency" that "they could cope" and were now feeling a failure;
- problems with the agency at the time of the adoption;
- wanting to talk to someone outside of the placing agency;
- not knowing if the placing agency had a post-adoption service.

Peer support for adults and children

From its inception, LINK had planned to hold events for adopted children and young people (Horne and Trent, 1998). At that time no national organisation was specifically representing their views and concerns. Many of those adoptive parents who would later attend the adopters' meetings encouraged their children's attendance at the early events. Initially, in the absence of any plan for peer support for adopters, Helpdesk staff (a qualified social worker and an adoptive parent) endeavoured to offer a listening ear to adoptive parents and to give advice. If the issue was one where counselling appeared appropriate, LINK staff could apply for a small grant for sessions with a LINK counsellor who had been specially trained. This is a service that LINK has developed in the region and which is filling a very obvious gap. While improved access to counselling and the Helpdesk advice line are valuable services, the need for peer support for adoptive parents became clear.

"Normal" family life

Helpdesk staff increasingly found themselves trying to reassure adopters that what they were living through could be said to be "normal" in an adoptive placement. One afternoon, following another call in which an adopter asked if it was they who had "the problem", LINK staff, who are largely part-time, unusually found themselves together discussing the concept of "normality of adoption". It was not long before the idea was mooted to bring together the families telephoning the Helpdesk. In this way they would be able to share their experiences and thereby better understand this "normality". This would act as a starting point for addressing their concerns.

One of the advantages of being a relatively small organisation is the speed with which staff are able to be proactive. In the spirit of being a service-user-led project, we had, within two hours that afternoon, set the date for a meeting, chosen and booked a venue, and drafted an invitation.

The meetings

In a region the size of East Anglia the obvious difficulty for LINK was that we had received calls from adoptive parents living in six counties. The logistics of getting a group of people together in a location convenient to all would be a challenge. The decision was made to look at an area in which there was a grouping of adoptive parents and to book a venue that would feel special and would be near to main access routes. There are only three or four main highways in the region and a hotel at the intersection of two of these roads in Suffolk was selected. Invitations were sent out to adoptive parents who had contacted the Helpdesk from across East Anglia, and to all adoptive parents who live in Suffolk where the meeting was to take place.

It was agreed that the meeting should be held on a Saturday to enable working mothers and fathers to participate; that it should be an all-day event from 11am to 3pm to allow sufficient time for discussion; and that it should be led by a Helpdesk staff member, and the LINK Counselling Co-ordinator, herself an adoptive parent.

The meeting was designed to be semi-structured. It started with an introduction to LINK, its framework and services, followed by adoptive parents introducing themselves, saying who they were, where they came from, how many children were in their family and sharing something about what had brought them to the meeting. From experience we felt that if we used this time to allow people to talk about what was going on in their lives, those parents more reticent in group settings would be encouraged to share their concerns through listening to others. We anticipated that there would be adoptive parents attending who would talk openly about their feelings from the outset.

After a good lunch, provided by LINK, the leaders introduced a topic for discussion: attachment. At the end of the day an evaluation form was used to inform staff of the needs of the group. Postcards were also supplied and people were encouraged to exchange names and telephone numbers with others with whom they felt further contact would be useful.

This first meeting led to the next step in the LINK style of support meetings, again user-led. Sixteen adoptive parents attended the meeting from five counties. Between them they had 30 adopted children. One adoptive father said that he felt disappointed that his wife had not been able to attend, as she had needed to stay at home with their three adopted children and one birth child. Many parents were describing the same difficulties that he and his wife were experiencing and he felt sure his wife would have felt encouraged by their words, had she been here. In response, another adoptive mother whose child had attended a LINK children's event asked, 'Why can't the children go to an event on the same day that we come to our parents meeting, then both parents can attend'.

The children's events

Three different types of events for children were in the original plan for the scheme. We aimed to run, annually, two one-day events for eight to

12-year-olds; a one-day event for black children and young people aged ten plus, and a weekend event for young people aged 12 to 17.

The purpose of all the events is to bring adopted children and young people together to have the opportunity to share experiences, reduce feelings of being different, address feelings of isolation (and the potential for later depression) and to have fun!

The very first event for children aged eight to 12 took place in July 2000. Ten children attended, from all over the region. Since then there have been eight events held throughout the region with 150 places taken up in total by children aged four to 15.

Barnardo's Black Emphasis scheme (Gittens and Tappin, 2000) was contracted in to organise the days for black young people. Two events involving a total of eleven black children and young people have taken place, one in August 2000 and one in September 2001. The days were co-ordinated by black social workers, and ATRAP (The Association for Transracially Adopted People) led a workshop on the first day. Black adopted children place the same value on meeting each other as do their white peers but, in addition, meeting as black children enables them to talk through the problems they encounter in establishing their sense of self both as black children and as adopted children in the face of racism and of ambivalence about adoption.

LINK staff have co-ordinated and led all other events, which have been held quarterly, on a Saturday from 10am to 4pm, in different parts of the region. They are supported by two young helpers who are themselves adopted and who have been involved throughout. We are also fortunate in being supported by a range of other volunteers including people attending the adopted adults support meetings and prospective approved adopters.

Adopted adults have been keen to offer their time to support their younger peers; they say that they would have welcomed such an opportunity when they were children. Prospective adopters have provided valuable help and it has given them hands-on experience with adopted children of different ages, as well as insight into some of their difficulties.

The age range of children attending these events has extended to include children as young as four who normally come with older adopted siblings. The needs of children born to the adoptive parents have recently come to the fore and, following a small workshop at an event held for all family members, we will be looking at how to develop peer support for this group of children and young people.

The popularity of groups for all adopted children has meant that we have yet to hold an event specifically for the older age group, but this remains an aim. The days follow the now established pattern of small group workshops in the morning, lunch, an afternoon walk and a further workshop or entertainment to end the day. All the children receive a certificate of attendance and a party bag. Workshops provide opportunities for play and skill development and have covered crafts, magic, balloon tying, juggling, trampolining, and drama. One of our local theatres has been very helpful in offering drama workshops.

Bringing any group of children together presents management issues; adult to child ratios are normally one to three. The children's parents complete consent forms for attendance, which give us basic facts about each child, but invariably we have no detailed information and have to be prepared to support individual children who may be nervous about attending or present challenging behaviour. In the main, children have responded enthusiastically to being together, rating the days as nine or ten out of ten on their feedback sheets. What we do on the days appears less significant than the chance to meet and make friends with other adopted children.

Linking the events for children and adoptive parents

The idea of running an event for children and a meeting for adopters on the same day in itself created some logistical problems. We decided that the two groups needed to be in close proximity but not in the same building. We wanted to maintain the separateness of the children's event in order to protect the notion that they would be more able to talk freely about their adoptive status if they did not feel they had to edit what they said to one another out of loyalty to, or concern about, their adoptive parents. In addition, the adopters needed their own space without fear of interruption. Venues in close proximity would provide a safeguard for the children's group leader and helpers in case of difficulties. The fact that the children's event started an hour earlier than the adopters' meeting and ended an hour later, would enable the parents to deliver and collect their children. It would also mean that parents could attend the entertainment and certificate ceremony with their children, providing an upbeat end to everyone's day.

The first joint events were held in Norfolk. There was good attendance from five counties including parents whose children were unable to join the children's group. Since then, there have been a further five joint children's and adopters' events in Hertfordshire, Huntingdon, Suffolk, Essex and Norfolk. Children's activities have been held in village halls, schools and countryside centres. Adopters' meetings have taken place in hotels, church halls, a village hall and in a religious retreat.

Changes made

The adopters' meetings have generally maintained the same format as devised for the original meeting but with two important changes. Adoptive parents are now asked on the booking form whether there are any topics they would like to discuss at the meeting. Leaders can then prepare any literature that they may need to take with them. The afternoon session now covers concerns raised on the booking form and during the morning. This can sometimes mean group leaders have to "think on their feet" but when they do not have the information or answers, they usually know "a person who does", and are happy to send out information on any areas they are not able to cover.

In May 2002 we included a "Talking Adoption" workshop at one of the children's events. The workshop was advertised and parents were asked to discuss the children's participation with them before the day of the meeting. Eleven children aged nine to 14 took part. A second workshop was held in June with six children attending. Plans are being made for further sessions.

This workshop is designed to give the children a better chance to talk in a semi-structured group about anything that concerns them. Most of the children and young people who have opted to take part have come to know one another over the months. However those children who had not attended an event with their peers previously do not appear to have been held back in sharing their views in the workshops.

At the end of each session the children and young people taking part agreed on points they felt strongly about, and wanted to share anonymously with adoptive parents and with "anyone else who wanted to know". This means of creating a dialogue between children and their adoptive parents had come from an idea used by After Adoption Manchester who operate a mail box for children at their events to write and post anonymous messages about their problems, as well as any questions they may want to ask their adoptive parents which they have not asked before. These are then shared at an adopters' meeting.

Adopted children

The issues raised by the children have included:
* the desire to have a better understanding about what had gone wrong in their families of origin: 'Why could they not look after me?'. For some, the reasons they had been given seemed simplistic.
* a wish to have information about their life histories written for the age they are now;
* a need to have up-to-date photographs of family members so that they would know them if they saw them on the street;
* the need to feel able to acknowledge and be open about their adoptive status without fear of bullying at school or what they perceived might be the "disapproval" of their adoptive parents.

It will come as no surprise that, as they enter adolescence, adopted children become more acutely aware of the "biological link of the generations" (Blum, 1976) and their desire for a more sophisticated understanding of their histories is understandable.

The need for up-to-date photographs came from both a natural curiosity, and to ease what appeared to be the burden of constantly wondering if new people they met were related to them. The same issue has been raised in the adopted adults' meetings.

Many of the adopted adults attending meetings have admitted to feeling angry; most have verbalised their self-doubt and a basic lack of confidence. Most of the children and young people have said they often feel angry but do not know why. Some children and adults have expressed strong punitive feelings towards their birth mothers in particular. The need to understand how any parent could agree to adoption, or get into a situation where their child was adopted, has been shared by adopted children and adults at their respective meetings. Whatever the quality of their relationship with their adoptive parents, the fact of being adopted was felt by many of the children and adults alike to mean that they, as vulnerable infants and children, did not inspire nurturing from their birth parents however much they understood the disadvantage of their parents' situation at the time.

In adoption work we talk about cover stories and maintaining confidentiality for children moving into adoption placements. We need to look at whether this approach, designed to aid and protect a child from unwanted intrusive questions, gives children the message we intend. Considering the issues raised by children attending our workshops, we will be asking ourselves, and adoptive parents, to explore with children how this approach is interpreted by the children themselves. We will be looking at how we acknowledge the child's status given that this goes to the heart of their sense of self.

Adoptive parents

During their meetings, adoptive parents have been clear about what would be helpful to them and many families make similar comments.

- They need respite care "to keep the placement going" but do not want to place their child "back into care to obtain respite".
- They need more information on the child's background, including access to letters written by workers for children to read as they grow up, sometimes referred to as later-life letters.
- They need support to work with contact agreements/orders as their children grow older.
- They want access to therapists who have a good grounding in adoption.
- They need help to have a better understanding of attachment patterns and to know what they as parents can do.
- They feel worn out with no time to recuperate after the "onslaught" of the placement.

The adoptive parents expressed a need for respite but shared their hesitancy in asking for help in getting a break. The fact that some agencies apparently could not accommodate children without technically receiving them into care, reinforced the anxiety many held that agencies would respond by taking over and ultimately excluding them as parents. Some agencies are addressing this problem. Schemes for respite for parents of children who have a disability are well established and ought to provide a model for other respite services.

Many people in the group felt they had insufficient information about their children's history with which to work. However, they commonly did not feel able to request additional detail. Some queried their entitlement to information. At the time of placement, an adoptive parent's concerns are manifold and most are unlikely to appreciate the gaps when trying to take on board all the different information they are being given. Agencies might usefully be pro-active after adoption by going back to the basic information and supplementing it at a time when families can better focus on what they have and do not have.

The adoptive parents largely felt excluded from the decisions about contact with birth family members and did not appreciate, at the outset of the placement, the impact contact would have on day-to-day family life. They felt that more detailed preparation was needed at the point of "working up" a contact agreement with them as the adoptive parents. For many, contact represented an aspect of their child's life which was out of their control and they felt frustrated by a system of review that they saw as too inflexible to accommodate their child's changing needs and wishes. It would be helpful for agencies to give more attention to contact plans in the early stages of discussing a prospective placement with adoptive parents. Plans for contact are often made before the adoptive parents come onto the scene and it should be self-evident that they need to buy into the plan consciously and wholeheartedly if they are to make it work. When considering an adoption placement, prospective adopters are likely to be preoccupied with deciding whether they can parent the child or children and, unless agencies emphasise continuity and contact as a significant factor throughout adoption, new parents could, at this stage, see it as a side issue compared with the enormous task of actually looking after the children day to day.

Several adoptive parents had sought and obtained therapeutic help. Most said that they had experienced the therapist as having little or no appreciation of the adoption factor. They felt the therapist's frame of reference applied more to "mainstream" families. Work had been done with the child, but the adopters felt they needed input so that they could also work with their children. Developing their understanding of the theory behind attachment patterns was a first aim, but the group, like many other adoptive parents, want support in applying the theory, together with opportunities to discuss the process and outcomes of their "work" as parents with the child (Archer, 1999).

Most of the adoptive parents in the meetings have adopted older children in sibling groups. They are managing multi-layered attachment and behavioural problems with more than one child and feel burnt out. Their dilemma is that, while they want to air and address their feelings in order to carry on, they fear prompting an unhelpful pathologising response from agencies. Regrettably, some feel this is the response they have already experienced. Adoptive parents need reassurance during their preparation and training, that any problems they face after adoption are predictable, and not associated with their competence as parents. Everyone involved in making adoption placements could helpfully review the messages given consciously, and more subtly, about what adoption will mean for children and adults. If we regard adoption as a solution, without addressing the pain the main protagonists bring to it, and the lifelong implications of dealing with the losses they have sustained, then we are in danger of setting up children and families to feel as if they are failing when they compare themselves to other "normal" families.

Conclusion

We all accept that people who have similar skills, vocations and interests, regularly come together as part of everyday life. Being part of a group or community of people who share our values, and our chosen lifestyles reinforces our sense of ourselves and what is normal, reasonable and right for us in our lives. Most people find this sense of communion with others within the family and friendship networks they have grown up with, as well as within the groups they join as they develop their belief systems and settle into their adult lives.

Family lifestyles develop in any society within a framework of some basic shared sense of what is expected and acceptable within family life, in other words, what is normal. The wider groups to which individuals belong, be it extended family, community, religious or political groups, daily reinforce that sense of normality. Human beings gravitate towards feeling part of a group who share similar experiences. In Western society people are encouraged to seek a sense of themselves as individuals, but they nevertheless also search for the security of feeling part of a group in order to feel accepted and to enjoy the mutual support the group offers.

Adoptive parents, and their children, are in danger of gravitating towards a potentially erroneous measurement of their success as a family from a desire to be the same as others; to return their lives to some sense of what they perceive to be normal, having been derailed by the pain of infertility (Brinch, 1990) and of rejection, real or perceived (Fahlberg, 1994). People cannot be blamed for seeing adoption as a way of getting "back on track", but it is a different road to parenting and family life for all concerned (Horne, 1999). The adoption road has elements in common with the road travelled by other families, but there are essential and key differences, which, if put aside or denied, can lead at best to dissatisfaction in relationships and at worst to placement disruption.

Providing opportunities for adoptive family members to explore their sense of normality with mutually supportive peer groups is offering reassurance to parents and their children that they are not alone, and that their experiences are within a normal framework as an adoptive family. Some adoptive parents have travelled great distances to attend the support meetings and take their children along to their own events. Many adopters feel that they have long ago used up the goodwill of local babysitters. Most say they would not be able to attend if there was not a children's event on the same day. Sometimes it is the simplest of ideas that lead on to significant service developments. Holding the events for children and adults on the same day may have been born out of practical need to enable each group to enjoy the benefits of being with their peers, but the developing linkage between the two events is now leading to a new and potentially liberating dialogue between adopted children and their adoptive parents and to a reframing of their sense of normality in family life.

References

Archer, C (1999) *First steps in parenting: Tiddlers and toddlers*, London: Jessica Kingsley Publishers.

Archer, C (1999) *Next steps in parenting: Tykes and teens*, as above.

Blum, L H (1976) 'Adoption and identity factors', in Brodzinsky, D M and Schechter M D (eds) *Psychology of Adoption*, New York: Oxford University Press.

Brinch, P (1990) 'Adoption inside out', in Brodzinsky D M and Schechter M D (eds) *Psychology of Adoption*, New York: Oxford University Press.

Fahlberg, V (1994) *A Child's Journey Through Placement*, London: BAAF.

Gittens, J and Tappin, E (2000) *Black Emphasis – Ten years on*, Unpublished report, Colchester: Barnado's (unpublished).

Horne, J (1999) 'The road to placement', in *Making Good Assessments*, Appendix IIIc, pp 142–48, London: BAAF.

Horne, J and Trent, J (1998) *Post Adoption in the Eastern Counties*, Unpublished report, Colchester: Barnardo's.

Howe, D (1995) 'Adoption and attachment', *Adoption & Fostering*, 19:4.

Hughes, D A (1997) *Facilitating Developmental Attachment*, New Jersey: Jason Aronson Inc.

Lowe, N, Murch, M, Berkowski, M, Weaver, A, Beckford, V and Thomas, C (1999) *Supporting Adoption: Reframing the approach*, London: BAAF.

6 The Nottingham Drop In: providing mutual support for birth mothers

Jenny Jackson

Support After Adoption, the Nottinghamshire post-adoption team, was set up in 1991 by Nottinghamshire County Council Social Services to provide a range of services to all parties connected with adoption who have a link with the county. Since 1998 a service level agreement has operated between the county and the new unitary authority in Nottingham City, whereby the team also continues to provide post-adoption services for that authority.

From the outset, approximately one-quarter of all annual referrals have come from birth parents (predominantly birth mothers). They have mainly received a service on an individual basis via our Phoneline and, where appropriate, through time-limited allocation to a named worker. A self-help group of relinquishing birth mothers, linked to the Natural Parents Network, has also existed locally for some time and provides a valuable additional service. However, this group generally perceives its needs and experiences as very different from those of more contemporary birth mothers whose children have been compulsorily removed and then placed for adoption from the care system. The Support After Adoption team shared this view and was therefore committed to establishing an alternative group for these particular service users.

Group work obviously offers a small team like ours, with a very heavy demand for services, a way of meeting the needs of more people more quickly. However, we strongly believed that a group would also provide particular benefits to birth mothers whose children had been in care. These women tend to be among the most socially marginalised and disadvantaged of our service users by most indices. Many have a significant level of learning disability and mental health difficulties. They also feel acutely the public stigma of having had their children permanently removed by the actions of welfare agencies and an adversarial judicial system. We hoped that such birth mothers would find meeting with others who had had similar experiences both therapeutic and empowering. We also wanted to ensure that these women's hitherto largely hidden voices would be heard within the department so that they could inform future practice and service delivery.

We considered offering a service to birth fathers as well as mothers, but quickly decided to limit ourselves to the latter. This in no way reflects our estimation of the impact of compulsory adoption on birth fathers compared to birth mothers. However, the number of non-consenting birth mothers known to the team, and therefore potentially service users, far outweighs the number of birth fathers. We also know that many of these birth mothers are survivors of sexual abuse and domestic violence and we felt that this would deter them from joining a mixed group. A final consideration was our belief that a mixed group would need a male as well as a female facilitator, something we could not provide at that time.

We discussed various options and liaised with colleagues in post-adoption services in Manchester and Leeds who had run groups for birth parents. We also learned from the experiences of the 1993–96 Parents Without Children project in the North East (Charlton *et al*, 1998).

One thing we were clear about from the beginning was that our service would be jointly delivered by a social worker and a volunteer. Since its inception, Support After Adoption has sought to involve in its work people who have themselves received a service from the team, and one such volunteer had already indicated her interest in the group work project. Having a volunteer as co-worker meant that the service benefited from the personal adoption experience of the individual concerned, which included an awareness of the issues many birth mothers face in relation to social workers and adoption agencies.

We opted for an informal time-limited group where participants could attend any or all of the meetings and where the content was mainly directed by the needs of the women themselves rather than planned by the facilitators. Our experience – like that of most other post-adoption services – is that this group of service users is particularly difficult to engage and we believed therefore that a formal group work agenda would be hard to sustain. Even more importantly, we felt that imposing a pre-planned agenda did not fit with the aims and values we were formulating for this service, which were to provide a warm welcome and a listening ear, a chance to talk about their child and what their adoption has meant for them and an opportunity to meet other birth mothers who have had similar experiences. The values which informed our work were broadly those of good social work practice, namely respect, empathy, empowerment, acceptance and validation.

In keeping with our choice of an informal group driven by the needs of participants rather than a pre-planned agenda, we also made a deliberate decision to keep boundaries and rules to a minimum. We were clear that language, which was offensive in terms of race or different abilities, would need to be challenged and that physical aggression would not be acceptable, but beyond this we did not formulate any rules for the group in advance and we did not find in practice they were needed.

Much effort went into finding an appropriate venue. Ideally, we were looking for a welcoming, comfortable city-centre location; we also felt it must not have associations with the social services department. In central Nottingham we were lucky to find a Women's Centre which had the additional advantage of a crèche and of being a women-only space.

Our work within Support After Adoption has highlighted the particular significance of endings for parties to adoption, so we aimed to provide a time-limited service with a clear ending built in. This also allowed for proper evaluation of the group and informed decision-making about whether and how it should re-convene.

The service was publicised by sending a flyer to every birth mother living in the Nottingham conurbation who was already known to Support After Adoption. Some had previously received counselling or other support from the team; many were known as a party to the Letterbox Scheme, which the team manages on behalf of the two local authorities. Further flyers and a covering letter were also sent to childcare, family centre, mental health and learning disability managers in social services and to relevant health professionals and voluntary organisations.

The Drop In, as we named the project, was launched with a cycle of six fortnightly meetings between January and March 1998. It has continued to thrive and we have offered seven similar series of meetings since then, usually at the beginning of the year and then again in the autumn. Approximately 15 birth mothers have attended in total – several have come very regularly, others more intermittently as circumstances and needs dictate.

All the women who have attended thus far have been white. We are aware of some of the factors underlying this. For example, both black birth mothers and black children have historically been under-represented in adoption in relation to the size of the black population in both the city and the county of Nottingham. While the numbers of black children in the looked after population has risen in recent years, with a corresponding rise in the number for whom adoption is the plan, the majority of these are children of dual heritage, with a white mother and a black father.

The women's adoption stories vary – some had children removed at birth or as babies, others parented for several years; the ages of their adopted children range from very young to over 18. The overwhelming majority has had no post-adoption order contact and we wonder whether the existence of a working letterbox reduces the need to make use of a service such as the Drop In. Only two birth mothers who have attended during the seven cycles of meetings run over the last four years have been party to a letterbox and of these, the only repeat attendee has been a birth mother whose letterbox was suspended following loss of contact with the adoptive parents. A couple of the birth mothers have had indirect contact initiated by their children's adoptive parents in recent years as the children have reached their mid-teens; this contact was facilitated either by Support After Adoption or by the adopters' own agency where this is different. One of these birth mothers has gone on, over the course of her membership of the group, to have a reunion initiated by her 17- and 19-year-old daughters and their adoptive parents that, two years later, is continuing successfully. Our perception is that this event has been accepted by the other women in the group in a surprisingly matter-of-fact way. Our impression is that those women with an unswerving belief that their adopted child will one day come looking for them view this birth mother's experience as confirmation of their expectation, while those who believe that adoption means they will never see their child again seem to view her experience as a unique event with no relevance to their own lives. What is unquestionable, though, is the absence of envy and the genuine pleasure the other women have expressed for this particular birth mother.

The women's current circumstances are as varied as their adoption stories. Some have or have had new partners, others are alone; some have had no further children while of those who have, some are managing to parent them while others have experienced the compulsory removal of a child more than once. Several of the women have physical disabilities such as epilepsy, many have learning difficulties and others have, or have had, involvement with mental health services. Often these characteristics are combined: the latter two seem particularly prominent.

What the women talk about and how they feel

The themes which come up time and again during the Drop In sessions can be grouped into three main categories.

Thoughts about their adopted child

- "Holding the child in mind" – all the women who attend have many and frequent thoughts about their child which are powerfully expressed and often accompanied by strong emotions such as tears and anger.
- Great anxiety about whether their child will know that they were born to another family – it is very important for the women to believe this but often very difficult, especially for those whose child was removed at birth or in infancy.
- Equally, there is great anxiety about what information will have been given to the child about their birth mother and whether it is accurate and anything other than unfailingly negative.
- There is also much worry that the child will believe their birth mother wanted them to be removed: our birth mothers have found it helpful to devise messages for their children, either in the form of an actual letter which we arrange to have placed on the adoption records or as a therapeutic tool we can use within the group. Jane has considerable learning and literacy difficulties typical of many of the birth mothers we have met. Her message to her daughter was also typical of the key messages most want to get across:

   Dear Christine, I still think about you. I still love you. I worry you might think I gave you away but it wasn't like that at all. I didn't want it to happen.

Feelings about the adoption process and professionals involved

- Powerlessness – this was a universal experience and also often seems to echo other aspects of these women's lives, past and present.
- Confused or patchy memories about events and dates, emotional trauma often being overlaid by physical disability and the effects of medication: Susan, who has severe epilepsy which, at the time of her daughter's birth in the mid-1980s was poorly controlled, says:

  It's terrible not having my own memories . . . I've read the adoption records but they're not my own memories . . . For me it's like I missed out on the memory of my daughter. If one day she comes to see me and asks 'What happened? Why was I adopted?' what can I tell her? I'm going to lose out again unless she can understand.

- Anger towards social workers who represent for them all the agencies involved in decisions leading to their child's removal.
- In particular there is strong resentment about "being told what to do" by workers who have no personal experience of parenting.
- Language – most said they had constantly struggled to understand what was being talked about. They asked: 'Why can't they [all parties, not just social workers] use plain English?'
- The adversarial nature of care proceedings are seen as focusing almost totally on weaknesses and failings, rarely acknowledging effort and achievement nor the strength of the birth mother's feelings for her child.

Reflections on their life post adoption

- The difficulties and risks of identifying yourself as a woman whose child has been compulsorily removed and is now adopted.
- The recurrent grief on universal anniversaries such as religious festivals and Mother's Day as well as individually significant triggers such as birthdays, family celebrations and dates of key events. Jean says: 'It's like a ball and chain dragging behind you all your life', which prompted others in the group to liken their situation to 'a life sentence with no parole and no remission'.
- Doubts about their entitlement to mark special occasions and, if so, in what form.

- Lack of informed understanding and support from people around them.
- A deep yearning for information, ideally ongoing, about the child.
- Fantasies about accidents – even death – befalling the child unbeknown to the birth mother; anger and disbelief at the realisation that they have no legal entitlement to be informed if the child should die. The unanimous view of our groups is:

  We as mothers have played the biggest part in bringing this child into the world by giving birth to it – how dare they tell us we have no right to know if they die before we do?

- Beliefs about reunion – there seemed to be an entirely random division between those who hold an absolute conviction that their child will search for them in adulthood and those who hold an equally strong and despairing belief that they will never see their child again.

What the birth mothers need

What then do these birth mothers need and what does a group offer them? First and foremost they need a chance to tell their story, sometimes over and over. In this respect the Drop In format works particularly well as the process of welcoming newcomers and introductions to existing members provides a natural opportunity for telling and retelling their story. The next most important need, in our experience, is to have their feelings and the impact of these acknowledged and validated – this applies particularly to the feelings of grief, loss and pain which are sometimes all pervading and always lifelong.

Other important needs which seem to us to be uniquely met through a group are the reduction of stigmatisation which comes from the concrete realisation that they are not alone in their experience of losing children to adoption through the care system; the opportunity to learn from other birth mothers who are at a different point in their adoption lifecycle and the chance to offer and have accepted expressions of caring towards others. Some of the things which we have seen our birth mothers learn from each other are coping strategies, confirmation that it *is* possible to feel the loss less acutely and less damagingly with the passage of time, and that moving on in your life does not equate with having fewer and less strong feelings for your adopted child.

On many occasions within the group, we have witnessed women accepting each other's expressions of anger and distress and offering each other physical and verbal comfort. The impact on them of being valued is often tangible: we know that most of these women have had little experience of being nurtured themselves and, of course, the nurturing they offered their adopted child was often deemed to be inadequate or, at best, scantily acknowledged amidst the public parading of their parenting failures. Their very different experience within the group can be powerfully therapeutic in itself.

The women's enduring relationship to their child as the biological mother and their continuing positive regard for their child is affirmed by the Drop In. It also enables women to work collectively on constructing a continuing role for themselves as a mother who holds their child in mind even though they are not parenting it.

Finally, the Drop In allows us to provide birth mothers, whose children were adopted some years ago, with the quality and quantity of non-identifying information about the child's adoption which current best practice allows. Where the child's adoption records are held by the city or county authorities for whom we provide post-adoption services, and if the birth mother has not already received this information by way of an individual service from our team, I will access the records and prepare a written summary to be shared with and kept by her. Where another agency holds the adoption records, I will liaise with them and generally we have agreed that they will prepare the written information and then forward it to me for sharing with the birth mother. When a series of meetings is in progress, birth mothers are offered the choice of receiving the information during one of the group meetings and in the presence of other women attending (which has been the choice of all so far) or of meeting me and my volunteer co-worker on their own. If the Drop In is between meeting cycles, we arrange a one-off session for the birth mother or mothers concerned.

All birth mothers who attend the Drop In are offered advice about how to leave a letter or other up-to-date details about themselves on their child's adoption records if they wish, and when necessary we have helped women write such letters. We do not usually offer any further help in terms of contact: birth mothers who raise this issue are given a clear explanation of what we can and cannot do and the reasoning behind this, but our focus is always on acknowledging the women's feelings and giving them as much time as they need, over as long a period as they need, to voice these feelings and to talk about the impact on their life of having no contact.

Outcomes

We have to acknowledge that it is not easy to provide concrete evidence of the benefits birth mothers gain from the group. We have tried in each cycle to encourage participants to give us feedback in a variety of forms, for example, through questionnaires, pictorial evaluations or numerical scales. But low literacy levels, learning and mental health difficulties mean it is a struggle for many to do this. Denise, one of our more articulate members, was able to tell us:

> I come along without being entirely certain why. I just feel I want to and that I find the meetings valuable . . . I know that adoption is something that is part of my life and that I have to deal with it. The group gives me space and time to think and talk about adoption rather than just pushing it away from me, although it isn't always easy to find the words for my feelings.

Barbara acknowledged that she has considerable problems controlling her temper but told us she felt a lot calmer after coming to the Drop In and that she and her partner were pleased because this meant she 'didn't beat him up so often'. Several of the women who have attended have said that they have made friends and feel they are with people who really care about them – again an experience which we speculate is a rare one for most of them.

We suggest that the best evidence we have for the importance birth mothers attach to the Drop In lies in attendance levels, especially the number of regular attenders during or across cycles of meetings, and in the often considerable lengths many women go to in order to attend. For example, one woman walks several miles from her home into the city centre while another makes great efforts to reorganise her shift work. There is also the importance the women attach to having Support After

Adoption's commitment to continuing the Drop In regularly reaffirmed. Finally, we have the evidence of direct observation by my co-worker and myself: over time we have seen a considerable improvement in the listening skills of many participants and consequently there has been less need to limit inappropriate interruptions and ensure turn-taking and adequate attention for all. We have seen improvements in self-esteem as shown, among other things, by several women starting or persevering with education, training and job opportunities which they had previously struggled to pursue.

Improved self-esteem and confidence have also been evidenced by the way some of the birth mothers – again very much taking encouragement from each other – have written poems, made cards or started journals and collections of mementoes which they hope one day to have the opportunity to share with their adopted children. Jean is a birth mother who finds reading and writing very difficult but she was able to devise acrostic poems for each of her adopted daughters which her present husband wrote down for her and which she eagerly brought to the group for us to read out. Jean is very proud of being part of the Drop In and feels it is extremely important for social workers and other people involved in adoption to hear what she and the other birth mothers have to say. She is therefore happy to be identified in the following poem which she wrote after she had been attending meetings for two years:

J is for Justice right or wrong
E is for Each memory that's strong
A is for Absent not from thought
N is for Now help I sought
B is for Beauty each child seeks
R is for Radiance which lasts for weeks
A is for Ambitious if we train
D is for Delight if we use our brain
L is for Love I have to give
E is for Each as they live
Y is for Yourself what you do

What works well

Finally, in terms of service delivery the following works well in our experience:

- An open group – this allows women to join the Drop In at any point in a meeting cycle and can accommodate differing attendance and participation patterns, times when women want to focus on their adoption experience and times when they want to talk about something completely unrelated.

- An unstructured format – this offers obvious advantages in relation to the amount of worker time needed for the project and, obviously, fits closely with the aim of providing birth mothers with time and space to use as they themselves choose. This has not precluded our occasionally suggesting particular exercises or topics to focus on.

- Having, in most cases, no previous knowledge of the women or of their history with social services does not, in our experience, hamper us either in terms of engaging them or in gaining their confidence, and may actually help these processes.

- Minimal recording (usually only of names of those attending and themes which emerge during sessions) likewise does not impede either engagement or establishing trust. It also keeps the amount of worker time needed for the project within manageable boundaries.

- A women-only group and the Women's Centre as a venue both combine to offer a safe space – a high proportion of the birth mothers known to Support After Adoption have unsatisfactory experiences of relationships with men and have survived domestic violence and/or sexual abuse as children and/or as adults.

- Support After Adoption's deliberate positioning of itself as somewhat "at arm's length" from mainstream social services helps reduce the reluctance many might otherwise feel at re-engaging with social workers, especially workers from the agency that also took the lead in removing their children and eventually placing them in an adoptive family. The fact that our service users only engage with the team voluntarily and mainly through self rather than third party referrals is also helpful.

- The combination of a social worker and a volunteer with personal adoption experience offers a broad range of skills, adoption awareness, knowledge and personal attributes for service users to draw on.

• Lastly, outreach is a crucial factor in the success we have had in engaging birth mothers in the Drop In (and this certainly mirrors the experience of the Parents Without Children project). Resources are strained within Support After Adoption and in the early days of the Drop In project constraints on social worker time and availability meant that it was not possible to offer much in the way of outreach. However, the volunteer involved for the last two years has been keen to give her own home telephone number on the Drop In flyer and to provide a listening ear to any birth mother who rings her. She has done invaluable work in engaging several women and in giving them the confidence and reassurance to actually come along to the meetings. She also provides much-needed support and befriending when the group is between meeting cycles. In turn, I provide support to the volunteer and also a sounding board for her to reflect on the boundaries she needs to maintain around her involvement.

At Support After Adoption we are committed to continuing the Nottingham Drop In. For some time now we have offered a similar service in Mansfield and we have recently piloted a series of "one-off" meetings in more distant areas of the county. The Nottingham birth mothers are keen to make their voices heard more widely and we are exploring a number of ideas ranging from a self-produced booklet to the longer-term goal of making a video.

Reference

Charlton, L, Kansara, K and Oliver, C (1998) *Still Screaming: Birth parents compulsorily separated from their children*, Manchester: After Adoption.

7 Youth work with adopted children and young people

Stephen Eccles

The West Midlands Post Adoption Service (WMPAS) was established in 1994 and went on to become a registered charity in 1996. WMPAS provides a range of post-adoption services to anyone involved in adoption. It is a user-led organisation that takes its starting point from the needs of people with personal experience of adoption, and is currently run on a part-time basis: the office and phone lines are open for three days a week. The work of WMPAS is funded through subscription by ten West Midlands social services departments as well as through grants from various local and national trusts and charities. All project work depends on fundraising.

A high percentage of the work WMPAS undertakes is with adults in the adoption triad. Advice, guidance and counselling are offered within a supportive, confidential environment to adopted adults and birth relatives who wish to begin the process of searching, contacting and reuniting with family members. There is the option of using WMPAS workers as intermediaries in this process.

WMPAS also had a brief from the beginning to support both children and parents in adoptive families. This work consisted of much listening to, and supporting of adoptive parents, both over the telephone and face to face. Parents needed to be reassured that they were not the only adoptive parents experiencing difficulties and that their children's attachment problems were rooted in earlier experiences. Adopters also needed periods of positive respite away from their children.

The WMPAS worker found that services for adoptive families demanded a far broader, more holistic approach than she was then able to offer. This thinking was backed by Beverley Hughes (1995) who commented that:

In relation to adoption, the over-riding aim of post-placement services must be to contribute to the maintenance of a successful and happy adoption, first to the child and second for the whole family. The primary task must be to provide adequate services and resources to enable adoptive families to negotiate such challenges successfully, while doing so in ways which do not pathologise the adoptive family and label adoption as another form of professional therapy for difficult children. (p 3)

After a period of exploration, it became obvious that more specific provision was needed for adopted children and young people.

Youth work

In autumn 2000, staff at WMPAS contacted the Birmingham University Department of Community Youth and Playwork. After some discussion with course tutors about the role of a youth worker and the curriculum covered in their training, the decision was made that a youth worker was required to complement the work of the Adoption Family Support Worker. A youth worker would have the skills and knowledge base to work with individuals and groups, have a good grasp of what it means to ensure equality of opportunity and, most importantly, have the ability to communicate and relate to young people.

It was seen as an advantage that a youth worker would move the provision away from the social work arena. Many adopted children and young people have had a heavy involvement with social work departments, over a number of years, and do not always view those services positively.

So what is youth work? If we look at a definition for the overall purpose of youth work, which was agreed at the Second Ministerial Conference on the Youth Service in 1990 (National Youth Agency, 1991), we can see that it offers a broad overarching statement of youth work aims:

The purpose of youth work is: to redress all forms of inequality and to ensure equality of opportunity for all young people to fulfil their potential as empowered individuals and members of groups and communities; and to support young people during the transition to adulthood. (p 16)

Within the National Youth Agency Statement of Values and Principles, the nature and purpose of youth work are described as:

> ... *to facilitate and support young people's growth through dependence to independence, by encouraging their personal and social development and enabling them to have a voice, influence and place in their communities and society.* (National Youth Agency, 2000, p 1)

From this statement the following aims for the youth service as a whole were developed:

1. Youth work should offer young people opportunities that are:
   - educative;
   - designed to promote equality of opportunity;
   - participative; and
   - empowering.

2. Youth work is based on the following elements:
   - It is voluntary in its participation.
   - It can take place in many settings.
   - It has a heavy dependence on the strength of relationship between worker and young person, so that conversation is a main tool.

To highlight the importance of conversation as a part of informal education, Jeffs and Smith (1996) conclude at the end of their chapter "Trusting in Conversation" that:

> *These elements make conversation a powerful focus for educators. Conversation in this sense is not simply a method that we may use; it embodies a number of emotions and virtues we may seek to foster. Through conversation we express concern by spending time with others; we show we are interested in them as well as in what they have to say. We also display trust and respect, we value the other person.* (p 23)

3. Youth work uses experiential learning and reflection (Kolb, 1984). Reflection means that we can all learn through recalling particular events from memories, highlighting the salient points within those events and connecting with the feelings we experienced at that time. We can then evaluate those experiences objectively in the light of our

present aims and knowledge. Any new knowledge can be slotted into our conceptual framework.
4. Youth work uses informal education as a method of working. Informal education is an accepted and established form of education mainly based on the work of Josephine Macalister Brew (1946) who wrote the first text in English.

An important aspect of informal education is that participants should have a "say" in the content of their learning, or the element of "negotiated learning". Some theorists suggest that negotiability be applied to both content and method (Jeffs and Smith, 1990).

Once the decision to employ a youth worker was taken, funding for the post was sought and found through "Children in Need". A job description and person specification were drawn up. The key tasks required were:

- to develop and be the lead provider of direct work with adopted children and young people;
- to work alongside the Adoption Support Worker to establish services to adopted children and young people;
- to work with adopted children and young people on a one-to-one basis dealing with issues of identity, separation and loss and the impact of early childhood trauma; and
- to develop activities on a sessional or weekend/holiday basis when groups of adopted children or young people can work together to build self-esteem and confidence.

Adopted children and young people

What are the specific needs of adopted children and young people? How do they differ, if at all, from mainstream children and young people?

The Ministerial statement on the purpose of youth work, referred to above, declares that 'the purpose of youth work is to address all forms of inequality'.

One of the largest groups of young people today, who are acknowledged as facing inequalities, are those young people who are "at risk" – risk of being excluded from society. The situations that put them at risk of being excluded, such as homelessness, lack of education and crime, have been brought to our notice through the work of the Government's involvement in the Social Exclusion Unit (SEU).

As a result, much of today's youth work has led to the development of a number of models designed to identify and engage with young people who are deemed to be "at risk" of being excluded from education or work, and are exhibiting what has been defined as "risk behaviour" such as:

- truancy and exclusion from the education system;
- drugs misuse;
- risky sexual behaviour;
- emotional/mental health problems leading to depression, self-harm and suicide; and
- involvement in crime.

It is generally understood and accepted that these "risk behaviours" are best addressed by supporting personal and social development. This can be achieved through:

- encouraging self-esteem;
- motivating young people to take responsibility for their own lives and effect change;
- developing a positive life view; and
- improving social skills to enable them to achieve their goals.

If you were to ask an average youth worker to offer a profile of a "young person at risk" they would probably come up with someone living in a deprived inner-city area, having been brought up in a broken home on a below average income, with perhaps a history of generations of unemployment and social support. Possibly some family members would have a criminal record.

Very rarely would they suggest that an adopted young person could be at risk. Yet the caseload of the WMPAS support worker has shown that a significant number of families have teenagers who have been adopted and are exhibiting the very "risk behaviours" described above, as they struggle to make the transition from childhood to adulthood while coping with painful and confused memories of their early years. They may also be living with identity problems while trying to integrate their family of upbringing with their birth family.

At present the Government and society like to view adoption as a solution for children who might otherwise be "at risk". But it could be argued on the basis of work on attachment by Bowlby (1971) and work on identity by Erikson (1968) that adopted children and young people by their very definition are "at risk".

'So what?' you may say. Well, difficulties develop when structural forces begin to impinge on adoptive families seeking support from existing services.

Once adopted children and young people start to exhibit these "at-risk" behaviours and because they often do not fit the generally accepted profile of a young person "at risk", the adoptive parents may be labelled as having poor parenting skills. This leaves them feeling isolated, unsupported and having to battle for help, while their adopted children will often charm strangers and outsiders at a very superficial level.

This ability of adopted young people to "get along" with others and be "charming" can also work in a positive way. It has allowed the Youth Worker to get to know and engage with the young people very quickly, far more so than would be the case in a mainstream youth club. The down side of this, of course, is that the relationship will only develop so far, and that when in-depth work begins, the barriers will go up. Many adopted children find it easy to make friends, but very difficult to keep those friends and deepen friendships to a significant level. We have found that friendships and allegiances change very quickly within the groups, even during a one-day session together.

Many parents who approach WMPAS for help are greatly relieved to know that they are not the only adoptive families who are struggling. They are shocked and amazed that no one else has informed them of Reactive Attachment Disorder (RAD). Often, after hearing about the recognised symptoms of RAD, they will say, 'Have you met my son/ daughter?' WMPAS workers have received much anecdotal evidence of how adoptive parents have felt let down, unsupported and misunderstood by education, health and social services departments which do not seem to appreciate why and how their children's behaviour can be symptomatic of their early life experiences and subsequent adoption. Instead they seem to lay the blame at the parents' feet. As a result many of the parents who contact WMPAS are at the end of their tether, with the placement on the verge of disruption.

Children who were adopted at a younger age, even those living in a quite "open" adoptive family with birth family contact, can suddenly be confronted with feelings of loss and grief. This can happen when their cognitive development is sufficient to process the fact that to gain an adoptive family, they have had to lose a birth family.

One adopted teenager told me, 'I don't know why I can't see my mother, my real mother I mean, I just don't understand'.

In some cases, many of the young people's early life experiences will have taught them massive distrust of adults and others. This was demonstrated quite graphically when a young person admitted to the worker, in a conversation about sharing problems in order that they may be resolved, '. . . I don't trust anybody, and never will do. I keep all my problems to myself.' This young person had been living in an adoptive family for some years.

For the adopted young person, adolescence can be a "double whammy" as they battle to gain adult status (and the independence and responsibility this brings) while, at the same time, on a conscious or subconscious level, they are still dealing with unresolved attachment problems.

The youth worker's role

The WMPAS Youth Worker is well placed to state very clearly that he or she is there to work solely for the children and young people's benefit. It is hoped that this explicit commitment can provide a solid foundation and an overall strategy for WMPAS on which all future work with adopted children and young people can be based.

A confidentiality statement and child protection safeguards have been drawn up in order to construct clear boundaries for WMPAS workers and, more importantly, as a method of assuring the children and young people that youth workers would not necessarily have to disclose everything that was talked about, to either adoptive parents or social workers; but that they would inform the young person if they were disclosing something that they were unable to keep confidential.

The role of the Youth Worker within the organisation has been clarified in order to support and complement existing work. Aims, objectives and responsibilities have been set down and developed into a mission statement. This mission statement can be used as a foundation for various elements of the work to be built on, as a rudder to ensure the project keeps to the original aims and objectives, as a benchmark to measure the success of the project over time, and as a tool for describing the purpose of the work to others.

The overall aim of direct work with adopted children and young people for this project was *to provide appropriate, safe environments where adopted children and young people felt able to explore their thoughts, feelings and experiences of adoption with each other and their workers.*

Parents often approach WMPAS with all the anxieties and concerns surrounding their children's behaviour, while the children's own perceptions may be quite different. As a result they may not see the need to modify their behaviour, or to engage in any "adoption work". Although it may require a good deal of time and effort, it is important to enable children and young people to tell their stories and to raise their levels of self-awareness in order to induce in them a "motivation for change". This will only come about in environments and relationships where they feel safe and able to trust. But it is also important to remember that all young people are unique and are at different levels of development and stages of their lives, and that their needs must therefore be individually assessed and addressed.

The project

An advantage and disadvantage for the project is that, to the best of WMPAS's knowledge, there is no other scheme of this type in existence. Although this has meant that there was no "specialist model" of work to follow closely, and no real guide to use for the early stages, it has also meant that interest in the project was generated very quickly because of the real need for such a service.

It was decided that as WMPAS already had a database of adoptive families, the project would target these families and initiate personal contact with the parents, children and young people. It was essential to consult with them as to the form of support and assistance that would best meet their needs:

- A personal letter of introduction from the Youth Worker described the aims and objectives of the new role and the services that would be developed. Comments were invited.
- The letter also offered the opportunity to meet the worker, either in their home or by appointment at the WMPAS offices.
- The aims and objectives of the new worker's role, as well as the project's mission and confidentiality statements, were written up as flyers and leaflets.
- Local facilities and youth centres were identified and budgets were projected on the basis of the number of potential and existing clients.

Once information on the project had been disseminated and interest in it had been expressed, the next step was to plan and organise an initial event. Careful consideration had to be given to the type of activity chosen, in order to offer equality of opportunity and to meet the needs of a wide age range.

The first event, in the spring of 2001, brought together a number of adopted children and young people to take part in a fun activity, to meet each other and, of course, to meet the new WMPAS Youth Worker. The activity chosen was a morning of "team-building exercises" in a local outdoor centre, followed by an afternoon at WMPAS for some direct work on the many issues that surround adoption.

From this initial event the project was developed into a monthly youth club session to:

- provide an arena in which the worker and young people could start building relationships;
- provide a place where adopted children and young people would feel able to voice their feelings and share their experiences, and where they are accepted, listened to and valued;
- provide group work that will be planned in advance, set within boundaries of mutually agreed "group ground rules" based on trust, confidentiality, respect and equality;
- develop strategies that use informal education processes and techniques to help children and young people to use their own

experiences and those of others in order to explore issues of identity, separation and loss and the impact of childhood adoption trauma;
- follow an agreed curriculum and develop a programme of task-centred or issue based sessions with specific aims and objectives, both for younger children, and young people (teenagers);
- encourage children and young people to put forward their ideas and interests, which will then be used to form the basis of some of the group work, such as art, crafts, sports and drama; and
- include games, exercises, activities and discussions to make sessions fun and to use different learning styles.

It became necessary for the WMPAS worker to develop a personal strategy for working with children and young people on a one-to-one basis by establishing the boundaries in which the relationship was to take place. Confidentiality and the aims and expectations of the relationship, such as "mentor", "counsellor" or "role model", had to be clarified.

The advantage of this work seems to be the independent nature of the youth worker but there are several disadvantages:
- the dependency on the specialist skills and understanding of the worker;
- the inefficiency of working on a one-to-one basis;
- the geographical spread of children/young people may lead to the running of two to three groups in different areas, using the same structure;
- the danger of assuming that the work could be a "magic cure-all". Can we expect any youth work undertaken with adopted children and young people to deal with the range of problems surrounding the whole spectrum of attachment disorders that may be manifested? Adopted children and young people may need more specialist therapies before traditional youth work models can prove successful;
- the difficulty in ensuring the work is meeting the needs of the children and young people – and not just the wishes of the parents or social workers. A huge factor in any youth work is making sure that the aims and objectives and the work undertaken do actually meet the needs of the service users.

Opportunities

- There is an opportunity to work with parents as well as children, whereas in more mainstream youth work the emphasis is totally on the children and young people, with youth workers having little or no contact with parents.
- Youth work skills, experience and knowledge of the Youth Service and other organisations can be used to develop a network of resources and agencies that are able to support, assist and enhance this new area of work.

WMPAS summer camp 2002

The camp took place during the week of Saturday 27 July to Saturday 3 August, and was held at the Ranch Outdoor Discovery Centre in Snowdonia, Wales.

The cost was £365.50 per head and was covered by contributions from parents, the Children's Fund and grants raised through trusts and charities. Subsidies were available for young people who would have been excluded from the camp for financial reasons only.

The camp had three specific main aims:

1. to enable a number of adopted young people to enjoy an active, adventurous outdoor residential experience in a safe and secure environment where it is openly acknowledged that all participants have been adopted;
2. social education through sharing new experiences and challenges in a reflective and supportive setting, to encourage personal growth and an increase in self-esteem and confidence through specifically designed group work exercises and games; and
3. to provide a positive form of respite care for a number of adopted young people and their families.

The Ranch offered full-board accommodation and provided the instruction and shared supervision for 20 different activities:

- high ropes
- kayaking
- hill & valley walk
- waterfall and nature trail
- crafts
- visit to slate caverns

- archery
- orienteering
- rock climbing
- abseiling
- gorge walking
- games night
- circus skills

- mini sports competition
- team krypton factor challenge
- woodland survival
- falconry display
- camp fire on beach
- day out
- video night

The camp was staffed by six WMPAS workers:
- Two were WMPAS staff members (the WMPAS Children and Young People's Worker and the Service Co-ordinator who is also a counsellor).
- Two were sessional youth workers (a black woman and a white man).
- Two were volunteers (teachers with experience of outdoor education). All workers and volunteers on the camp were police checked. The WMPAS Family Worker came for the last two days to be available for adoptive parents arriving to collect their children.

Twenty-one young people attended the camp. Their ages ranged from ten to 15. There were ten boys and eleven girls:
- 1 boy aged 11
- 2 boys aged 12
- 2 boys aged 13
- 2 boys aged 14
- 3 boys aged 15

- 2 girls aged 10
- 2 girls aged 11
- 2 girls aged 12
- 3 girls aged 13
- 2 girls aged 14

Particular efforts were made to recruit black leaders, as we anticipated many of the young people would be black or of dual heritage. However, we were largely dependent upon our subscribing agencies for promoting the camp to adoptive families. All children who applied were given a place but only two children of dual heritage were among them; all the other children were white/European. The young people came from throughout the West Midlands; two young men were referred through The Children's Society adoption service.

The subject of ethnicity did come up during the week, when one of the older boys made a racist comment. This was challenged and addressed by the worker at the time and discussed within the larger group later in the day.

At the end of the week some of the children were being collected from a local community centre in Birmingham and racist remarks were made by some of the parents because a large number of black people were attending a function at the centre. This has highlighted the fact that we should not make assumptions about the attitudes of adoptive parents, and that we may be working with children and young people from families where racist attitudes are the "norm".

Although, during the planning stage, it was anticipated that there might be difficulties due to the eight-day length of the event and the wide age range of the young people, it can be said that, overall, the camp was a success on many levels.

- During the period of the camp there were no real crises, injuries or organisational disasters.
- A full week of respite was enjoyed by a number of adoptive families.
- Many in-depth conversations took place between workers and young people around the topic of adoption.
- Twenty-one adopted young people were able to feel part of a group where, for once, adoption was what they had in common and not something that set them apart.
- Relationships between WMPAS workers and the young people improved.
- The workers benefited from a greater understanding and integration of theory and practice.
- New friendships were made, and existing friendships between adopted young people were re-enforced, ensuring a vital form of peer support.
- Many of the young people were able to try new activities and stretch their own boundaries by overcoming certain personal fears and apprehensions. The workers saw previously shy and introverted young people come out of their shells, while in a new and different environment, and become more confident and assertive.

The camp has certainly proved a useful tool in bringing together all the young people who attended and forming them into a core group on which the WMPAS children and young people's project can build in the future.

Unfortunately, due to a number of reasons, the planned daily group work sessions were more difficult to hold than anticipated. The large size of the group, the wide age range, the practical difficulties of finding the most suitable time in the day to fit in with other activities, and the tiredness of both workers and young people, all militated against running support groups. Even so, the importance of having been in a "safe" environment where all the young people were adopted should not be underestimated. One young person said, 'It was great to spend time and get to know other adopted young people like me'.

Although the staff team was thoroughly exhausted, we all felt that the camp had been a very worthwhile undertaking. The young people appreciated the time and energy given to them: 'I think everyone had a brilliant week. When can we go again?' (from a young person's report of the camp)

The WMPAS Service Co-ordinator and the Family Support Worker have given some of their own impressions:

When I arrived, I noticed that the young people were very emotional and dramatic in the way they interacted with each other and with the adults around them.

The following morning the children and young people were leaving. There were huge waves of emotion around. Most, if not all, were in tears. Small groups of three or four were hugging or embracing. They appeared to find it hard to "let go".

Some youngsters were totally distraught at leaving friends they had only met a week earlier. Is this some indication of how each loss compounds previous losses?

During a walk with three girls, one of them asked me how old I was. She seemed surprised when I told her and commented, 'Gosh, you can run quite fast can't you?' (given my great age!). The conversation between the girls then went on something like this:
'My Mum can't run that fast.'
'How old is your Mum?'
'Do you mean my first Mum?'
'No, your adopted Mum.'

'She's about 50 I think, but my other Mum is younger – how old is your first Mum?'

This conversation developed quite naturally into talking about why the first girl's Mum could not look after her, with total acceptance by the other two girls. While I listened I thought, 'I can't imagine this happening in the school playground.'

Since the end of the camp the WMPAS office has received a number of thank-you letters and phone-calls both from young people and parents saying how much they enjoyed the camp and the respite time respectively. One parent reported that their daughter had happily informed them that the camp had been "the best week of her life". Many parents said that although they did have concerns about sending their children to the camp, they now felt that it had been a positive experience for them. One parent said that she was more confident in her child attending the WMPAS summer camp than other kinds of camp, as she felt the workers would understand and be better equipped to deal with her child's background and difficult behaviour.

In future years, WMPAS will organise two summer camps for different age groups: 10–14 and 14–18 with a maximum of 14 young people and a minimum of six workers/volunteers in each group. Also the camps will be for only five days midweek, as a whole week away was deemed to be too long. It is envisaged that these changes will foster a more focused group atmosphere, prevent over-tiredness and allow young people and youth workers to concentrate on adoption issues.

Targets and ideas

We have identified some priorities for the future:
• to find and train more sessional youth workers who are sympathetic to the needs of adopted young people;
• to develop a successful model for working with adopted young people alongside their families, such as residential weekends for "lads and dads" and "mums and daughters";
• to develop an adopted adult/adopted child and young person mentoring scheme;

- to organising family days;
- to develop an adoption website offering support, advice and information run by adopted young people for adopted young people;
- to establish a WMPAS users' forum in order to evaluate the work; and
- to develop an advocacy/support/advice/information scheme for adopted young people who wish to contact birth parents.

Conclusion

The project must continue to balance the logistical problems of being accountable to so many families over such a wide area, with its role in meeting the very many and varied needs of adopted children and young people. Should the project remain essentially a "youth work" project? Or should it aim in a more therapeutic direction?

Although these questions have yet to be answered, the youth club sessions and the summer camp have so far fulfilled the main aim of the project: to provide appropriate, safe environments where adopted children and young people can feel able to explore their thoughts, feelings and experiences of adoption with each other and workers.

If this important aim can continue to be met, the time and resources committed to the project will have been justified, and any other outcomes will be a bonus.

References

Bowlby, J (1971) *Attachment and Loss, Volume 1: Attachment*, Harmondsworth: Penguin.

Erikson, E (1968) *Identity: Youth and crisis*, London: Faber & Faber.

Hughes, B (1995) 'Post-placement Services of Children and Families', Department of Health, Social Services Inspectorate.

Jeffs, T and Smith, M K (1990) *Using Informal Education as an Alternative to Casework, Teaching and Control*. Milton Keynes: Open University Press.

Jeffs,T and Smith, M K (1996) *Informal Education, Conversation, Democracy and Learning*, Ticknal: Education Now.

Kolb, D A and Allen, D (1984) *Experiential Learning: Experience as the source of learning and development*, London: Prentice Hall.

Macalister Brew, J (1946) *Informal Education, Adventures and Reflections*, London: Faber & Faber.

National Youth Agency (1991) *Towards a Core Curriculum – The next step: report of the Second Ministerial Conference*, NYA: Leicester.

National Youth Agency (2000) *Ethical Conduct on Youth Week – A statement of values and principles*, NYA: Leicester.

8 "Am I alone in this grief?"
User support for transracially adopted and fostered people

Perlita Harris

> *. . . the loss of my birth mother through adoption has meant the loss of my birthright; of a way of life within the Indian community; of a rich and beautiful culture; of knowledge of my maternal history and ancestry; and of my ability to speak my mother-tongue with birth maternal and paternal relatives . . .* (Shobha, 2000)

> *I feel like my feelings haven't really been recognised . . . for example, I think losing, you know, your birth family, your parents, and your country and culture, and community and everything, and people don't think it's very relevant because you've never known it, and so I don't think people think you have a right to actually grieve any of that.*
> (Lyn, intercountry adopted adult, South East Asian)

> *I can't be alone in thinking that being transracially adopted, we have lost something: lost our languages, traditions, cultures, and most importantly the subtleties and nuances of those cultures. We have lost something we never had which we may not have even valued had we had it and, yet, we continue to mourn. Am I alone in this grief?*
> (Anderson, 2000)

Introduction

Adoption and long-term fostering of black children by white families has been known in the UK for over 40 years, and yet the voices of transracially adopted and long-term fostered adults are rarely heard or listened to. Indeed, very little is known about the adoption support service needs of this diverse, heterogeneous and hitherto silenced group. This chapter focuses on the Association for Transracially Adopted and Fostered People (ATRAP), a black user-led and user-controlled organisation, and the experiences of its members. I begin by briefly examining the context within which the practice of transracial adoption has arisen and continues to flourish. I then focus on the reasons members give for joining ATRAP, and the difference that being a member of ATRAP has made to their lives. Finally, as the opportunity for transracially adopted and fostered people to voice their experiences and concerns is extremely important, I highlight some common themes and issues that arise in conversations between ATRAP members.[1]

Setting the context

Although there are no figures available on the number of children who have been adopted transracially in the UK (either domestically or from another country), we know that there is a direct correlation between social factors and the increase in domestic transracial adoption. With the decline in white babies available for adoption from the late1960s onwards (from 14,000 in 1968 to 1,400 in 1988) (Prevatt-Goldstein and Spencer, 2000), transracial adoption became an established practice. Prior to this black children, including children with one black parent, were generally considered "unadoptable" or "hard to place", although a small number of black children were adopted by white families in the 1950s and early 1960s. Intercountry adoption in the UK has a different history. Although it is only recently that government figures have started to distinguish between intercountry and domestic adoption in the UK, we can reasonably assume that intercountry adoption began in the late 1950s/early 1960s (Kinsara, 2002a). This adoption of children from the poor countries of the developing world to the rich countries of the developed world is an extension of global inequality that has its roots in colonialism (Kinsara, 2002b).

Despite the politicisation of adoption and "race", and in line with the more recent backlash against same-race placements epitomised in the Department of Health circular LAC (98)20, *Achieving the Right Balance*, the practice of transracial adoption has continued. In a national survey

---

[1]The quotations are from an ATRAP focus group held on 8 May 2002, and an ATRAP Committee Meeting discussion on 25 May 2002 attended by Committee and other members, unless otherwise indicated.

with a response rate of less than 50 per cent, BAAF (Dance, 1997) found that, overall, 17 per cent of minority ethnic adoptions were transracial (reaching 50 per cent in shire counties). A Social Services Inspectorate report (1997), using a smaller sample, found a higher rate with 53 per cent of children adopted transracially. With an absence of recruitment strategies to ensure a sufficient supply of black adoptive families (Social Services Inspectorate, 2000), and the current emphasis in government policy on increasing the percentage of "looked after" children who are placed for adoption, the practice of transracial adoption is likely to continue, perhaps at even greater rates than in recent years.

There is a dearth of literature concerning the experiences of transracially adopted children and adults in the UK. Research by Gill and Jackson found that transracially adopted children 'saw themselves as "white" in all but skin colour' (Gill and Jackson, 1983, p 130), and Kirton (2000), in his pilot study involving interviews with ten transracially adopted adults (some of them ATRAP members) found these adults had 'an uneasy . . . relationship with "whiteness" and an equally ambivalent one with "community of origin", characterised by a powerful gravitational pull but also by distance and discomfort' (p 90). The black adopted adults felt basically unsupported regarding racism, and had protected their parents from learning about their experiences of racism. The Children's Society study of search and reunion (Howe and Feast, 2000) found that transracially adopted adults are more likely to feel different from their adoptive families, but also less likely to feel "at home" with their birth relatives than their white counterparts. It has also been found that many children adopted from other countries display symptoms of Post Traumatic Stress Disorder (Hoksbergen and van Dijkum, 2001). Furthermore, not all placements that last are successful when other outcome measures such as satisfaction or "racial" and cultural pride are taken into account (Moffat and Thoburn, 2001).

Personal accounts by transracially adopted adults in Britain and in other countries, and the body of creative writing that has emerged from intercountry adopted adults and other transracially adopted adults provide further insight into the day-to-day experiences of those black people brought up by white families. Together they bring out the common themes of difference, belonging, loss, gratitude, loyalty, racism, racial abuse, childhood depression, adult mental distress, loss of birth relatives, culture and language; visiting countries of origin, and search and reunion with birth relatives.

Current service provision

The paucity of adoption support services for those who have been transracially adopted, both children and adults, including intercountry adopted adults, is of great concern. In 1988, the Post Adoption Centre in London was the first agency in the UK to provide a service specifically for transracially adopted adults. This took the form of a series of groups with two black facilitators (Dagoo, undated; Sheckleton, 1990). More recently, in 2001, After Adoption (Manchester) started a monthly group for transracially adopted adults. Following a study of the views of service users of the West Midlands Post Adoption Service (Harris, 2002), this agency is establishing a similar group, having made an earlier unsuccessful attempt in the mid-1990s. It is an indictment of the lack of importance attached to the needs of transracially adopted people that there is not one comprehensive adoption support system tailored to meeting the needs of this group of children and adults.

Many ATRAP members have had no previous contact with any post-adoption services, and are unaware of their statutory rights, and the services that do exist. Some of those who have had contact with other services, report difficulties including:

- long waiting lists for accessing adoption records, birth records counselling and counselling services;
- finding a counsellor or therapist, particularly a black therapist, skilled and knowledgeable about transracial adoption, search and reunion; and
- lack of information and guidance about searching for birth relatives who may live in other countries.

What is ATRAP?

ATRAP is run by and for transracially adopted and fostered people. ATRAP seeks to centralise the views and experiences of transracially adopted and long-term fostered people, and values user experience as a basis for essential knowledge. ATRAP believes that members can take action to benefit themselves, learn from each other, explore and analyse their experiences, and identify action and strategies to bring about change to improve the quality of their own lives. Established in 1993, ATRAP evolved out of the series of groups held at the Post Adoption Centre for transracially adopted adults. Over the past nine years ATRAP has grown steadily, becoming a registered charity in 1996, being relaunched in 2000, and in 2001 securing (minimal) three-year core funding from the Department of Health. Although London based, regional groups and networks of ATRAP members have developed in Leeds, Brighton and Bristol.

The primary aim of ATRAP is to provide peer support in order to reduce the isolation that transracially adopted and fostered adults feel. ATRAP aims to create a safe place for members to meet and talk (in person, in the newsletter and online), as well as social and educational opportunities to empower members. ATRAP seeks to provide a welcoming, supportive and non-judgemental space for all transracially adopted and long-term fostered people irrespective of (1) their views about transracial adoption and fostering, intercountry adoption, search and reunion, and (2) their sex, class and whether they are mental health service users, psychiatric system survivors, disabled, lesbian, gay, bisexual or have experience of the criminal justice system. Creating a safe environment where all members will be accepted and valued by each other has not been without difficulties, but reflects a commitment to challenging discrimination and oppression.

ATRAP membership is open to people who have been adopted transracially both domestically and from another country, to those who have been "looked after" in long-term transracial foster care, or have been privately fostered. The Bristol ATRAP group (LAFTA) is also open to those who have grown up in all-white residential children's homes. The ATRAP membership reflects the diversity of transracially adopted and fostered people, including those whose placements disrupted, and those who were abused or neglected by their adoptive or foster families. Members range in age from late teens to mid-40s, and include people who have grown up in both rural and urban areas. Associate membership is available for interested professionals, family members by birth, foster care or adoption, local authorities, and voluntary sector agencies.

Services provided by ATRAP for transracially adopted and fostered adults:

- ATRAP social events:
  - to meet other transracially adopted and fostered people;
  - to give and receive peer support;
  - to share and value experiences;
  - to socialise and share food.
- ATRAP workshops and informal discussion groups with guest speakers and trainers;
- the ATRAP website (www.atrap.org.uk) including a discussion forum;
- an ATRAP email list;
- the quarterly ATRAP Newsletter of articles, poems and letters by members;
- support with establishing regional ATRAP groups;
- advice and information on legal rights, counselling, post-adoption and post-care services available;
- volunteering opportunities;
- linking members who share a common experience, parentage, or live in the same geographical area;
- an informal friendship and support network.

In addition, ATRAP has produced a video, *Love is Not Enough: Experiences in transracial adoption*.[2] We also undertake training and public speaking, and work with the media upon request.

Why do people join ATRAP?

People join ATRAP for a variety of reasons. One of the main reasons cited is to reduce isolation through meeting someone else who has been adopted or fostered transracially. ATRAP gives them the opportunity to talk about their experiences without fear of being ridiculed, silenced, judged, dismissed, disbelieved or pathologised. Although some members have had contact with other transracially adopted and fostered adults in

---

[2] *Love is Not Enough* is available from Infactuation Productions on 020 7503 0500 or email: infactuation@btinternet.com. A percentage of all sales go to ATRAP.

their childhood, including siblings, they say they were never enabled to talk about the experience itself, or to question the practices of intercountry and transracial adoption. Many members report negative reactions when they attempt to speak about their feelings with adoptive and foster family members, friends or acquaintances:

... I've told most friends that I go to ATRAP, and they, they really can't understand why, and I think they find it quite hard to understand that there is actually racism ... I just think it's really hard for them to understand ... you've got all these OK things in your life, so why should you be feeling down, depressed, can't make sense of your life? So it's ... it's something that they've got no sort of conception of ... Then you end up feeling that you're just making a mountain out of a molehill. (Lyn, intercountry adopted adult, South East Asian)

The only person that fully understands the experience is the person that's going through it. Everyone else has a different position from which they look into and upon that experience, and should your description ... not match with what they see ... then you'll get that reaction; that kind of hush, or that kind of, you know, ridicule, or you'll just be told to shut up, you know, what are you talking about, that's just ridiculous, that didn't happen, that couldn't have happened, it's obviously your problem. (Abayomi, transracially fostered, Nigerian)

Others have spoken about feeling alone in their experience, or wanting to know what other black people feel about being raised by a white family:

I suppose I was hoping it might offer support in a way, that I felt like I was the only person that felt the way I did. I suppose reduce that feeling of being alone ... (Lyn, intercountry adopted adult, South East Asian)

I originally became a member of ATRAP because I was interested in hearing the opinions of other people who had similar experiences to myself, and I was desperate for a space to express what I felt about my experience without fear of suddenly feeling completely out of place or like an alien, or like I am from, you know, like I was suddenly on a different planet ... (Abayomi, transracially fostered, Nigerian)

The process of talking about these experiences is made more complex by the multiple losses, pain, guilt, shame, self-hatred, confusion, gratitude, loyalty, and fear that so many members speak of:

> *I sometimes have a feeling of indescribable sadness of losing my country, culture and family and wish I had the courage to shed this burden of feeling grateful. I want to express these feelings without fearing that people would reproach me for such contradictions and disloyalty since I don't deny having had a wonderful family, happiness and more.* (Mylien, 2000)

Why is ATRAP needed?

The experience of meeting another transracially adopted or fostered person is profound and powerful; for some exciting, for others overwhelming, and ultimately, the experience can be healing. For many, it leads to the realisation that they are not the only one, the "alien" they had previously considered themselves to be. Meeting others normalises the experience of transracial adoption and fostering, with the potential to transform feelings about the self:

> *[It's] that initial realisation you're not the only one that's been through this strange circumstance.* (Imogen, transracially adopted adult, unknown parentage)

> *I finally realised, after half a lifetime, that I was not ET, and my feelings about myself had been a normal reaction to the abnormal events I had experienced.* (ATRAP website)

Some ATRAP members describe how meeting others has made a positive difference to how they feel about themselves and their ability to heal. This in turn has enabled them to feel more optimistic about the future:

> *It confirms your identity. When you've had an experience different from other people you feel bad about yourself. When you meet other people [like yourself] you feel normal again . . . it helps to affirm yourself and get on with your life.* (Peter, transracially fostered, Barbadian/English)

One's identity is affirmed by being with people who've had a similar experience, and that can help with my self-acceptance . . . I feel wounded but the wound doesn't show . . . that wound is taken care of somehow while I'm with those other people . . . I can be myself, so it's healing. It's also part of myself that doesn't get a venue anywhere else . . . (Folusho, transracially fostered, Nigerian)

Discomfort about being in foster care and discomfort about being Black . . . get addressed in ATRAP. . . I wish I'd found ATRAP earlier. (Peter, transracially fostered, Barbadian/English)

Members have also highlighted the important space that ATRAP creates in terms of a forum to talk, to share and express views, and to create a perspective that challenges self-blame and pathological views of transracially adopted and fostered people:

. . . I guess that it provides a space where you are a member, and there's other people who feel like you even if everyone's got completely different experiences, there is that common thread . . . (Lyn, intercountry adopted adult, South East Asian)

When I'm talking about the space that ATRAP creates, I also mean the information that you come into contact with through ATRAP, and . . . the philosophy that you . . . can be exposed to as a result of having contact with ATRAP. That philosophy is one of: it's not your fault, you know, you are not responsible, you should not feel guilty, you should not feel bad about anything. (Abayomi, transracially fostered, Nigerian)

Some members report that for the first time they do not have to explain who they are and their circumstances:

You just spend your life having to explain yourself and evading the need to explain yourself, and so you're not under that pressure when you're with people who've been through a similar experience. (Jo, transracially adopted adult, Kenyan/English parentage)

Others have spoken about how ATRAP has helped them to maintain their mental health:

For me it's important because there's very little alternative. Without this opportunity I would probably have gone insane or be staring severe psychiatric problems in the face . . . (Abayomi, transracially fostered, Nigerian)

Veronica Dewan (2001), a psychiatric system survivor and an adopted adult of Indian and Irish parentage, has written about her involvement with ATRAP:

In 1993 I met a group of Black adopted and long-term fostered adults who, like me, had been brought up in white families. Feelings we shared included loss, desolation, confusion, rejection and abandonment. When I heard parts of my story being recounted by other people I realised I was not alone . . . As our journeys converge we are gradually working out different ways to support each other without getting overwhelmed. This has been a starting point for me to learn what it feels like to belong and draw strength from being part of a community.

Sue Jardine (1999), a Chinese adopted adult who was brought to the UK from Hong Kong, has described the learning that has gone hand in hand with her involvement with ATRAP:

From listening to other people's experiences and being able to voice my own I have come to realise how much, from an early age, we felt it was necessary for us to take responsibility for our adoptive status. This situation was perpetuated because many of us had grown up in isolation and we also felt we had to protect our adoptive families from having to deal with our experiences.

An involvement in ATRAP may also help members to move from feeling powerless to identifying strategies for maintaining positive mental health and improving their life. Personal difficulties are reframed as common concerns, while new explanations and perspectives may lead to a change in perceptions and renewed hope. Members receive collective affirmation of their experiences, and collective action may result in personal growth and increased self-confidence. They are able to listen to people at different points on their journey, to empathise with each other, and learn from each other:

It's helped me to come up with my own ideas, to sort of make my own situation a bit better, or to how I can improve my own situation ... Perhaps you listen to someone else's story and you identify with several, you know, several parts of their story, and it just shifts your perspective, because when you are not hearing stories that are similar to your own ... personally, I tend to see every door as being closed ... whereas when I hear a few more stories that are similar to my own, I tend to start to think a bit more positively, and I can rationalise, and ... I can at least attempt to make a difference ... (Abayomi, transracially fostered, Nigerian)

Common issues

Despite differences in situations, members share a common experience of loss of birth family, community and country; and racism, as well as questions about their "racial" and cultural identity.

Identity

"Racial" and cultural identity is a key issue for transracially adopted and fostered people who have grown up in a white family:

There was a big shock coming to London. I felt dispossessed ... I wasn't cool with whatever Blacks were meant to be ... I'd grown up in all respects to be white. (Folusho, transracially fostered, Nigerian)

I think just walking around as a transracially adopted person you are struggling with that ... with liking yourself as a Black person ... it's been planted in your mind that to be Black is bad ... you have to adjust to what you are despite what you may have been brought up to think you are ... you go around assuming you're white perhaps, so ... you have to adjust to how people see you are ... (Peter, transracially fostered, Barbadian/English)

There is an identity crisis that arises for most of us ... It's about remaking something of myself. (Folusho, transracially fostered, Nigerian)

Loss of culture

> . . . I feel that the Black part of my culture has been denied . . . After all, how were my parents [. . . white, middle class adopters in their late 30s] supposed to know how to introduce me to my Black culture? (Eldred, 2000)

Emotional distress

Members have spoken about racism within the adoptive and foster family, as well as in the wider community; about having panic attacks around their racial identity, engaging in self-harming behaviour, self-hatred, trying to commit suicide, and becoming involved in the psychiatric system:

> I had first contemplated suicide at the age of seven, and such thoughts continued to haunt me throughout my childhood. I needed to get back to my roots . . . (Dewan, 1996)

> Witness the high preponderance among us of feelings of self-hatred because we believed our white parents who, while telling us we were "special", simultaneously demonstrated racist attitudes to other Black people in public and as portrayed in the media. Who wants love, if it's at the cost of low self-esteem or eventual suicide? (Anon, 2000)

Lack of support around racial abuse and racism

> It's there constantly as a child but you can't possibly acknowledge it if you're brought up by people that are white. (Jo, transracially adopted adult, Kenyan/English)

> . . . maybe it was that my mother didn't recognise or understand racism, and so after the age of seven I would never mention it, and so that's something I would live with alone and never say to somebody until I don't know maybe early 20s. And, I think that's really damaging. (Lyn, intercountry adopted adult, South East Asian)

Lack of self-esteem

> The process whereby in order to be accepted by the family the transracial adoptee has to accept and take on i.e. internalise

[the adoptive family's] possibly deeply racist attitudes . . . Thus, in order to survive, the transracially adopted child has to grow up hating itself (for being black) – the price for "love" (by [even unconsciously] a racist family who doesn't respect his or her culture and colour). The self-esteem damaged at such an early age is difficult to recover throughout life . . . self-esteem . . . is behind everything we do and achieve, and affects, for example, our relationships with others and our ability to love others and feel "lovable" by others. (Peter, transracially fostered, Barbadian/English, personal communication)

The impact of the fostering or adoption experience on day-to-day life

The simple fact is that most problems that I face nowadays one way or another I can pinpoint back . . . to being fostered . . . It has almost made me, I'm going to say proud of my ability to live without forming connections . . . Other problems stem with separation from culture of birth parents and having to confront that on a day-to-day basis and having to think about that . . . and just continuously sort of having to suppress that and then having it erupt all over you again, and then suppress it . . . (Abayomi, transracially fostered, Nigerian)

Gratitude and guilt

Feeling grateful towards adoptive and foster families, and feeling guilty for saying what the experience of being raised in a white family was really like:

That because I feel grateful, I don't want to say anything negative to Mum or my siblings about the life that I've had, and because of that you feel, you end up feeling angry or you end up feeling alone, and you end up feeling as if you're living . . . a sort of fictionalised life because everyone's seeing you in a light . . . I suppose you're not being honest with people because they're not allowing you to be honest . . . and you feel guilty if you say anything negative . . . (Lyn, intercountry adopted adult, South East Asian)

All in all there is a lot of guilt and it does, it does get in the way, and it manifests itself in different, different ways, but there is a great deal of guilt. And it's quite hard to shake off. (Abayomi, transracially fostered, Nigerian)

I don't ever say how I feel because I'm afraid they [other intercountry adoptees] are going to think I'm some traitor . . . (Lyn, intercountry adopted adult, South East Asian)

I don't talk to my family ever about this. I managed to pluck up the courage to tell my mum that I was going to ATRAP and that was an experience . . . she got quite indignant and defensive . . . (Lyn, intercountry adopted adult, South East Asian)

Racism and abuse within the adoptive and foster family

Racism within the family may be violently interwoven with physical and emotional abuse. For example, Linda wrote about physical and emotional abuse by her adoptive mother:

All those years of humiliation, being beaten up and called Black this and Black that, and then asked how much I loved her. (Linda, 2001)

Experiences of sexual abuse may be racialised. 'L' (2002), an adopted adult, has written about what she calls the "sexualisation of ethnicity":

. . . for me there was being touched due to the curiosity that my ethnicity generated but then there was also the "access all areas". This never involved another child; it was just me on my own, though at times stuff happened when other children were present. The culprits in the main were parents, relatives, school teachers and sadly parents of friends . . . my ethnicity seemed to provoke a response in adults that made them want to touch, stroke, feel, paw, maul, grab and hold onto [me] . . .

Charmaine (personal communication) has spoken about emotional and physical abuse by her adoptive mother, and sexual abuse by her Godfather, older adoptive brother and a teacher:

My memories of sexual abuse go back as far as I can remember. I couldn't tell you when it first happened.

I went from being very clever at school . . . to playing truant all the time, self-abusing, taking overdoses.

As a teenager, Charmaine ran away repeatedly. A social worker visited and Charmaine asked her to find her a new family, telling her that she did not feel safe there. She was not listened to.

. . . there is no help. I've always been quite an assertive person and there was nothing. I was screaming out for help and all the signs were there – in church, in school, social services. (Charmaine, transracially adopted, African-Caribbean)

Only as an adult has Charmaine received help through her faith, which has enabled her to start to heal from her abusive experiences and to understand how they continue to affect her life today.

Search and reunion

I am yet to meet my birth mother. Each year Mothering Sunday comes around, I often wonder if I ever will. I do not feel able to celebrate my birth mother's life or properly mourn her death and may go to my grave without either experience. (Mary, 2000)

. . . but there is hardly a day that goes past when I do not think of Vietnam or about my difference as a Vietnamese person . . . I am left wondering afresh about the family that I may have in Vietnam and what my life could have been like if I'd stayed. (Anthony, 2001)

Yet, most of all she [birth mother] rejected me as a Black woman and I rejected her for her racism. (Dewan, 2001)

But speaking to other people, it seems as if one of the reasons why they can't build a relationship with their parents is because they don't speak the same language . . . (Lyn, intercountry adopted adult, South East Asian)

Meena, a transracially adopted adult of Indian parentage, has written about concealing from her birth mother that she is a lesbian:

> *I am guarded about what I write too. There is so much I wish I could tell you about myself, but everything I do is censored from my correspondence with you . . . if I told you what I really do, perhaps you would disown me, and I am not ready to lose you again.* (Meena, 2000)

Survival

> *. . . I can assure you there are many transracially adopted and fostered adults attempting on a day-to-day basis to put back together the pieces of their broken lives, attempting to make sense of their place in the world, attempting to unravel what the hell has been inflicted on them – above all, attempting to survive.* (Anon, 2000)

Conclusion

Despite forthcoming changes in the legislation regarding adoption support, the shift towards user involvement in social care, and the growing number of user-led organisations, adoption is one area where users, especially Black users, remain marginalised. The experiences of transracially adopted and fostered people, as told in their own words, have not been noted. Yet, as the experience of ATRAP shows, transracially adopted and fostered people have the ability to define their own needs, to set goals, to take action for change, and to work together to challenge injustice and oppression, and to strengthen, support and empower each other. It is time that the social work profession paid due attention to the analyses and discourses of this group, and respected and valued their perspectives. The experience of ATRAP demonstrates unequivocally the vital role of Black user groups for transracially adopted and fostered people. Transracially adopted and fostered people must play a key role in the development of adoption support services if these services are ever to meet their needs. Unless professionals value Black user "knowledges", they will fail to create adoption support services that are responsive to the needs and concerns of transracially adopted and fostered people, including intercountry adopted adults.

References

Anderson, M (2000) 'Fish outta water', *ATRAP Newsletter*, No. 3, pp 3–5.

Anon (2000) 'Dear Editor', *ATRAP Newsletter*, No. 2, pp 11–12.

Anthony, G (2001) 'Orphans of the airlift', *ATRAP Newsletter*, No. 7, pp 3–4.

ATRAP (2001) *www.atrap.org.uk/html/issues.html*

Charmaine (2002) Personal communication, 22 August.

Dagoo, R (undated) 'Getting together: groups for transracially adopted adults, and for birth mothers', in Burnell, A, Reich, D and Sawbridge, P (eds) *Adult Counselling and Adoption*, London: Post-Adoption Centre.

Dance, C (1997) *Focus on Adoption: A snapshot of adoption patterns in England – 1995*, London: BAAF.

Dewan, V (2001) 'Life support', in *Something Inside so Strong: Strategies for surviving mental distress*, London: The Mental Health Foundation.

Dewan, V (1996) 'The pressure of being a human chameleon', in Read, J and Reynolds, J (eds) *Speaking Our Minds: An anthology*, Hampshire: Macmillan Press Limited.

Dewan, V (2001) 'Losing and choosing', *ATRAP Newsletter*, No. 5, pp 6–8.

Eldred, F (2000) 'Farrah talks the talk', *ATRAP Newsletter*, No. 1, pp 2–3.

Gill, O and Jackson, B (1983) *Adoption and Race: Black, Asian and mixed children in white familes*, London: Batsford.

Harris, P (2002) *'It Changed My Life Completely': User views on the delivery of post-adoption services (Summary)*, Birmingham: West Midlands Post Adoption Service.

Hoksbergen, R and van Dijkum, C (2001) 'Trauma experienced by children adopted from abroad', *Adoption & Fostering*, 25:1, pp 19–25.

Howe, D and Feast, J (2000) *Adoption, Search and Reunion: The long-term experience of adopted adults*, London: The Children's Society.

Jardine, S (1999) 'Transracial placements: an adoptee's perspective', in Barn, R (ed.) *Working with Black Children and their Families*, London: BAAF.

Kinsara, K (2002a) Personal communication, 22 August.

Kinsara, K (2002b) Unpublished paper presented at an ATRAP social, 3 February, London.

Kirton, D (2000) *"Race", Ethnicity and Adoption*, Buckingham: Open University Press.

Kirton, D, Feast, J and Howe, D (2000) 'Searching, reunion and transracial adoption', *Adoption & Fostering*, 24:3, pp 6–18.

L. (2002) 'Transracial adoption – an experience', *ATRAP Newsletter*, No. 9, pp 6–7.

Linda (2001) 'Untitled', *ATRAP Newsletter*, No. 6, pp 3–5.

Mary (2000) 'An overwhelming impact', *ATRAP Newsletter*, No. 2, p 8.

Meena (2000) 'Letter to my mother', *ATRAP Newsletter*, No. 3, pp 10–11.

Mylien (2000) 'Orphans of the airlift', http://www.atrap.org.uk/html/newsletter.html

Moffat, P J and Thoburn, J (2001) 'Outcomes of permanent family placement for children of minority ethnic origin', *Child & Family Social Work*, pp 13–21.

Peter (2002) Personal communication, 26 June.

Prevatt-Goldstein, B and Spencer, M (2000) *"Race" and Ethnicity: A consideration of issues for black, minority ethnic and white children in family placement*, London: BAAF.

Shobha (2000) 'Mother's Day service', *ATRAP Newsletter*, No. 1, pp 3–5.

Sheckleton, J (1990) *'A Glimpse Through the Looking Glass' – a summary of personal experiences and reflections of a group of transracially adopted adults*, Post Adoption Centre Discussion Paper No. 8, London: Post-Adoption Centre.

SSI (2000) *Excellence not Excuses: Inspection of services for ethnic minority children and families*, London: Department of Health.

SSI (1997) *For Children's Sake: An SSI Inspection of local authority adoption services*, London: Department of Health.

9 Working with black adopted children and their families: the Post-Adoption Centre's experience

Monica Duck

The placement of black children with adoptive parents continues to evoke considerable debate and anxiety for social work professionals. The newly established Adoption Register, which uses a computerised database to help place children more swiftly, has brought renewed interest to this debate. It is striking that "race" or ethnic background is not seen as one of the main criteria to be used by the Register for matching a child with a good enough substitute family whereas geography, for example, is to be taken into account. Most professionals would welcome the consideration of geography, which could prevent black children from being placed in isolation, many miles away from their communities. However, after more than a decade of discussion about the rights of black children to be placed in a family of similar ethnic background, why is this still considered a contentious matter, while for white children it is simply not a matter for consideration at all? This continuing denial of the importance of black and minority ethnic children's identity needs only serves to marginalise prospective minority ethnic adoptive parents.

The opportunity to explore and pursue some of these issues has been made possible by a recent Department of Health and Access 4 grant to the Post Adoption Centre (PAC). PAC was the first independent post-adoption agency in the UK and is a leader in the provision of specialist services to anyone affected by adoption.

When I started working at PAC over five years ago, one of the things I soon became aware of was the low take-up of the child and family services by minority ethnic groups. This was not altogether surprising to me as my own experience of over 15 years as a social worker in a range of settings suggested that black families are less likely to seek help from social service agencies. However, given PAC's independence from social services departments, I was interested to explore how black and multiracial families cope with some of the complex and difficult problems of caring for children with a history of deprivation and abuse and to find out where they go to seek help or support for these problems.

Soon after taking up my post at PAC, I had the benefit of working with my first black family at the Centre.

Case example

Like many families that contact PAC in desperation, this couple was considering whether to end the placement of two siblings after three hard years of trying to integrate them into their family. The children were placed with a view to adoption but, because of the children's difficult behaviour, the parents became diffident about proceeding to adopt. The purpose of the referral to the Centre was to work with the family to improve family relationships, enhance understanding of adoption, and ultimately save the placement. The issue of "race" or ethnicity had not been overtly identified as an aspect of the therapeutic work. However, it soon became clear that, in order to work with the family in a meaningful way, it was important for the counselling team to reflect an understanding of the family's culture and ethnicity. What was significant about this case was that the parents had very strong links with their Caribbean culture and with their extended family and church with which the children had also become closely involved.

Working with the family on the children's past soon revealed the high level of trauma, abuse and multiple losses that the children had experienced prior to placement with their new parents. The parents seemed overwhelmed by the level of grief the children had suffered and the impact of it on the older child in particular. They were encouraged to examine information about the children's early history, some of which they had not been aware of prior to placement, and to make sense of the effect on their children's development and behaviour. It also became evident that the older child, Fay, had maintained a strong commitment to her birth mother even though the birth mother had previously been unable to protect her from serious abuse. Due to Fay's fantasies about her birth mother and a lack of understanding about the circumstances leading to her placement in a new family, she projected a lot of anger towards the adoptive mother and other authority figures such as her schoolteacher.

In addition to the complexities faced by all adopted children and their adoptive families, there appear to be specific challenges for black and multiracial families. One continuing theme that emerged from the work with this family in question concerned the parents' own personal grief resulting from their separation from, and loss of, their country of origin and extended families. This is not to suggest that such an experience prevents black and minority ethnic parents from becoming "good-enough" parents. On the contrary, it can be of positive benefit if they are able to explore and manage their own feelings of loss. An important task, therefore, was to work with the parents to enable them to share some of their own experiences of loss with their children and to help them identify strategies for dealing with the emotions that might be triggered for them by caring for very hurt children. It is also important to recognise that black parents may be reluctant to speak openly with strangers outside their networks or communities about personal matters or indeed acknowledge difficult feelings which they have faced as a result of separation, or the absence of key family members, or through immigration.

It soon became clear that these parents did not find this way of working easy but, as they began to trust the team and to feel empowered by the process, they gradually became more comfortable and less defensive about providing information. They completed the programme we planned together at the Centre, and they were subsequently able to adopt the children with some ongoing support from the PAC team.

It should be emphasised at this stage that black and minority ethnic adoptive parents caring for traumatised children are faced with exactly the same problems as white adoptive parents, with the added dimension of race and all its ramifications. It is misguided to imagine that simply by placing black and minority ethnic children with adoptive parents who share their ethnicity, the children's emotional needs will be automatically addressed. Likewise it is equally unwise to deny the importance of a child's "race" and ethnicity when considering placing a child in a "good-enough" family. Working with black and multiracial families, therefore, requires an integrated approach, which includes a thorough understanding of racism and its impact on the psychological well-being of black children. These general principles have inspired the development of an innovative project at PAC that offers a therapeutic service to black and multiracial adopted/fostered children and their families. The majority of the referrals to this project involve older children and families in crisis. The children invariably come with a history of dysfunctional relationships and chaotic and abusive parenting; they are likely to have led an uncertain and fragmented life prior to placement, resulting in a sense of mistrust or insecurity that will remain throughout their life if help is not sought and healing does not occur.

Working principles of the programme

The new PAC programme aims specifically to address the psychological needs of black and minority ethnic adopted children and to provide comprehensive advice and support to their families. The project is not restricted to adopted children and parents as some of the children referred are in permanent foster families. The work is based on Bowlby's theories of attachment (1969), Brodzinky's psychosocial perspectives on adoption, and the work of a number of attachment therapists from the USA, namely Nancy Verrier, Greg Keck and Joyce Maguire Pavao. Despite their lack of focus on cultural or ethnicity issues, we have drawn from these theories to adapt our programme to respond to the specific needs of black and multiracial families. For example, where possible we have attempted to involve significant extended family members in the therapeutic process. Counselling sessions are directive and action orientated rather than focused on the individual. Family members are encouraged to interact, relate, listen and be listened to within the group. The concept of empowerment is therefore an important element of our work. Nancy Boyd-Franklin (1989) emphasised this as a process of helping people to gain the ability to make and implement basic decisions in their own lives and in their children's lives. The culturally diverse team of counsellors and therapists working on this project maintains a position of adoption expertise and authority. We offer support and practical advice on special parenting techniques and on child development. In addition, an external child and adolescent psychiatrist and a clinical psychologist supervise the team regularly. This provides a supportive forum that enables the team members to reflect on their roles and therapeutic techniques, to acknowledge success, take risks and to learn about their own cultural values and those of the families with whom they work.

Take-up of the therapeutic service

Initially, it was difficult to know how widely to advertise the service given that it was a pilot project with limited resources and we did not want to raise expectations that PAC could not fulfil. Our target was to provide intensive therapeutic support to six black or multiracial families per year for a period of up to six months. We decided to target our subscribing local authority social services adoption and fostering units. This proved a fruitful source of initial referrals although, as the service became more established, an increasing number of self-referrals were received from individual adopters or foster carers. The main reasons adopters/foster carers gave for seeking help were:

Child's behavioural problems	96%
Need for help on "race"/identity issues	4%
Need for advice and information	100%
Placement nearing the point of disruption	5%
Adolescent problems	44%
Wish to attend advertised groups or workshops	60%

During the first three years, 56 black or multiracial families were referred for face-to-face counselling at the Centre. Out of these 56 families, two families failed to keep their appointments and the remaining 54 families visited the Centre for an initial parents' consultation. For a small number of parents this consultation session was sufficient to address their concerns. However, in the majority of cases, further intervention was required and a range of services was offered depending on each family's individual situation, as illustrated in Table 1.

Table 1
Family take-up of services

	1999/0	2000/1	2001/2	Total
Parent consultations	18	21	15	54
Failed appointments	0	1	1	2
Family sessions	0	8	8	16
Family assessments	7	5	2	14
Intensive programmes	7	4	2	13

It was important to maintain some flexibility in responding to the families' needs. For example, we found that, during the second and third years of the project, more than one family session proved effective if families accessed the service early on in the placement, before reaching the end of their tether. It also became evident that there was a need to offer some follow-up support to families who had used the intensive programme. Consequently, by allowing time for additional family sessions and follow-up support, we curtailed our capacity to maintain our target of offering six intensive programmes each year.

It is interesting to note that a discrepancy exists between the ethnicity of the children referred to the project when compared with their adoptive parents. The largest group of children (43 per cent of the total) was of mixed parentage. Of the other 57 per cent, 15 per cent were African-Caribbean, 7 per cent Black African, 12 per cent Asian and 21 per cent were described as "others", some of whose ethnicity was unknown. The remaining 2 per cent were white children within a sibling group. In contrast, white parents, parenting children of minority ethnic backgrounds, account for 34 per cent of the parent referrals, while 28 per cent were of mixed ethnicity, 25 per cent African Caribbean, 7 per cent Asian and 2 per cent were described as "others". These figures suggest that significant numbers of white adoptive parents are involved in transracial adoption.

Everyone referred to the project was invited to an initial consultation session, which aims to demonstrate an understanding, knowledgeable and non-judgemental approach. A large proportion of these families often voice a deep level of dissatisfaction about the support that they have received from the placing or supporting local authority we usually show a new appreciation of how the child's problems have impacted on all family members and thus the need to work with the family as a whole. Particular attention is given to what the parents convey about the child's behaviour and how they have been trying to manage their day-to-day family life. What we offer to these families is an exploration of feelings, rather than an investigation. This method has proved successful with parents and they have commented that, rather than feeling blamed for failing, they have been given real consideration and understanding about adoption-related issues and how these affect black families.

In working with black and multiracial families, the counsellors assume that change is possible and that the essential ingredients of change lie in the creation of a more positive relationship between the children and their parents. However, in order to help them understand what is happening in their lives it has been important to focus on the psychological adjustment of the child as well as on the coping strategies of the parents. For some parents, one or two consultation sessions are enough to assist with special parenting strategies and to help them to respond empathically to their child's specific needs. A comprehensive family assessment is normally offered in cases where the parents have expressed concern about a wide range of problems including excessive defiance, aggressive behaviour, problems at school, hoarding of food, self-harm, running away from home, difficulty in making friends, and lying and stealing.

Case example

Mrs Granger contacted our advice line at a crisis point. She was extremely anxious about the behavioural difficulties of their adopted children, Nathan aged 11 and Samantha aged 13. Mrs Granger was particularly concerned about Samantha who seemed very depressed, spending a lot of time in her room and refusing to speak to the rest of the family. She was excessively jealous of her brother and was prone to stealing and lying. After a lengthy telephone discussion with a counsellor, Mrs Granger was offered an appointment for a parents' consultation. The consultation offered the parents an opportunity to meet with two counsellors in order to discuss their concerns. When Mr Granger, who is African-Caribbean, and Mrs Granger, who is white British, arrived for their initial session, they seemed quite overwhelmed by the problems that they were experiencing with their adopted children. Samantha, who is of mixed heritage, was placed with the Grangers at the age of three after experiencing several moves of carers. She was subsequently adopted by them at the age of five. Soon afterwards, Nathan, also of mixed heritage but not related, was placed with the family and adopted two years later. Both children came with a history of severe neglect due to the mental illness of their birth parents. Mr and Mrs Granger were advised of the potential risk of the children developing mental illness as adults, but were also assured that a stable and healthy environment would significantly reduce this risk.

During the consultation session it transpired that the Grangers were feeling exasperated about both children. Nathan was described as always acting out, at home and at school, hurting other children and having major temper tantrums if he did not get his own way. Mrs Granger confided that she was on the point of shutting off from their daughter while Mr Granger was ambivalent about wanting Nathan returned to care. However, despite their despair, they felt committed to the children and this session gave them the opportunity to offload their concerns openly without the children being present.

As well as listening to the parents, the counsellors observed that Mrs Granger sounded more optimistic about the children, but Mr Granger seemed disheartened and was extremely disappointed about Nathan's failure to respond to discipline and his lack of success at school. Nathan's frequent rejection of Mr Granger's authority as a parent was particularly difficult for him to come to terms with because it challenged his cultural model of fatherhood. This situation illustrates a common dilemma for black and multiracial families where the experience of powerlessness resulting from racism and victimisation has impacted on their ability to make basic decisions about their lives. It was, therefore, important for Mr Granger to feel that he could not only provide for his family but also maintain an authoritative role within the family. Following this session at the Centre, the Grangers decided to take up the offer of a comprehensive assessment with the aim of providing some recommendations for future therapeutic support.

Prior to the assessment, which usually takes places over a three-and-a-half hour session, the parents are asked to complete detailed questionnaires. These are important in giving a full picture of the child and of the adoptive parents' own personal experiences. There is often some initial reluctance from black families to complete the questionnaires, as parents are mindful of not wanting to say anything negative about their child and appear to worry that anything written may further label themselves and their child adversely.

The family assessment is normally followed by a comprehensive report that is prepared primarily for the benefit of the adoptive parents. A copy is also made available to the agency or agencies if they have made the referral and are supporting the family. A "network" meeting with the parents and professionals is offered if additional work is deemed to be necessary so that specific issues can be explored. If the parents wish PAC to undertake a programme of therapeutic work, it is necessary for the family to give a strong and positive undertaking of commitment to the work. In cases referred by the local authority, it is crucial for the local authority worker to remain actively involved in supporting the family through this difficult process. In the case of the Granger family, the assessment revealed that the parents' concerns were justified and that the family needed urgent intervention to sustain the placement of their younger child. Additionally, the assessment indicated that their daughter had severe attachment difficulties and that she also needed ongoing therapeutic help. The assessment report provided a detailed outline of the various areas in which the children and their parents needed further therapeutic support and included specific strategies for maintaining the parents' authority.

Following the comprehensive family assessments, 13 families have proceeded to an intensive programme. PAC offers treatment over a series of three-hour, fortnightly sessions for a period of four to six months, depending on what is involved and the composition of the family. Where black children have been cared for from infancy by a series of white foster carers and have developed negative feelings about themselves or about black people generally, it is crucial that the therapeutic work will encourage the current carer/s to nurture the child's racial identity. Careful consideration is also given to whether the extended family may have a valuable contribution to make in supporting the adoptive family. Attention is given to the choice of play materials, toys, images and models in the counselling rooms to ensure that they reflect racial diversity. The Child and Family team at PAC is a multiracial, multidisciplinary group. Workers are encouraged to be mindful of how they conduct themselves during sessions and how they communicate with black and multiracial families, particularly when dealing with questions of authority. For example, during sessions counsellors try to employ strategies to encourage the parents themselves to negotiate and set appropriate boundaries for their children. A range of creative activities is used to facilitate interaction between parents and children in order to enhance family relationships. We use a mixture of methods that include working with the whole family together, individual child sessions, and sessions with the parent or parents.

Sessions may include the following activities:

- making a family tree of the adoptive family to include the adopted child's birth family members, clearly depicting their "race" and culture;
- painting a life-size self-portrait paying specific attention to skin colouring features and hair texture;
- acknowledging and validating differences within a family to enhance self-esteem and develop trust;
- discussing a child's life story with parents and child together, whereby emotional impact is explored;
- special parenting strategies and communication exercises;
- sharing of adoptive parent's own life stories including experiences of racism or being visibly different.

These activities encourage communication, listening, modelling and mirroring of strategies for dealing with dysfunctional behaviour. During the sessions, the family is given a full explanation of the rationale for the activities.

Infertility

Informal adoption, when relatives or friends take care of a child if parents are unable to care for them, has been an integral part of black communities for centuries. However, it cannot be assumed that formal, legal adoption is therefore problem-free for black families. There are issues for black families concerning infertility. Many black families are embarrassed to admit to infertility to their friends and extended family, and remain secretive. Even though close friends and relatives may be aware of the problem, it is rarely discussed openly and is likely to surface only when a child's difficulties begin to emerge or when there are subsequent losses. A lack of preparation and foresight in assisting parents with their painful feelings about their infertility can affect acceptance of their adopted child.

Case example

Mrs and Mr Brooks referred themselves to the Centre after receiving information about PAC from their local authority. They had not been able to have their own child and decided to pursue adoption as the next best option for building a family. They are both African-Caribbean and after the usual preparation process, Leo, a three-year-old African-Caribbean boy was placed with them. Prior to placement, Leo had experienced two changes of carers and there were concerns about possible sexual abuse within the foster home. He was described by his social worker as a bright and engaging child. However, Mr and Mrs Brooks soon began to realise that they had taken on far more than they had been prepared for.

When Leo first arrived he seemed irritable, he would scream all night, never settled easily and there were feeding problems and aggression towards other children who visited the home. After two years, Mr and Mrs Brooks seemed exhausted by the demands that Leo continued to make on them. He was still very controlling and could go wild, throwing and breaking things if he did not get his own way. His parents were genuinely committed to him. However, they were very worried about his future well-being and in need of specialist support to help them manage his behaviour.

During the parents' sessions, Mr And Mrs Brooks were encouraged to share their feelings and disappointments about the child that they had dreamed of parenting and were helped to gain a more realistic understanding of parenting a child with serious relationship problems. Mrs Brooks at times became quite upset as she tried hard to come to terms with their situation. She felt particularly burdened by her inability to speak freely to her friends and close relatives about the difficulties that they were experiencing with Leo as she feared that she would be criticised for having failed as a natural mother. After an extended period of work, including some "couple sessions" that focused on working through Mr and Mrs Brooks grief about their infertility, they were able to begin to recognise small improvements in their son's behaviour and build on the progress they had made. And with support from a supportive headmistress and relatives, the placement began to flourish.

Conclusion

Significant features and factors have emerged from this programme over the last three years. The project has demonstrated, by the numbers of referrals, that minority ethnic families will access therapeutic services that specifically address their needs. The work has provided us with an opportunity to develop our understanding and awareness of the added complexities involved in working with black and multicultural families. Although there is still some way to go, team members have become more confident in taking risks in discussing difficult issues regarding "race" and ethnicity and acknowledging differences of opinion. Having regular meetings with our external consultants has been very helpful in keeping the focus on the outcomes for the children and the families.

The feedback from families has been extremely positive and indicates that, in a significant number of cases, the quality of the placement has been much enhanced. In a small number of cases parents have decided to end a placement, and support has been given to deal with the painful outcomes in a way that is least distressing for the children. The majority of families that approach the Centre do so at a point of crisis after many years of struggling to maintain their commitment to their children. For some of these families, follow-up support has been crucial in maintaining the progress that they have made during the therapeutic work. With the recent expansion of the PAC Child and Family team, we are hoping to develop our work further with young adopted black people and to take a more pro-active role in empowering black parents to support their children in their education. Most importantly, we have learnt the need for flexibility in our approach regarding the support of black families and hope that our learning and model of working can be disseminated more broadly to provide minority ethnic families with easier access to similar services.

References

Banks, N (1992) 'Techniques for direct identity work with black children', *Adoption & Fostering*, 16:3, pp 19–24, BAAF.

Bowlby, J (1969) *Attachment and Loss*, London: Hogarth Press.

Boyd-Franklin, N (1989) *Black Families in Therapy*, New York: Guilford Press.

Brodzinsky, D (1987) *Adjustment to Adoption: A psychosocial perspective*, Oxford: Pergamon.

Keck, G C and Kupecky, R M (1995) *Adopting the Hurt Child*, Colorado Springs: Pinon Press.

Maguire, P J (1999) *The Family of Adoption*, Boston Mass: Beacon Press.

Verrier, N (1993) *The Primal Wound*, Baltimore: Gateway Publishing.

10 Support for intercountry adopters in the Jewish community

Jacky Gordon

'I didn't come out of your tummy, I came out of a Chinese lady's tummy!' announced Lucy Beth loudly in the middle of the swimming pool changing room, to the great embarrassment of her adoptive Mum. At least she had absorbed the basic details of her adoption story, but this was certainly not the place Mum would have chosen to discuss it!

Norwood Jewish Adoption Society applied to the Department of Health to become an adoption agency in 1989 and was approved in 1990; but we were not registered as an intercountry adoption agency until 2000. In the intervening ten years we undertook home studies referred to us by a number of local authorities.

It is important to stress that our applicants for intercountry adoption are not confined to the Jewish community. They come from any culture or religious persuasion and, if our staff are not equipped to deal with a particular family, we obtain the advice we need. However, for the purpose of this article I will concentrate on issues for Jewish families.

For the Jewish community, intercountry adoption has extra difficulties because only a tiny minority of children who are brought to this country for adoption will have been born to Jewish parents. The Jewish families with whom we work come from right across the spectrum. Some families and individuals are culturally Jewish but do not practise their religion; others are reform or liberal Jews; others are modern orthodox; and yet another group manage their daily lives strictly according to religious Jewish law. Many overseas adoption agencies will not understand the nuances of the Jewish religion and will have little understanding of the differences among these groups.

Jewish families considering adoption of non-Jewish children need to grapple with a host of dilemmas about assimilation, acceptance into the community, and possible prejudice. Jewish people often "know" another person is Jewish when they meet. They "sense" it. White non-Jewish children may look very different from the children who have been born into these families, and transracially adopted children will almost certainly have different physical features. Acceptance within the wider family and by the friends of the families who adopt is vital if these placements are going to be successful. But in a close knit community, acceptance of adopted children by that community is also important, if the adoptive parents and the child are going to play a full part in it.

If you are born into a Jewish family you have a sense of history which goes back often many generations. Victims of persecution and holocaust survivors remember the horrors of what has gone before. The following generations will have that sense of history from the stories told to them by their parents and grandparents. There is a responsibility for every next generation to continue the Jewish line, and to make sure that the memory of suffering is not forgotten and will be passed down to future generations. Will the children adopted from overseas who do not have a sense of the past even be interested in all this history?

. . . when I look at my son I'm reminded that he isn't biologically linked to any of this particular history. (Steinberg and Hall, 2000 p 174)

Children who look different cannot easily blend in. They will frequently be objects of speculation and, because people are naturally curious, questions will be asked about their origins or – even worse – insensitive comments will be made. Unless children know how to respond if Mum or Dad are not there to help, they will become confused and troubled.

We know from the work that we do in placing children domestically, how hard families struggle to assimilate their adopted children. Steinberg and Hall (2000) comment on the experience of adopted siblings:

Though they could read Torah and adored matzo balls, their acceptance depended on having Jewish parents. Without us with them they felt like outsiders. (p 175)

Was this because they were adopted or because they were trans-culturally adopted?

All adoptive parents, and particularly Jewish adoptive parents, need to understand the possible prejudice that their children may suffer in order to prepare them for what they may have to face. Children can be cruel to each other or may report comments from their parents about the new boy or girl in the class. Children may feel connected to other children in school or in the community because they look like them or share a sense of the past in some way. Children adopted from overseas come from a different ethnic group, may be a different colour, were born to a different family and are being brought up in a minority religion. When we consider that children will pick on others if they notice even very small differences, we must realise what these children have to live with and help them to manage to cope somehow. In other words, if we want good outcomes for these children we have to invest, not only in support for the parents, but in support for the children too.

How we offer preparation and support to parents

Support in intercountry adoption is a vital part of the process of managing adoption programmes. Prior to the home study, we run preparation groups for our intercountry adopters which include the major issues affecting everyone in the adoption circle. However, we have learned that there are so many factors relating to intercountry adoption in general, and Jewish adopting families in particular, that many of the areas covered in the groups are very specific to the task. There has, for example, been discussion about circumcision – most Jewish baby boys are circumcised at eight days old. But if there are medical concerns about the child, circumcision must wait until he is well. Problems arise when an older child arrives from overseas and has not been circumcised. If the parents decide not to carry out the procedure, he will be different from his father and his peers. If they have their child circumcised they must decide when to do so. In theory it could be any time after the Adoption Order has been made (or earlier with parents' consent). However, it is important to wait until the child is settled so that the trauma of the change of environment is not compounded by what could be experienced as a painful invasion of his body. Converting a child to Judaism is another major topic to which I refer later. Discussion about these and other "Jewish" issues could probably only happen in this unique group.

Support starts from the day we initially interview our families. Before they embark on the journey towards their quest for their child, they must think about helping the child to deal with ethnicity, assimilation and identity problems. How possible is it for Jewish parents to enable their adopted child to be part of Jewish culture and religion, while at the same time promoting pride in the children's own ethnicity and culture?

It is vital that support is offered in easy stages. We know from research into adult learning that, during a lesson or lecture, we absorb only a small proportion of what is taught. Our applicants are excited about the prospect of having a child, nervous in case they don't succeed, wanting to impress and therefore may absorb very little at the preparation stage. We hope they will learn the basics and, like all good adoption agencies, we give them written material to take home, experiential exercises which make adoption more "real", and visits from outside speakers and from experienced adoptive parents.

The gap that exists at present is the support we offer to intercountry adopters between approval and placement. Good practice would dictate that we offer a seamless service from referral to adoption and beyond. The Adoption (Intercountry Aspects) Act 1999 Draft Regulations and Guidance for England and Wales – in draft at the time of writing – impose a duty on adoption agencies to receive information about the child to be adopted from overseas, and to discuss the details with the prospective parents – as we would in domestic adoption. If they decide to go ahead and travel to see the child, the agency will also have a role in helping during the final decision-making process. The Department of Health will expect to hear from the agency regarding that decision. This level of continuing support will be expensive and the question of who pays for this service will need to be addressed.

One of our families was told at 10pm the night before they flew to see the child they wished to adopt that the birth mother was a heroin user. If there had been close communication between the overseas agency and the adoption agency one would hope that this important piece of information would have been shared in advance. Fortunately they were able to obtain some advice even at that late hour and travelled the following day prepared with the appropriate questions to ask the agency. The picture could have been different if the new Regulations had been in force.

Another role of a "full service" agency might be to monitor information on the child's health. Some of our families have travelled to their chosen country and found that the child, who they were told was healthy, had serious physical or learning disabilities. We encourage our families to travel to their chosen country with BAAF medical forms to be completed locally. But the quality of the information they are able to get at that stage varies considerably. When they return home they need good paediatric advice in the initial stages of placement and immediate practical support.

After adoption

Peer group support after adoption is invaluable as each parent can help others who are going through the same process. The 17 Jewish inter-country adopters in our support group tell us that the group makes them feel less isolated. The "founder members" have been together as a group for years – others have joined and none want to give it up. It seems that the bond created by the existing group of Jewish intercountry adopters has grown over time and that the Jewish factor is important and "glues" the members together.

It was hard to anticipate the Jewish issues that would arise; schooling is one. There are some excellent Jewish schools, many of which combine a good academic standard with the teaching of Jewish studies. Our parents struggle with the decision about the best sort of education for their child. Is it better to attend a school where they will meet children who belong to different religions and ethnic groups, or one where the children will all be Jewish but mostly white? The decision about the right school for a particular child is dependent on so many variables, but the group will help the parents to weigh up the pros and cons and reach a balanced decision. If the application to the school of their choice is not successful, there may be another meeting where they can get support for that disappointment too!

We have recently run a support group consisting of domestic and inter-country adopters. This has had a mixed reception, as the group comprises parents who have children of a wide age range. In discussion with the current support groups, we have decided to try groups that relate to the ages of the adopted children – whether the parents have taken the domestic or the overseas route. This will mean that there will be three support groups with children in the age ranges: 0–3; 4–7 and 8–18. In this way we hope to focus first on the needs of the child.

The adoption story

Both parents and children must feel comfortable with the adoption story before it becomes part of the family ethos.

The adopted child has a history of origin that involves her with the world apart from her parents right from the beginning, whether or not she knows it. (Watkins and Fisher, 1993, p 23)

Children need to feel established and secure in their new families whilst still being allowed to value and embrace their birth heritage. Children adopted from China, for example, almost without exception know nothing of their birth family and have little history to help them to build a healthy self-image. When they get older, they will want to find explanations and inevitably their parents will find it hard to help them. We encourage our families to gather every little fact or story that could possibly be helpful to their children as they grow up. The orphanage can often help – if a child was left on a doorstep it may have been the doorstep of a frequently used building where the birth mother could be sure the baby would be quickly found.

The support we offer to our families aims to help them to be open and honest about their child's adoption, however painful the story may be. Children no doubt wonder about their birth parents at a very early age. Sophie was playing happily in the bath when the phone rang. 'Was that my Mummy on the phone from China?' was her question when the call had been answered. Another child was playing with a sibling when suddenly she exclaimed, 'I want to go and see my real Mummy in Chile'. Various ways of talking to children about their origins are often discussed in the group. This helps parents to understand that there are many ways to cope with the "telling" process and that children at different ages need progressively more information.

Our support groups explore ways to help parents find the right words to explain painful details about their child's origins. Ideally, before the children actually reach the stage of asking, the parents will have practised their answers so that they are ready. Parents who are going through the same struggle can help each other. One adoptive mother commented:

I wouldn't have known what to do otherwise – the support group is where I get my ideas . . .

Most Jewish parents, even if they are not religious, plan to bring their adopted children up as part of the Jewish community. Many will want their children to be formally converted to Judaism. When children are initially brought to this country they will be introduced to the family's community. The process of conversion and the ceremony that follows have helped some communities to be more accepting. The child is now the child of the family, and the parents have demonstrated that they have given serious consideration to the child's future. The amount of preparation that the family must undergo before the child can be converted will vary depending on the family's degree of religious observance. Families who have not been practising previously but want their child to convert to orthodox Judaism, will need to undertake a course of study in order to be able to learn more about the religion. They will need to demonstrate how they will practise the religion themselves in the future, and teach their child about Jewish family life. The process may take years. Families who belong to orthodox communities and are observant, sometimes find the process is shorter. Those who belong to reform or progressive synagogues will have a different experience – the expectation of their observance will be limited, but will vary according to the culture in the community to which they belong.

Helping children with identity and self-image

We have some evidence that young children adopted from overseas "feel Jewish". The predictable nature of the year with its regular routine and special holy days gives a feeling of security to children whose lives have been chaotic. The Sabbath is an opportunity for families to get together and, for most, the Friday night meal is particularly important. When the candles are lit and a special meal is served, the atmosphere is warm and welcoming. Children value this opportunity to eat and talk together with parents and siblings who may have been busy at work and school during the week.

Some of the festivals are child-focused – for example at Purim the children have the opportunity to choose fancy dress to celebrate the occasion. Other festivals have tasks for children – there is a special part in the service at Passover which is an opportunity to receive praise from the adults. As the children learn to participate they will, we hope, enjoy these special occasions as part of being Jewish.

It will probably be somewhat later that the child starts to ask questions – 'Why was I placed in a Jewish adoptive family when my birth parents were Christian, Catholic or had no religion?' What do parents answer then? This topic is frequently raised in the support groups because it is hard to know how best to tackle it. Discussions about different religions at appropriate times will help to clarify the similarities and differences between Judaism and the religion into which the children were born. Parents will need to have their answer ready because no thought may have been given by the orphanage or adoption agency to religious or cultural matching. They will have to rely on their feelings for the child at that stage, and on the relationship they have built by that time.

It is quite possible that, like many questioning adolescents, the young person will reject the family religion and want to explore the one into which he or she was born. Agency support will be crucial at that stage, especially if it is not forthcoming from family and friends. Children joining Jewish families who have been converted when they were very young, will be asked at 12 or 13, when they have their Barmitzvah or Batmitzvah, to formally confirm their acceptance of their conversion. By that relatively early age they will need to have quite a sophisticated understanding of their background, adoption story and conversion in order to make the commitment. Balancing this commitment with their birth culture may be a life-long task.

Families raising a child adopted transracially will not manage alone. As children grow they will need role models from their own culture to help them to feel good about themselves. Laura, aged nine, was desperate to know *exactly* where her birth father was born so that she could identify with his culture and language. It was very hard for her not to have details – what she really needed was a photograph for her life story book. Laura's birth father was unknown and her birth mother did not give information about him. We do not know whether, in the future, Laura will come to terms with her birth mother's inability, or unwillingness to disclose what she knows. We hope that Laura will gain support from other children who may be struggling with similar problems. If all the children in her school know, for sure, the identities of their birth mother and birth father, the fact that another adopted child does not, may help her to feel less isolated.

Laura's story demonstrates that support groups are not only for adoptive parents. The children need each other too and will do so increasingly as they grow, question and try to build a strong and healthy self-image – perhaps on shaky foundations.

Although the group of children with whom we are working at present are all under eight, we are beginning to learn what is helping them identify with their culture of origin. Artefacts brought back from their country of origin, foods cooked from local recipes, pictures of their village or town (perhaps even pictures of their birth family or people from their community) will help. Lucy Beth's father found some oranges imported from China in his local Sainsbury's, which happened to be the sweetest and juiciest oranges anyone had tasted for ages – well spotted! Some families use every opportunity to attend festivities which acknowledge and celebrate the child's culture – Chinese New Year in London, for example. Learning the language of the child's country of origin is a good idea so that when she or he returns to the country for a visit, the family can communicate with the people who live there. Return visits can be very difficult for adopted children. It is a good idea for as many family members as possible to accompany the child in order to give support and comfort.

But however hard the adoptive parents try, they cannot know what it feels like to be a child from a culture which is different from their own. Acknowledging difference in a positive way is best if they wish to give their child maximum opportunity to feel secure. Hoksbergen (1997) says:

> ... the best way for parents to respond when they notice their child is being frequently teased because of his different looks [is to] make their child aware of the fact that he is different as far as appearance is concerned [because] he belongs to a different race and that is certainly not a reason to feel inferior... (p 84)

We encourage parents to meet adults from their child's country of origin so that the child may have role models who look like they do. Observing acceptance and friendship will give the child an added sense of worth. If the family live in a multicultural area this will be much easier to achieve. Most importantly though,

> ... *each child needs to be placed in a family where he or she can feel that all aspects of themselves are valued.* (Prevatt-Goldstein and Spencer, 2000, p 14)

Social events

Twice a year a party is held for our families. The summer party is an opportunity for all our adoptive parents and foster carers and their children to join us for a social occasion, children's entertainment and tea. In the winter there is a party for the intercountry adopting families. These are very important events where children can meet each other and their parents can chat in a relaxed (if noisy) atmosphere.

Conclusion

In our work with intercountry adopters and their children, it has become clear that adoption support is essential if the placements are to succeed. The delivery of this service by the agency is time-consuming and costly, but we have learned a tremendous amount over the years from the users of the service.

The unique position of a Jewish agency supporting Jewish families gives rise to a fascinating task and we feel it is with this small group that we can deliver a particular and special service.

The support of the agency and peer group support go hand in hand. This is helping our adoptive parents to raise their children's self-esteem to a sufficiently high level for them to function well at home and in school. It is only as they become old enough to ask more searching questions that we will know what support we need to provide directly to the children. The parents of the oldest group feel that we should be starting that support now and therefore this will be the next stage of our development.

References

Evans, K (2000) *The Lost Daughters of China*, New York: Tarcher/Putnam 2000.

Harnott, C and Robertson, R (1998) *Adoption & Fostering*, 23:4.

Hoksbergen, R (1997) *Child Adoption*, London: Jessica Kingsley Publications.

Prevatt-Goldstein, B and Spencer, M (2000) *Race and Ethnicity*, London: BAAF.

Selman, P (2000) (ed.) *Intercountry Adoption*, London: BAAF.

Steinberg, G and Hall, B (2000) *Inside Transracial Adoption*, Indiana: Perspectives Press.

Department of Health (1999) *Implementing the Adoption (Intercountry Aspects) Act 1999 Draft Regulations and Guidance For England and Wales (Draft)*, London: Departmetn of Health.

Watkins, M and Fisher, S (1993) *Talking with Young Children about Adoption*, New Haven CT: Yale University Press.

11 Adoption support for disabled children and their families

Hedi Argent

Unless a mother is completely off the wall, she knows what her child needs and doesn't need. Like an electric wheelchair; someone once thought that Adam should have one, but I thought whatever do they think he's going to do with it?

Adam was adopted. He was unable to do anything for himself. The well-meaning social worker, aware of the overwhelming day-to-day management problems faced by Adam's single parent, was surely trying to offer the latest and most expensive available equipment in a misguided effort to provide the best support. In contrast, Margaret's adoptive mother really did want support to sort out her daughter's electric wheelchair, but she didn't always get it.

*Getting the wheelchair right has been the biggest problem – we haven't got it right yet. They make standard wheelchairs for standard people who aren't standard. I go on fighting the same battle. And there's so much that can go wrong with powered wheelchairs – I'm still struggling after 15 years. (*Whatever happened to Adam?* Argent, 1998)*

All children with disabilities have a right to specialist services and children who are fostered or adopted retain that right. All adopted children and their families also have a right to adoption support services. Furthermore, adopters or birth parents may themselves be disabled and require special consideration. The National Adoption Standards for England (2001) state that 'The particular needs of disabled children will be fully recognised and taken into account when decisions are made'. Both disability and adoption remain life-long factors. Should adoption support for disabled children and their families be different from other adoption support? Is special expertise required? Can family placement workers be expected to know about the many aspects of living with disability? Can workers from a disability team be expected to know about adoption issues? Should the responsibility for disabled adopted children be transferred to an adult disability team when they reach the age of 18 or should adoption support continue for as long as the young person needs it? Would it be possible, perhaps, for adoption and disability teams to work out a joint support package with and for each family? Whatever the policy of social services, families should be given clear messages about who will do what and who is qualified to do what; they should never be left to disentangle the procedures and practices of various departments or be made to feel that they are making unreasonable demands from the wrong people, as happened to this adopter of a child with muscular dystrophy:

The adoption people expect us to slot into all the local services for children with special needs, and our local authority tells us to go back to the adoption people if we ask for anything.

Elements of support

The elements of adoption support for all children and for both their adoptive and birth families can be itemised:

- accurate, appropriate information, clear lines of communication and liaison with other agencies;
- counselling for the adoptive family; providing a sounding board and mirror whereby families can measure progress;
- counselling for birth relatives;
- negotiating and managing contact arrangements;
- financial and practical assistance;
- health and education advice and guidance;
- speedy referral to experts as and when required;
- short breaks as and how families want them;
- access to mutual support groups for adopters, adopted children and birth parents;
- training opportunities;
- preparation for disruption (see Chapter 21).

A daunting list, perhaps, but a list we disregard at the peril of the placements we make. Adopted children who are disabled, and their families, require the best of the same services as *all* families and children involved in adoption. But perhaps they also need a little extra care (Argent and Kerrane, 1997).

Accurate, appropriate information, clear lines of communication and liaison with other agencies

Adopters must be able to trust that every bit of information known about the child and birth family, now or later, will be shared with them. It is vital for all adopters to know everything there is to know about their child. They must also be able to rely on the placement agency to share all necessary information with schools, GPs, health visitors, and relevant local authority departments. The agency medical adviser should take responsibility for transferring medical records. If the child has disabilities, there will be more information to pass on and it will be more important that it is passed on in good time; it can take longer to line up special schools and health services.

Families need to know who will be offering them which element of the service, when and how; what the arrangement is for out of hours; where the managers are to be found. There are too many stories of frantic telephone calls, at crisis point, to overworked social workers who are giving reactive adoption support as and when they can fit it in. Families who adopt disabled children can be very discouraged by having to explain, over and over again to a variety of workers and administrators, that their child has special needs and what they are.

Information has no end. There is no point at which giving information stops. Information has to be reissued for families in step with their progress, just as it has to be recycled for children to fit their stage of development. The timing is as important as the content. Information can only be absorbed when people are ready,

> Joan and Lesley came to the office and read all four volumes of files about ten-year-old Ben before he was placed with them. Ben was deaf and quadriplegic and they were confused by the wealth of detailed reports, reviews, and expert opinions. After the child had been with them for three months they asked to read the files again. This time they knew what to look for.

Adoption has life-long implications for all involved and requires life-long commitment from many different organisations, professionals and individuals who have to work together to meet the needs for services of those affected by adoption. (National Adoption Standards, 2001)

Children with disabilities may attract many experts. The family GP, a health visitor, a paediatrician, a child development consultant, a speech therapist, an occupational therapist and a physiotherapist, one worker for the deaf and another for the blind, an educational psychologist and specialist teachers, and both adoption and disability social workers and family rights workers, can all give valuable advice and guidance and opinions about the same child, but can leave families feeling overwhelmed, confused and invaded.

The Davies family adopted three children with multiple disabilities. They used a special diary to note down all the appointments they had to keep. Some days they had to travel from one end of the county to the other in order to take two of their children to different hospitals; on other days, visiting experts arrived one after the other, hardly giving the family time to eat. There was no liaison between services and information had to be repeated and duplicated. The parents were grateful for the attention their children were getting and were afraid to offend anyone by complaining. But Jan Davies said, 'It feels like the family is becoming disabled because we don't have a minute left just to be a family'.

No one would wish to discourage support from wherever and by whomever it is offered, but a post-adoption worker can effectively help the family by co-ordinating services so that families can make the most of them and feel in control. The Davies' adoption worker finally organised an annual meeting of all the professionals to share information, to listen to the parents and to plan a comprehensive joined-up service for the whole family. The meetings also offered an opportunity to acknowledge the parents as the greatest experts as far as their children were concerned.

Counselling for the adoptive family: providing a sounding board and a mirror whereby families can measure progress

However thorough the preparation and training have been, the real work starts when a child is in placement. How many times have adopters said that nothing and no one could have told them what it was really going to be like? In the only study of post-adoption needs of disabled children and their families, Catherine Macaskill (1985) found that families were critical of professionals without experience in both adoption and disability. They valued the continuing support of the adoption worker who had placed the child and who could appreciate the progress made and the effort involved. They wanted to be listened to and they wanted help when they asked for it. They wanted support that was pro-active, regular and theirs, as of right.

Relatives, neighbours and friends, faced with a disability, may be too much out of their depth or too anxious to give the informal support families with children usually give each other; or they may be simply unaware of the progress and problems which seem minor to the casual observer but are momentous for the family living through them. It is not helpful if adopters are told that there is nothing really wrong with their disabled child or that they shouldn't worry because the child will get better. Adopters with disabled children have described their family worker as a welcome mirror and a sounding board, lending a listening ear and giving back a true reflection of what they hear and observe. Some parents like to have pre-planned visits, others prefer to know that their worker will telephone regularly and a few want to be free to make arrangements to fit in with the life stages of their child and family.

Lynne, a single parent, had adopted a ten-year-old girl with severe learning difficulties and communication problems. Although she had a very supportive family and many good friends, she waited eagerly for her adoption worker to call her on the first Monday evening of every month. She talked almost non-stop for the best part of an hour and always finished up by saying, 'That was great, now I've re-charged my batteries'. Lynne also relied on her worker to tell her, honestly, how she perceived the placement when she visited twice a year.

Families need to have it pointed out that their disabled child has better concentration than she had six months ago and that she seems to be making more eye contact; they also have a right to know if a worker sees warning signs – that the child has less energy or is more destructive than he was. It is no good to say or even to think, when it is too late, that we saw the problem coming. At the same time, families must have enough trust to be able to tell us themselves when something is not working, even if there is no solution except disruption.

On the whole, adopters are the best people to work with their disabled children to explain adoption, to develop life stories, to talk about disability and to find strategies to modify behaviour and to encourage attachment. They may need some guidance, they may like to have some useful tools, they may want to know that they are doing right and they may, occasionally, ask to have expert advice. It is then essential to find a person or a service used to working both with adopted and with disabled children.

Most disabled children can achieve some degree of independence although it will almost certainly take longer and require more effort. Disabled young adults may not be ready to make a move away from home until they are in their twenties or they may need help in order to become more independent at home. This is the time when families could do with support but when adoption workers will nearly always be out of the picture. Adult disability teams are rarely aware of the dynamics of adoption and families can be made to feel that they are hanging on when they should be letting go.

Nina's social worker wanted her to go into a residential home when she was 18. He didn't seem to understand that she didn't come to us till she was 12 and she still had a lot of catching up to do. We knew she wasn't ready. This worker put words into Nina's mouth without even knowing her. He said, 'You want to come and stay here, don't you Nina?' and of course Nina said 'yes' but she didn't know what she was saying 'yes' to. That's when we went back to the adoption agency and they sorted it out for us. And when Nina did leave home, she was 21 and we chose the place she went to and the timing was right and it was good for Nina. (Adoptive parent of an adult with severe learning difficulties)

It was not only good for Nina, it was a good lesson for the workers. Adopters should know that adoption workers learn from families at the same time as offering a supportive service. The principle of giving as well as receiving helps families to acknowledge their vulnerability (Macaskill, 1988).

Members of minority ethnic groups are generally under-represented as adopters of children with disabilities. Consequently disabled black children are more likely to be placed transracially than other black children. Perhaps this is due to a tendency to disregard the significance of ethnicity and culture if the child is disabled, or perhaps the special needs linked to the disability obscure the need for a sense of identity. But disabled black children may need the protection and guidance of "same race" parents even more than non-disabled children do because they are probably even less well equipped to deal with the racism they will inevitably encounter. Prospective black carers should be assured of regular expert adoption support if they adopt a disabled child; the enormous contribution they can make to the lives of even the most disabled children should be more widely acknowledged and valued.

Jade was a black two-year-old with cerebral palsy. She could not move unaided or communicate verbally. She had lived with white foster carers for most of her life. When she was placed with her black single adopter, she became fascinated by her face. She would sit on her lap and stroke her face and then touch her own cheeks.

If disabled children have been placed transracially, adoption support must offer particularly sensitive mirrors and sounding boards to pick up ethnic issues which may be overlaid by the demands of the disability.

Counselling for birth relatives

Unresolved feelings may remain for parents who have not only had to cope with a birth trauma but have also had to face the double tragedy of having to relinquish their child. (Macaskill, 2002, p 144)

The majority of birth parents of adopted children with disabilities have been unable to care for them and have agreed to adoption. Some birth parents have had their disabled children removed because they were neglected or abused. A very few parents have injured their children and caused the impairment. Whatever the circumstances, birth parents of children with disabilities have a heavy load to carry and they have a right to post-adoption support.

It is often desirable for birth relatives to have their own social worker who has not been involved with the placement. The National Adoption Standards in England require that:

> *Birth parents will have access to a support worker independent of the child's social worker from the time adoption is identified as the plan for the child.*

However, if parents have made an informed decision to have their disabled child adopted, it may be helpful to have a support worker who can give them first-hand reports on their child's progress, even if it is painful to know that other parents are able to manage better than they did.

Serena and Steve, a very young unmarried couple, could not face bringing up David, their new baby with Down's Syndrome. They really wanted him to live in residential care and found it hard to accept that other families were eager to adopt him. But they met the prospective older parents and agreed to the adoption. The same support worker stayed in touch with both families and, in due course, they exchanged information directly and began to meet occasionally. David is now growing up with a sense of being connected to his birth family; Serena and Steve have come to terms with his disability and with their own inability to be his parents. The adopters feel validated as David's parents because Serena and Steve appreciate what they are doing for him.

Of course, work with birth families of disabled children is not always as straightforward. Anger, guilt and grief for the loss of the child who might have been are frequently very much to the fore. Birth parents may wish to cut off and "bury" the child – they may literally say that their child has died. Other children in the family may carry the sorrow for their parents.

Raza's older brother, Akram, remembered seeing Raza in the hospital before he was adopted. His parents would never talk about him and Akram didn't know where he was. Raza had a rare fatal syndrome and Akram became obsessed about knowing whether Raza was dead or alive. Raza's adoptive mother tried to make contact through the social worker – she wanted his birth family to know that he was doing better than expected and that she talked to him about them. The social worker replied that the family had had another healthy child and that it was better not to upset them with unsolicited information. When Akram was 18, he traced Raza's family and made contact but he kept it a secret from his parents. When Raza died, aged 20, Akram mourned alone.

Birth siblings of adopted disabled children need special attention. Sometimes the parents can be encouraged to help themselves by helping their remaining children. Raza's birth parents and their worker might have reacted differently if they had noticed Akram's needs.

Negotiating and managing contact arrangements

Contact with birth families is as important for children with disabilities as it is for all children who have been separated from their parents (Russell, 1995). It may be more difficult to find the right words or the right way, but it is never good enough to presume that children are too disabled to comprehend the meaning of continuity and that therefore, contact has no significance. On the contrary, it could be argued that a child with learning disabilities can only make sense of her world if contact with her birth family is maintained, or a child with physical impairments can only accept himself as he is, if his birth parents also accept him (Argent, 1996).

Both families should believe that continuity and contact, if it is at all possible, will enhance the placement and the life of the disabled child. They should not agree to contact as a condition, as an inducement or out of a feeling of guilt. Sometimes a child can only register a little more or a little less contentment, but the adults may find other rewards.

Joanne was adopted by a family who already had six disabled adopted and birth children. She could not walk, talk or hear. This was an open family with truly open adoptions. All birth relatives were welcome and came and went with varying regularity. Joanne's mother had moved to another country and letters were exchanged at Christmas and just before Joanne's birthday in July. Her father, a local teacher, visited every week and looked after Joanne for the evening to give the family a break. Then he started coming more often in the holidays and at some weekends. He liked being useful and the family was grateful for the help. One might have said that Joanne did not react to her father's visits but the adopters felt sure that she was calmer when he came and that she benefited from the good atmosphere when he was there. They said, 'On some level she knows. It doesn't have to be on our level, she finds her own level in her own world.'

Contact arrangements are not always as comfortable. The same disabled child who caused shock, pain and distress for the birth parents, arrives as the precious special child for the adopters. Later, as their attachment to the child strengthens and they have to struggle and fight on the child's behalf, adopters may also go through stages of grieving, but the two families will rarely be at the same point at the same time. It then requires sensitive preparation and support to avoid tensions and conflicts during contact meetings.

If face-to-face contact is put off for a long time, birth parents may get stuck with their image of the child. If Jimmy was an immobile, mute four-year-old when they last saw him, they will need to be ready to meet a large, fully developed adolescent with a deep voice and a shambling gait who gives indiscriminate bear hugs. Birth parents have admitted that they have frightening fantasies about meeting their disabled child after a lapse of time because they do not know what they will find. Though adopters may be proud of Jimmy's walking ability and see it as an unexpected achievement, the birth parents may regard it as a shocking reminder of his impairments.

When birth parents have injured their children, even letterbox contact can be problematic. As one adoptive mother said,

I want to be forgiving, I want them to know that Leah is surviving but then I see the other children play outside and I think, that could have been Leah but for you.

This mother did manage to sustain the letterbox exchange and even went to meet the birth parents, but she did not want them to see Leah and they did not ask to see her.

There can be no rules about how often contact should happen if a child is disabled. Frequency has to be negotiated to be as meaningful as possible for each child and it has to be manageable for all those involved. What is comfortable in one situation can be full of stress in another. The adoption worker is best placed to mediate, to support and review and to act as a barometer to measure the satisfaction level of the outcome.

Financial and practical assistance

It costs three times more to bring up a child with disabilities than a child without special needs. (Baldwin, 1985)

People who adopt children with disabilities should have every possible financial assistance. But people who are good at bringing up children with special needs are not necessarily as good at filling out forms, finding out about benefit changes or claiming what is their due. A welfare rights worker, available as part of the adoption support team, can guide adopters who do not have the time and energy left at the end of the day, let alone the expertise, to pick their way through the complicated benefits, allowances and grant systems for disabled children and young people. One single parent puts it very clearly:

> *I know Adam hasn't got all the benefits he's entitled to. He should have the Disability Benefit – I've got the forms but I hate filling them in, I've half done it. And I should have applied for Income Support when he left school but by the time I got around to it, it had all changed. I've had conflicting advice from Social Security and we've had some hard times but now I've got a Welfare Rights Officer to sort things out.* (Argent, 1998, p 14)

Dealing with practical problems can obscure deeper issues as the long-term implications of a disability become more apparent but, nevertheless, the overriding importance of aids, adaptations, special equipment, an incontinence laundry service, a competent babysitter, transport and wheelchair access should never be under-estimated. 'I don't pay much attention to the social workers coming in and out as long as the nappy service is working,' said an exhausted adopter.

Some families can fight for everything they need but others cannot and would prefer to have a support worker who will fight for them.

Health and education advice and guidance

It has to be self-evident that children with disabilities have many health and educational problems. All adoption agencies have medical advisers who oversee the medical aspects of every placement; it is good practice if the medical adviser can also be called upon to see families and children after adoption. Very often adopters are confused by assessments and opinions and they need a "medical interpreter" to explain what they have been told. They may also need the medical adviser to alert consultants to the adoption factor.

We had all these doctors and students standing round and asking questions, half of them we couldn't answer. They knew Matt was adopted but it didn't seem to make any difference. They talked right over him as though he was just a disability, not a child. But he isn't stupid. We got so flustered we couldn't really understand what they said about him. They wrote it all down but it was more written for doctors than for parents. (Parent of a multiply disabled child)

Education can make or break a placement. A good special school or department within a mainstream school can be of immense support to adopters. But no available school or the wrong school can cause endless problems for any adopted child; for a disabled child it can mean that their placement is put at risk. If parents do not agree with a Statement of Educational Needs, if they do not want their adopted child to be sent to a boarding school, or if they want a different school from the one allocated, they may have to handle a long process of appeals.

Elli, who was nine years old, had been physically abused by her ambitious father because she would not learn. She was partially sighted and had a significant learning disability; she also had severe epilepsy and cerebral palsy. Her mother was a long-stay patient in a psychiatric hospital. Elli was placed for adoption with two nurses in a small country town. The local education authority said that Elli did not fit the criteria for any of the special schools in the area – she would have to go to a boarding school 100 miles away. The parents objected and tried to explain that Elli's greatest need was for security rather than learning, which she associated with being beaten, and that being sent away would feel like another rejection. The adoption worker supported the family but Elli was out of school for a year; one of the nurses had to give up her part-time job to look after Elli full-time and to teach her at home as best she could. Finally, the adopters made a personal appeal to the head teacher at one of the special schools and Elli was admitted.

It is not obligatory for adoption agencies to appoint education advisers, but if such an expert had been available as part of the adoption service, to guide Elli's parents through the educational maze, much anger and frustration would have been avoided and Elli would certainly have been the winner.

Speedy referral to experts as and when required

One of the tasks of an adoption support worker should be to refer adopters and their disabled children to experts and special services when appropriate. And "when appropriate" should usually mean, "when the adopters ask for it". If a disabled, non-verbal young person discloses that a member of staff at the day centre has sexually abused her, the adopters want expert help *now*.

She couldn't tell us what happened, she only made signs and she went mad – punching herself and throwing herself about and ripping off the wallpaper. The doctors from the practice were coming day and night to sedate her but they couldn't help her. I've found out since that other disabled children have been abused but you find it so hard to believe. There's nothing for young people like that, at least not in our area. We'd have to come to London to see anyone who knows about disabled young people who have been sexually abused, and then they probably don't know much about adoption.

(Single parent of three adopted teenagers with Down's Syndrome)

Disabled children and young people may be powerless to protect themselves, may not be able to tell and may not even understand what is being done to them. If they carry a history of abuse or emotional deprivation, they are "doubly disabled". It can be difficult for families to track down support services if their child has several disabilities or if their child's disability doesn't have a label, as in the case of Matt above and below.

Because Matt is blind, they won't take him at the playgroup and because he's so disturbed they won't take him at the nursery for the blind. He falls between two stools all the time. And then he may be autistic, but he's not been properly diagnosed yet so he doesn't qualify for their special services.

Ideally, every post-adoption worker should cultivate a pool of experts who are knowledgeable about, and interested in, both disability and adoption. For instance, there are now several kinds of therapists and therapies to help adopted children; there are also a few therapists who work with disabled children, especially with disabled children who have been abused. Disability and adoption are linked life factors which do not generally fit together but which require very special consideration in treatment situations. Agencies would do well to share information about any experts and services they find to meet this double demand.

Short breaks as and how families want them

Adopters often say, before a child is placed with them, that they will not want to have short breaks away from home for their child. But if short breaks are always on the adoption support agenda, they will feel free to change their minds later.

> Catherine, a single mother, adopted Janine who needed day and night attention. Catherine was a trained nurse and felt sure that nothing would faze her. But two years later Janine became acutely and seriously ill; when she recovered, Catherine was exhausted. She found the piece of paper with the details of the short breaks scheme and she used it. She said she would never have asked otherwise in case social services thought she was a failure.

It is equally important to tailor the short breaks to individual needs. One couple found it impossible to plan a year ahead as their agency expected them to do; they had adopted three blind children and they wanted to have relief when they most needed it. In contrast, a single adopter of two children with Down's Syndrome liked to feel that she could book her holidays knowing that the children would be looked after.

Access to mutual support groups for adopters, adopted children and birth parents

It is generally accepted that peer support is enjoyable and effective. If agencies can offer mutual support groups as part of their adoption service, there will be many benefits including less demand for other elements of adoption support. Practical matters like finance and equipment as well as deeper issues of adoption and disability are usually well handled by groups. However, it is not really successful to have mixed groups. Families who have adopted children with disabilities may have little in common with parents who have adopted older children; birth parents of disabled children will not easily share experiences with relinquishing birth parents of healthy infants or with birth parents who have contested their children's adoptions; and many disabled children would not be able to join other children in a group. Support groups for disabled children and their families therefore require special arrangements and skilful leadership.

It is often suggested to adopters that they should join a group or association for parents of children with specific disabilities. This can work for some families but not for others.

They don't seem to realise we've got the same problems as they have. They treat us like we're saints or else mad because we chose to have Mark. It makes it hard to join in with them. And in a way, I think they resent us. They don't seem to like it when we say we're happy with Mark's progress. (Adoptive father of a boy with Down's Syndrome)

An economic way for adopters to support each other is by telephone link. One voluntary agency invited all adopters and permanent foster carers of disabled children to join a telephone directory scheme. Information about each family was entered on separate sheets and collected in a loose-leaf folder. Families had their own books and could add or take away sheets as people joined or withdrew from the scheme. The information sheets included details about the child and the disability, about schools, playgroups or nurseries attended, about medical and domiciliary services and about anything else that one family thought would interest another (Argent and Kerrane, 1997).

Sarah discovered wonderful but expensive incontinence aids for her adopted teenage daughter. She put it down on her directory page and was inundated with enquiries. The families then got together and persuaded their local authorities to give a special allowance to families with incontinent older children.

The Smith family rang the Prior family when their daughter was due to start school because they saw in the directory that the Priors' son, who had a similar disability, went to a mainstream school in their area. After some negotiation, and with the Priors' help, their daughter was admitted to the same school.

Training opportunities

Sexual development, special education, medical conditions, alternative treatments, behaviour problems and welfare rights are the topics most adopters with disabled children want to learn more about. Study days and workshops for groups of adopters are popular events in adoption support programmes. It is not always necessary to hire guest speakers – there is sometimes enough expertise among adopters and it makes for a better day out if families can learn from each other and perhaps bring food to share for lunch.

One adoptive father was a reflexologist. He taught the other adopters how to make physical contact with defensive, distant children who avoided closeness. Gently massaging feet is not threatening and can begin to build trust between parent and child. This father also demonstrated, very movingly, how giving real, concentrated attention to a child was not at all the same as half listening while we peel the potatoes or think about the next day's dinner. All the people who attended this workshop, including the adoption workers, took away new ideas to put into practice.

Many adopters would not be able to come to training events unless their disabled children can come too. Some kind of reliable care for the children is therefore essential.

Conclusion and checklist

Finally, there are some questions to be asked: Does the adoption support on offer suit the service users? Does it fit in with the adopter's lifestyle, ethnicity, culture and religion? Does it take account of each child's specific disability and is it consistent? Are the birth family's needs acknowledged? A checklist may be useful:

Services and experts Are they working together in the interests of the child and the adopters? Should other referrals be made?

Information Are both families being kept up-to-date as planned and agreed?

Statutory benefits and adoption allowances Is the family claiming and receiving everything to which it is entitled?

Short breaks Are they available as, when and where the family needs them?

Life stages Going to school, changing and leaving schools, births, marriages, deaths, additions to the family, significant separations, moves to independence; is adoption support sufficiently responsive to the impact of change on a disabled child?

Contact and continuity Are contact arrangements working and are they regularly reviewed? If there is no contact how is continuity maintained?

Aids and adaptations Does the adoptive family have all necessary equipment as the child grows and the needs change?

Education Are educational statements up-to-date and do parents agree with the recommendations?

Health Do the adopters and the child have access to relevant treatments, assessments and therapies?

Birth relatives Are they being offered a post-adoption service they can use?

When all has been said, there is still a last word, which must go to an adoptive parent of two children with severe physical disabilities:

> *First we're a family with two children. Then we're a family with two adopted children. Last of all we're an adoptive family with two disabled children. Please remember that.* (Argent, 1996)

References

Argent, H (1996) *Post-adoption Services for Children with Disabilities* (Practice paper), London: Post-Adoption Centre.

Argent, H (1998) *Whatever Happened to Adam? Stories of disabled people who were adopted or fostered*, London: BAAF.

Argent, H and Kerrane, A (1997) *Taking Extra Care: Shared, respite and permanent care for children with disabilities*, London: BAAF.

Baldwin, S (1985) *The Cost of Caring: Families with disabled children*, London: Routledge & Kegan Paul.

Department of Health (2001) *National Adoption Standards for England*, London: Department of Health.

Macaskill, C (1985) *Against the Odds: Adopting mentally handicapped children*, London: BAAF.

Macaskill, C (1988) 'It's a bonus – families' experiences of adopting children with disabilities', *Adoption & Fostering*, 12:2, pp 24–8.

Macaskill, C (2002) 'Managing contact arrangements for children with learning difficulties', in Argent, H, (ed.) *Staying Connected: Managing contact arrangements in adoption*, London: BAAF.

Russell, P (1995) 'The importance of contact for children with disabilities – issues for policy and practice', in Argent, H (ed.) *See you soon: Contact with children looked after by local authorities*, London: BAAF.

12 Adoption panels and adoption support

Alan Johnstone

In view of the emphasis put on adoption support in the Adoption and Children Act 2002, it is timely to reflect on how adoption panels can influence adoption support services. How effectively have panels exercised influence in the past and how might panels extend their influence in the future?

What do adoption panels do?

We know that panels have a duty to make recommendations as to:
- whether adoption is in the best interests of a child;
- whether a prospective adopter is suitable to be an adoptive parent;
- whether a prospective adopter would be a suitable adoptive parent for a particular child; and
- associated issues such as freeing applications and adoption allowances.

Adoption support is relevant to each of the three main recommendations and to adoption allowances.

In approaching all these life-changing matters, a panel considers information and plans submitted by the agency. When focusing on the adoption support element of each issue, a panel will wish to be very clear that the child's possible future needs have been identified; that prospective adopters being put forward for approval appear to be people with the capacity and willingness to recognise when the family really needs support and will then seek it; and that the agency's matching proposal contains a specific adoption support plan for this child and this family.

In general terms that is what should happen and, by various means, often does. However, whether the adoption support aspects in matching proposals are always identified and presented in a systematic manner that guides and enables purposeful discussion is open to question. What do panels use to evaluate the adoption support needs in a specific case? How do they seek consistency of approach and operate within written policies agreed with the agency? Have the adoptive families been heard?

If panels are to discharge their duty towards the children and families affected by their far-reaching recommendations, then the need to influence both the general and the specific provision of adoption support services is surely axiomatic. If a panel is to recommend that the intended matching is a viable proposal, then some confidence about the likely availability of support is essential.

What else are panels meant to do and be?

The invaluable BAAF guide, *Effective Panels* (Lord *et al*, 2000) comments that:

> *This diverse group of people, pooling and sharing their different experience and expertise, can speak from a very informed perspective and with an authoritative voice, providing a vital scrutiny as well as a validation of the agency's work.* (p 1)

In *For Children's Sake* (Department of Health/Social Services Inspectorate, 1996), the inspection of local authority adoption services described panels as having a vital and expert role, and also pointed out that their legislative role invites them to act as the arbiters and shapers of good practice.

Fine words: however, the report found that some panels did not act in this way, partly due to a lack of awareness or practical involvement in wider issues affecting provision of adoption services. It found that most panels had no tradition of developing an overview and were not well placed to comment authoritatively on the general adoption business of the authorities they served. In 1997, *For Children's Sake Part 2* (relating to adoption support services) (Department of Health, 1997) found that the majority of panels considered adoption support to some extent, but that panels could make a greater contribution to strategic planning. All agencies were aware of the need to provide adoption support, but few had defined explicitly the range and nature of this support. Some excellent best practice was noted, but the message from these two important reports was a timely wake-up call for many local authorities. Given that adoption panels should, by regulation, have been involved in the process of drawing up policies in relation to adoption support, it was also a wake-up call for some panels.

Three years later, a further report provided some information on how the call had been heeded. In *Adopting Changes* (Department of Health, 2000) the comprehensive SSI survey and inspection of adoption services found that in many councils general adoption practice was good. The Devon adoption support policy provided for plans presented to the adoption panel to include details of arrangements for offering the necessary support, with confirmation that resources would be available. Procedures guided staff in writing these plans and in getting financial agreement.

However, this excellent example of best practice had to be considered alongside the fact that, in the ten councils directly inspected, there were few references to adoption support in children's individual placement plans. Many adoptive families were left vulnerable with varying levels of service, and varying attitudes towards eligibility and priority. Less than half the councils in the national survey had written information for adopters on available adoption support and how it could be accessed.

Many voluntary adoption agencies and their panels have been pathfinders in adoption support practice for a number of years. Increasing numbers of local authorities and their panels have, particularly in recent years, also developed innovative approaches. More local authorities have a specific post-adoption team, or post(s) dedicated to this work. But it is also the case that some adoption panels have not been as successful as they would have wished to be, in encouraging and influencing their authority to develop policies and resources for adoption support.

The Adoption and Children Act (2002), National Standards for Adoption (2001) and the *Providing Effective Adoption Support* consultation document (Department of Health, August 2002) that will lead to the Regulations governing adoption support provided for in the Act, provide an unrivalled opportunity for all of us involved in adoption panels to review our performance and strengthen our influence on new policies on adoption support.

How can panels gain more understanding of the issues in order to exert influence on agency policies and service provision?

New panel members (and perhaps some of us longer serving ones!) need to build on the experience and knowledge that led to our appointment. All panel members must have access to their agency library service where one would hope to find, in among some of the excellent relevant research and practice publications, a good selection of BAAF anthologies and articles. In addition to the vital Department of Health (DH) Guidance and consultation papers, *Adoption Support* (DH, 2002a), issued by the Adoption and Permanence Taskforce, provides useful practice materials. Some panels have negotiated with their agency to use the minimum one-day-a-year training commitment to organise a panel conference with agency staff and to invite speakers on topics such as adoption support.

An absolutely vital source of information comes from adoptive families themselves. Essex Post Adoption Service has completed phase one of a planned three-part research project, *Developing Co-ordinated and Comprehensive Post Adoption Services* (Plenty, 2002). A central element in the research was the participation of 73 adoptive parents. From this total group, direct interviews took place with 35 adoptive parents.

Of the 73 adoptive parents, over 90 per cent felt that the involvement of adoptive parents was "very important"; almost 55 per cent agreed to participate in the advisory/consultation adopters' group. Comments included:

The adoptive parents are receivers of post-adoption services and their experiences must say it all. (p 63)

The views of adoptive parents could help local authorities to improve the transfer of children from the care system back into family life. (p 64)

They are the ones living it, eating it, sleeping it – living with the practicalities. The service presumably is for their benefit so limited resources shouldn't be wasted on something they don't want. (p 64)

Placing service users at the heart of strategic service planning can be key to its success in terms of bringing "real life" experiences into the operational arena. Adoption panel members bring personal and professional experience and knowledge gained from research and reading to the task, but any opportunity to be involved in listening to adoptive parents' views on local adoption support services should not be missed. Some agencies, by reason of scale or other circumstances, may not be in a position to establish an advisory/consultation group, but most will have formal or informal adoptive parents support groups and, where it has not yet happened, panel members may well wish to seek a meeting or find some means of hearing their views.

Adoptive parents' views can lead to fresh perspectives on policy statements that appeared entirely appropriate when written. A small informal group of panel chairs recently reviewed agency policy documents on adoption support. One statement headed "problems and difficulties", while intended to assure adopters that there would be help at times of stress could, with hindsight, lead adopters, agency staff and social services councillors to see adoption support as a response to failure rather than as a response to an anticipated need. Another statement more helpfully began by saying that:

Placing children in adoptive families is only the beginning, supporting the placement and recognising the ongoing needs of the child and their adoptive family, and those of the birth family, are equally important.

Adoptive parents and adopted persons on panels bring their practical experience and need to be heard when adoption support policies are being developed. *For Children's Sake* (Department of Health, 1996) recommended, among initiatives that would promote panels' awareness of the context in which their work is set, observational visits by panel members to other panels. This has not become common practice, but the welcome growth of cross-authority adoption consortia ought to lead to an exchange of ideas and joint panel training including sessions on adoption support. Trying to be the "arbiters and shapers of good practice", as the DH expects adoption panels to be, need not be a solitary business.

How can panels influence adoption support services for individual children and families?

The first building block for an adoptive placement is when a panel recommends that adoption is in a child's best interests. The quality and range of documentation available for panels has improved in recent years. The BAAF Form E, LAC documents, school report, specialist reports (including those obtained by leave of the court) and, critically, the views of the child's current carer, can provide the panel with a clear picture of why the child may need an adoptive placement. The more recent introduction of Core Assessments should also be of value.

However, panel members must ask themselves, do I really have a sense of what it might be like to live with this child? If I were a prospective adopter, would I have sufficient information to feel confident about going forward? While agency staff devote their working lives to tackling such issues, the panel has a vital duty, at this initial stage, to ask the right questions. Once the recommendation is made, the process begins and it may be too late.

Listening to adopters helps us to focus. Quinton *et al* (1998) found that significant numbers of adopters were dissatisfied with some aspects of the information about the child, e.g. only half considered it to have been sufficient or up to date.

Panels should note, at the initial "best interests" recommendation, any clear indications for adoption support such as:

- attachment patterns;
- likely contact needs;
- impact of abuse and neglect;
- child's life experiences;
- behavioural problems;
- health, education and disabilities; and
- probable financial requirements.

All these issues are important, especially the complexity of contact. Figures from the Essex research (Plenty, 2002) show that the largest single group of referrals to the post-adoption team involve contact arrangements.

While formal recommendations in relation to adoption allowances will be addressed at the matching stage, panels will wish to give preliminary consideration to this question if the child has special needs.

For Children's Sake (Department of Health, 1996) commented that:

Adoption panels have a clear interest in ensuring that plans for adoptive placements are progressed effectively. It was disappointing how little involved they were in reviewing implementation of such plans. This is a proper responsibility of panels. (p 39)

Panels must set regular review dates for children, at three-or four-month intervals, so that the identified issues can be monitored. While minutes of panel discussions are useful, some panels have developed an "action sheet" approach. At the conclusion of the "best interests" recommendation meeting, the panel sets down the agreed tasks with timescales for the agency. Throughout the reviewing process and critically at the proposed matching stage, these action sheets can serve as a panel check on how thinking and work have progressed to a point where, hopefully, the panel can be clear that adoption support needs have been fully addressed.

One example involved an older girl and her brother who were presented to panel for an "adoption is in best interests" recommendation, during care proceedings.

The initial information indicated that the young woman had very complex needs, unlike her much younger baby brother. The panel requested a comprehensive sibling assessment including the girl's immediate and longer-term therapeutic needs; the timescale was agreed and set out in an action sheet. The assessment resulted in a decision to place the children separately, with direct contact, particularly as it was clear that the girl needed a period of care in a therapeutic community. Reviews over 18 months and subsequent action sheets addressed such matters as direct preparation work and the emerging long-term therapeutic needs. The agency was requested to find a family taking into account the key requirements for adoption support. The panel met with the proposed adopters and everyone found the sequence of action sheets and outcomes of great value when focusing on the range of financial, educational and therapeutic adoption support that was critical in enabling the placement to proceed. A recommendation was made only on the understanding that this support as well as respite care would be available.

The second building block for an adoptive placement is when a panel recommends that a prospective adopter is suitable to be an adoptive parent. Among the many important factors regarding suitability are those that influence the potential effectiveness of adoption support plans at a later matching stage and in the longer term. Panels will take into account the response of applicants to the preparation groups, the ways in which they, as individuals, acquire information and how open they are to the need for future agency or other adoption support.

The manner in which preparation groups are undertaken can have a major impact, as they can lay the foundation for a positive working relationship that empowers prospective adopters and encourages confidence in continuing adoption support. This is only the start of training, as parenting adopted children requires a constant accumulation of skills and knowledge. The benefits of continued training as an effective aspect of adoption support should be introduced at this stage.

Panels will wish to note and discuss the prospective adopters' openness to establishing buddy/mentor links with experienced adopters: for instance, if they are being recommended for a large sibling group, then a link with other adopters who have practical experience of the support needs would help at the matching stage. Panels may check that prospective adopters are fully aware of organisations such as Adoption UK and of the *It's a Piece of Cake* training package. As for children, panels may do well to have a mechanism for monitoring the position of approved adopters while they await a placement.

In the 1980s and early 1990s, many voluntary agency panels met with applicants, but relatively few local authority panels did so. That position will change, as the National Adoption Standards require panels to invite all applicants to attend. In five years as an independent panel chair with a number of agencies, I have met over 350 prospective adopters. All my panel member colleagues would agree that the individual and collective learning from this experience has been invaluable. The reality of, for example, meeting with second-time prospective adopters and discussing with them the adoption support they have received (or not received) enables panels to be clearer at the time of matching about what support is likely to be needed for this child and this prospective adopter.

One couple had been linked with a child by the panel two years previously and had faced real difficulties in relation to direct birth parent contact. While this had been, and still was, agreed as desirable in the child's long-term interests, the pressure on the child, adoptive parents, a birth child in the family and on the adoptive grandparents was significant. The panel had underestimated the potential difficulties at the time of linking and it was important for panel members to hear, at first hand, how the whole family and post-adoption services had addressed the issues. A post-adoption team worker had been introduced prior to the adoption order being made so that a working relationship had been established. The involvement and actions of the post-adoption worker in helping negotiate more positive contact arrangements and responding to the differing perspectives of members of the extended adoptive family and the birth parents had been crucial. In discussing their second application directly with the panel, the adopters were very clear how they would wish to negotiate contact in advance of a future placement. The panel's understanding of contact issues developed through the impact of direct discussion with the adopters who were "living it".

The third building block and the stage at which panels can and must exercise most influence over adoption support services is the proposed matching stage. No panel will wish to consider an agency proposal without first reviewing all the documentation relating to the child and the adopters. In addition the panel should have action sheets and panel review reports and a clear account of the direct preparation work undertaken with the child. The most up-to-date reports on the child's current and likely future needs are essential, as the panel must be very clear about any changes and must check on the comprehensiveness of the information provided to the prospective adopter. Any relevant developments in relation to the prospective adopter will be noted. Panels should receive a detailed account of the proposed adopters' views on the information about the child, which must have been discussed with the agency. Their views at this stage about adoption support needs are critical.

Effective Panels (Lord *et al*, 2000) contains useful guidance on the central importance of adoption support issues at the matching stage.

This is likely to be crucial to the success of the placement. There will almost certainly be some limitations and risks in any match as well as strengths, and panel members need to check on the particular help that is planned to compensate in these areas:

- *What help is proposed and from whom, both after placement and after adoption? It is particularly important to check this in inter-agency placements and where the family may live outside the child's home area.*
- *What is the family's attitude to seeking help and to working with others, for instance, specialist therapists, whose help the child may need?*
- *Are the agency and the family aware that support and help may be needed in the future even if it is not apparent at the time of placement?*
- *How will a need for help in the future be met? Panel members should check on the availability of specialist educational and medical facilities which may be necessary.'* (p 55)

At this stage the panel involvement in, and ownership of, the agency adoption support policy becomes very real. If the policy has been properly constructed and panel members understand the full range of adoption support services that can and should be available, then maximum influence can be exercised on the future arrangements for a particular child and their prospective adopter.

Those panels that do not meet prospective adopters can keep in mind the comments made to the Essex research team (Plenty, 2002) by adoptive families:

- Adoption services should be seamless so that rapport and consistency are maintained.
- More information should be given about adoption support services during the assessment and placement stages; adoptive parents are not usually focusing on the future but more on the here and now; encouragement should be given to consider adoption support issues and the services that are available.
- If you ask for help you should not be made to feel you are being judged.
- Adoption support services should offer practical and emotional support.
- Advocacy, especially in the school arena, should be available.

- Families need access to counselling services that understand adoption.
- It's important to identify the needs of existing children within the family and support other family members such as grandparents.
- We need to be reminded that you are out there and that we need to feel we can approach you without fears that our children will be whisked away or that we will be labelled incompetent.
- Now that we have been able to meet with you and learn more about the service, it has become "real" and we would have no hesitation in contacting you if we felt we needed help in the future for the benefit of our children.

The recommendations at the matching stage cover adoption allowances, a vital part of adoption support services. The history of adoption allowances is confused and many panels will have struggled to find the best way forward in an inconsistent system. The wildly differing levels of availability and amounts involved, along with the outrageous reported examples of panels recommending allowances and agencies not paying the allowance for budgetary reasons, have clearly presented real ethical dilemmas for some panels. However, there is overwhelming evidence that allowances enable adoptive families to meet the needs of children who require extra care. For example, the value of short breaks for some families is clear and allowances can be used for this purpose among many others.

Other financial means of support could be on the agenda at this stage. Creative plans have been made, with a panel's encouragement, for loft conversions, house extensions, second bathrooms and bigger cars as well as extra beds and furniture so that large sibling groups could be placed together. It is up to the panel to ask, every time a decision is made to split siblings, whether a sizeable grant could be raised to keep them together. Not many families, however committed and capable, can afford to take on four, five or six children all at once, without a hefty financial boost.

After adoption

Panels should, at the matching stage, build in reviews so that placement progress can be monitored. In the unhappy event of a disruption, all panel members should receive and discuss disruption reports. The learning from reviews and disruptions can be an affirming or very painful experience, depending on the circumstances, but either way it will help to develop better-informed decision-making skills for the future. It is worth noting here that inadequate support and or inappropriate support are the most often listed causes of disruption. The daily experiences of families living adoption and the kind of support they want was usefully captured by an adoptive parent in the Essex research:

> *Adoption support is important and it should be about allowing adoptive families to function, about teaching strategies for coping, but also about absorbing those elements of having adoptive children that take an ordinary family beyond the point where it is reasonable to expect ordinary families to cope. Children being placed today come with baggage, if as a society we are asking ordinary people to look after these children then as a society we also owe it to these families to give them the necessary support.* (Plenty, 2002, preface)

References

Department of Health, Social Services Inspectorate (1996) *For Children's Sake: An SSI inspection of local authority services*, London: Department of Health.

Department of Health, Social Services Inspectorate (1997) *For Children's Sake Part 2: An SSI inspection of local authority services*, London: Department of Health.

Department of Health (2000) *Adopting Changes: Survey and inspection of local council's adoption services*, London: Department of Health.

Department of Health (2001) *The National Adoption Standards for England*, London: Department of Health.

Department of Health (2002) *Providing Effective Adoption Support*, London: Department of Health.

Department of Health Adoption and Permanence Task Force (2002a) *Adoption Support: A workbook for commissioners of services*, London: Department of Health.

Lord, J, Barker, S and Cullen, D (2000) *Effective Panels* (2nd edn), London: BAAF.

Plenty, J (2002) *Developing Co-ordinated and Comprehensive Post Adoption Services, Phase 1: Surveying post adoption service need with agency staff and adoptive parents across the county of Essex*, Essex Adoption Agency Post Adoption Service.

Quinton, D, Rushton, A, Dance, C and Mayes, D (1998) *Joining New Families: A study of adoption and fostering in middle childhood*, Chichester: John Wiley.

13 **An after adoption panel:**
reopening closed adoptions

Maureen Crank

Increasingly, agencies are recognising the sadness and sense of loss that relatives, particularly birth parents, have experienced over the adoption of their children, and in recent years there has been a move away from the "closed" model of adoption towards a more open approach.

In August 2000, the Department of Health published guidelines encouraging local authorities and adoption agencies to offer a more sensitive and proactive approach to birth relatives who are attempting to discover what has become of the sons and daughters, brothers and sisters who were placed for adoption years previously (Department of Health, 2000). As a response, and in partnership with After Adoption, some agencies are now offering a service that is more supportive to birth relatives.

Background

Since 1992, After Adoption has worked in partnership with Manchester Social Services to provide post-adoption services including birth records counselling.

Due to the huge number of family members returning for information about their adopted relative, social services agreed to fund a pilot intermediary service for birth relatives and After Adoption began this work in 1994.

During the course of the pilot scheme, 31 adopted people were searched for, found and contacted. Of these, 29 were happy to have been found and to receive information from their relative, although not all went ahead with a face-to-face meeting. Two, however, turned into complaints and one of these became extremely complicated, drawn out and litigious.

The service was suspended for about 18 months while the complaint was investigated. The formal complaint against After Adoption was made by the adoptive parents, who had not been consulted before an approach was made to their daughter. Their daughter, in her mid-30s and married with three children, was approached by us on behalf of her full birth sibling. The excited daughter had immediately shared the information with her adoptive parents who were angry that the approach had not been made through them and that information about them had been passed on by the local authority to a third party, i.e. After Adoption. We believed, at the time, that we were acting in the best interests of an adult adopted person living independently. We have now taken on board the recommendations of the Inquiry. We accept that some of the distress caused to these adopters could have been avoided if they had been made aware, as a matter of policy, of the changing practice in voluntary agencies and some local authorities, to make approaches on behalf of birth relatives.

When the decision was made to resume this work, After Adoption and Manchester Social Services agreed that there needed to be a joint process of decision-making and a simple policy and procedure were designed. A leaflet was also produced to explain the process to those making a request for information.

The panel

A panel was set up to meet monthly and examine requests. The panel consists of senior managers from both agencies, who are permanent members, and usually two other workers involved in the cases as well as an administrator. This demonstrates joint ownership of the decision in the light of the request.

Initially the work consisted mainly of dealing with requests made by adults seeking adults, but as time has moved on and the work has developed, around one-third of the requests are in relation to adopted children and young people whose adoptions have so far been "closed".

In the case of children and young people under 18, the panel looks at the options in relation to the request and the available information. Is it to open up letterbox contact or to have face-to-face contact? Who may be around who knew this child or family at the point of reception into care or adoption?

The remit

1. *Intermediary services for birth relatives (approaching adult adoptees)*

- In the case of "straightforward" relinquishing birth mothers, requesting an intermediary service, there is no need for matters to be considered by the panel. Manchester Social Services will provide After Adoption with access to the adoption records. Any particular difficulties noted (e.g. inconsistency with birth mother's account, child suffering disability) would then be brought back to the panel for consideration.

- Where there is a history of care proceedings/abuse/neglect, the matter will be considered by the panel.

- Where the birth family presents particular difficulties (e.g. mental health issues, birth parents married to each other but one is acting without other's knowledge) the matter will be taken to the panel.

- Progress of the search or proposed method of approach do not need to be considered by the panel except where there are particular problems (e.g. suspected learning difficulties – adopted adult living with adoptive parents).

2. *Cases involving under 18s*

- In all cases where an approach to a child under 18 years – via the adoptive parents – is being considered, the matter will be taken to the panel.

- All cases involving approaches to sons/daughters who are over 18 but where there are adopted siblings under 18 years of age, will be considered by the panel.

- All cases where a child is accommodated or subject of a care order or where there are questions about legal status will go to the panel.

3. *Other issues*

- In cases where there may be a social worker (who is still in the employ of Manchester Social Services) currently involved with or previously known to the birth or adoptive family, the matter will be considered by the panel in order to decide who is the most appropriate person to undertake the work. Where appropriate the social worker will be invited to attend the panel.

- In situations where a death has occurred in either the birth or adoptive family and we are being asked to inform the other party, the matter will be considered by the panel.
- Cases involving complex inter-agency working will be taken to the panel.
- If in doubt about whether a matter needs to be considered by the panel, do so!
- In all cases, including "straightforward" requests from relinquishing birth mothers, a brief summary of outcome will be given to the panel for monitoring purposes and placed on the adoption records.

The process

The panel's service is offered in each appropriate case and the emphasis of the panel's work is to negotiate contact, but if the decision is to not proceed, a worker will make a home visit to explain why. All situations are seen as new referrals and following each request, a worker will be appointed to that case. They will research to see if any previous workers are able to give further background information. If they are, then it may be deemed best that they contact the family. The worker will report progress back to the next panel and an agreement about how to approach the family or individual is then made. Each situation is fully discussed and, where there may be a relevant person available, they will be invited to the panel.

In one such case we discovered that the non-searching sibling, Ian aged 17, had mental health problems. His mental health worker attended the panel to help with the best method of approaching Ian. Jack and Darrel, his twin brothers, aged 14, had requested contact and were supported in this by their adoptive families. The worker's input was invaluable in helping to make a successful plan, and it was the same worker who eventually approached Ian about his brothers and facilitated their meeting.

Another recent request was from a birth father named Harry.

Harry asked for a photograph and information about his two daughters who had been adopted. He was serving a prison sentence for sexual abuse of his eldest daughter and was due for imminent release.

The panel invited the social worker who had been involved, although she was now working for another authority. She was happy to attend and filled the panel in with additional facts that were not clear from the file. The decision was made to not support Harry's request.

A worker was sent to see Harry to explain this to him but was also able to let him know that the girls were well and thriving. The girls' family were told of Harry's request and of the panel's decision. Harry has had several counselling sessions in the prison about his situation.

All cases are recorded in a way that, should the adopted person want to know why a decision has been made, they can see and read the steps taken. At the end of the panel meeting, a summary is made and placed on the adoption file.

Re-opening closed adoptions

The panel meets monthly to discuss requests made to the local authority to re-open closed adoptions. It deals with approximately 20 to 30 requests a month.

The value base of the panel is to approach each case in a positive light and to proceed towards mediated contact between families, clearly protecting the anonymity of the adopted child or adult, but giving that adopted person's birth or adoptive parents an opportunity to open up contact in a planned way, should they wish. The safety of the child is always a consideration.

The panel makes decisions, minutes how they have reached that decision and plans a way forward. Actions are monitored at each meeting. If the response is not to proceed, a visit will be made to the person concerned and full reasons given.

Many discussions are carried forward to the next month if the panel is seeking more information to help them reach a decision.

Examples of requests considered by the panel

- A birth mother whose letterbox contact has not happened over the last two years (she had sent letters and cards and received no response).
- A white adoptive family in Wales wanting face-to-face contact for their 11-year-old adopted daughter with her birth mother. The adopted girl is of African-Caribbean origin and wanted to meet her mother who she knew was a popular black pop singer. The situation was complicated as the adoptive family's first language was Welsh.
- A case was brought to the panel by a birth mother's sister, Rita, who wrote explaining that her sister, Mary, was in the late stages of cancer. Mary had had a daughter, Jane, now 16, adopted when she was two. The doctors had advised that the medical information should be passed to Jane and her family. Rita felt they should be given the information before Mary's death to allow Jane to meet her birth mother should she wish. When Jane's family was approached they decided that Jane should not have the information about Mary at that time as she was in the midst of her GCSEs. However, they did tell her some two months later and she met Mary twice prior to her death, supported by her parents. Jane and her parents also met Mary's doctor and were given full medical information.

Conclusion

Trust is an important component in the successful working of this panel, and the excellent professional relationship between the two organisations helps. It is also relevant that there are enough specialist workers available to unravel the complexities in these post-adoption situations and to mediate where necessary. It is essential that social workers, families and other professionals understand the process of the after-adoption panel and the reasons for it.

This innovative after-adoption panel appears to work for those concerned. It is open and it is transparent. People receiving the service express high levels of satisfaction. Birth families, adopted people and adoptive parents say their need for information was dealt with and responded to in a timely and humane way.

Thank you so much . . . we all feel whole . . . said three sisters in their 20s, who had been separately adopted and reunited through the panel.

References

Department of Health (2000) *Intermediary Services for Birth Relatives: Practice guidelines*, available from Department of Health Publications, PO Box 777, London SE1 6XH, ref 220905KCHI.

14 Therapeutic approaches in adoption

Stephen Scott and Caroline Lindsey

This chapter discusses some practical therapeutic approaches intended to benefit adopted children. But first, the context in which adoption occurs and recent advances in the understanding of children's mental health are described. These considerations inform assessment and the planning of interventions.

The changing world of adoption

Until 30 or 40 years ago, the majority of children adopted in the UK and USA were white, born to healthy single mothers, and were developing in a typical way: they had no developmental delays or major mental health problems. There were enough babies or infants to meet the demand for them. Most were placed in the first two years of life with married white adoptive parents, who were told very little about the birth families (in the USA birth records were sealed), and had no contact with them (Brodzinsky *et al*, 1998). Now, in contrast, there are not enough infants to meet demand. The children come from ethnically diverse backgrounds, are older, and in the majority of cases have significant psychiatric problems or developmental delays. Many have experienced inadequate parenting to meet their needs, which are often complex. Many will have been subject to neglect and emotional abuse with scapegoating. Some will have been seriously physically and sexually abused by their birth parents or other members of the family circle, who frequently have psychiatric and personality disorders themselves. The adopting parent, who will come from as close an ethnic match as possible, may or may not have a partner, and in England and Wales legislation has been passed to allow unmarried and same sex couples to adopt jointly.

All these factors mean that adoption has become a more complex process. Assessments have become more difficult, and then deciding whether a child would be best served by removal from the birth family is often hard to judge and painful. Good evidence for what works in providing therapeutic benefit is scarce. Post-adoption support services are often sparse, with the adoptive parents sometimes feeling abandoned by local authorities, which no longer have immediate legal responsibility.

Defining good outcomes

Sigmund Freud defined mental health as the capacity to love and to work – *lieben und arbeiten*. If the adopted child can grow up able to enter into satisfying relationships and to take part in work or constructive activities, that is indeed a good outcome. One might add a secure sense of their identity and freedom from distressing psychiatric problems as further evidence of a good outcome. From the adoptive parents' point of view, the adoption process should have been satisfying (if hard at times) and sustainable – breakdown of the relationship with a return of the child to the care of the local authority is perceived as the final index of failure.

Relevance of recent genetic and environmental findings

Emotional and behavioural difficulties

When a young person has emotional and behavioural difficulties, the question often arises whether the problems can be wholly attributed to poor parenting, or whether the child might have developed the same problems anyway, due to their inherited personality or makeup. This will affect the degree of improvement that might be expected through the influence of being placed in a favourable adoptive family environment.

Recent Swedish and Danish adoption studies are illuminating. For example, Bohman and Sigvardsson (1996) looked at the adolescent outcomes of children who had been adopted before the age of two. The genetic risk was allocated to a high or low category according to whether either *birth* parent had a criminal record or had alcohol dependence disorder. If genetic influences were important, one would expect the children of alcoholic or criminal parents to have more difficulties than those from untroubled parents despite both groups being brought up in adoptive families. The researchers then went on to categorise the environment in which the children were brought up as more or less favourable, according to the same criteria applied to the *adoptive* parents.

Thus if either adoptive parent had an alcohol problem or a criminal record, this was taken as likely to indicate a less favourable upbringing (in an ideal world, one might hope that the screening of potential adoptive parents might pick up these difficulties).

The measure used for child outcome was whether or not they had a criminal record by the age of 17 years. This measure was chosen as it could be applied to the whole sample without the need to interview them. It is also a good proxy measure for a range of associated difficulties, such as less good academic performance in school examinations, poorer social skills, and drug and alcohol misuse. The results are shown in Figure 1.

Figure 1
Outcomes of early adopted children according to inherited risk and quality of adopting family

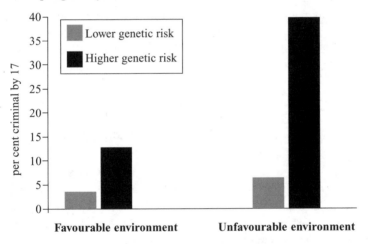

A number of conclusions may be drawn from these results. Firstly, the two left hand bars show that when raised in favourable conditions, children with higher risk parents did indeed have significantly increased rates of criminality (12 per cent vs. 3 per cent). This indicates a substantial heritable component to the amount of difficulties young adoptees have, despite a reasonable upbringing.

Secondly, the third bar in the figure indicates that children from low risk backgrounds who are raised in less favourable family environments also exhibit higher rates of antisocial behaviour than when they are raised in more favourable families (7 per cent vs. 3 per cent). This indicates the impact of the less favourable upbringing.

Thirdly, and perhaps most remarkably, the far right hand bar shows the rate of criminality at 17 years of children from high risk backgrounds who were brought up in less favourable environments. Here the rate is 40 per cent, far more than would be predicted by the other results. In other words, there is a strong interaction whereby temperamentally more difficult children do far worse than expected if they are brought up in less favourable circumstances. Other adoption studies confirm these findings.

A conclusion from this research is that, although genetic factors play an important part in children's outcomes, the greater part of poor outcomes may be prevented by ensuring a good upbringing, even in children of high risk parents. In practice, this means it is important to get as full information as possible on an adopted child's parents' psychiatric and criminal history. Since the majority of children put forward for adoption nowadays are from high risk backgrounds, it follows that they will be especially sensitive to both their original and their new family environment. Therefore, to maximise good outcomes for the child, the adoptive parents need to become skilled in managing child behaviour in favourable circumstances that do not expose the child to further risk.

Despite optimal upbringing, however, some disorders are highly genetic and not susceptible to a lot of improvement. For example, if both parents suffer from schizophrenia, the chances that the child will do so too are 50 per cent. This information would be important when assessing paranoid thoughts and decline in self-care in an 18-year-old adopted girl. Other highly genetic disorders include manic-depressive disorder, autistic spectrum disorders including Asperger's syndrome, and severe hyper-activity/ADHD (Attention Deficit Hyperactivity Disorder; hyperkinetic syndrome). On the other hand, milder hyperactivity/ADHD often has a socially determined component and is common in children who have spent a period in care (Roy et al, 2000) as well as severely deprived adoptees (O'Connor et al, 2000). Likewise, if an adopted young person is self-harming repeatedly and seriously, while the problem may be mainly in the current environment and predicament, there may be a substantial constitutional predisposition if this was a characteristic of a birth parent.

Intellect

The findings for genetic influences on IQ are in many ways similar to those for psychiatric problems. For example, Duyme *et al* (1999) found that the IQ of birth parents strongly predicted the eventual intellectual level of the child, but being raised in a stimulating household that encouraged learning also improved IQ considerably. In practice, therefore, it is again important to establish the level of functioning of the birth parents as this is a reasonable guide to the potential of the child. Often children with behavioural problems turn out on testing to have a low IQ, and not infrequently frank generalised learning disability (overall IQ less than 70, called mental retardation in the USA; see Scott, 1994 for further descriptions). This is more likely if the birth parents were of limited ability, which should raise serious consideration about having the child assessed before placement decisions are made. If adoptive parents are high achievers, and if the birth parents of the child to be adopted are of limited ability, it may work out well if the parents can accept a child who turns out to be a low achiever, but often it can lead to some disappointment and rejection when the adopted child, through no fault of their own, turns out very differently from how the adopting parents had hoped.

Effects of poor early environments

The impact of severe early deprivation has recently been illuminated by studies of Romanian adoptees, which show that remarkable "catch up" in development is possible following extremely severe early deprivation. Many of the children were left in high-sided cots with absolutely no stimulation or social contact; they were underfed and infrequently changed. Despite this, those who were adopted before the age of two have made remarkable gains in intellectual development, mostly testing within the normal range and performing satisfactorily at school. But the gains in social understanding and relating ability have been less good. Many of the children are proving to have subtle gaps in their ability to read social situations. When they were young and mainly looked after by their adoptive parents, these difficulties in social understanding may not have been too impairing, since the parents were largely able to cope on their behalf. But as the children grow older and have to cope at school with peer relationships, serious limitations are emerging in their ability to understand social rules and how to form relationships (O'Connor *et al*, 2000). In practice, therefore, it is important to be aware of the duration of any severe deprivation, and to know that this may be followed by social deficits.

Characterising accurately the impact of abusive, as opposed to deprived, upbringing remains elusive. Harsh, inconsistent parenting has for a long time been shown to be associated with under-performing children who are frequently oppositional and defiant and lack relationship skills, and are subsequently at high risk of social exclusion with all the concomitant risks including drug and alcohol abuse, teenage pregnancy, crime, and suicide attempts (Rutter, Giller and Hagell, 1998). Whereas some children were previously thought to be able to survive this sort of experience intact and be "resilient", closer inspection of how they are doing suggests that, sadly, few remain unscathed in one domain or another (Cicchetti and Toth, 1995; Rutter, 2000). Also, where several different types of abuse are occurring simultaneously, (which is the rule rather than the exception), the effects may be cumulative. For example, sexually abused children whose parents were also violent and harsh are more likely themselves to become sexual abusers as they grow older (Skuse *et al*, 1998).

Prevalence of mental health problems in adopted children

Adopted children show increased rates of mental health problems compared to children raised in their birth families. However, this statement has to be firmly qualified by taking into consideration the timing of placement. Children and adolescents adopted in infancy (under two) who were not subjected to unduly abusive or neglectful parenting have only moderately increased, if any, rates of difficulties compared to children raised by biological parents. There have been a number of good longi-tudinal surveys to show this. Maughan and Pickles (1990) followed up adopted children from the British birth cohort born in March 1958. At age seven, according to school reports, the adopted children were as well adjusted as children living with married birth parents, and better adjusted than children whose parents were not married. At age 16 the adopted teenagers' level of difficulties was in between those who were raised in birth families within marriage, and those whose parents were not married. By 23 the adopted group had no more problems or distress than those raised by married parents. The follow-up study of over 500 children by

Bohman and Sigvardsson (1980) in Sweden compared (1) adopted children with (2) children initially registered for adoption whose mothers then changed their mind and raised the children themselves, and (3) children registered for adoption who were raised in foster families. All groups were compared with children in the community for whom adoption had never been considered. In childhood, at age 11, the adopted children had raised rates of emotional and behavioural difficulties compared to controls, but not as high as either the children who were with their birth mothers (group 2) or those who were fostered (group 3). At age 15 the adopted children were as well adjusted emotionally as controls, but had somewhat worse school grades, whereas the other two groups were doing considerably worse on all fronts. At 18 a similar picture was found from military service records (compulsory then in Sweden) but by 23 a search of police records for criminality and alcohol abuse found no difference between adoptees and controls, nor for the children raised by their birth mothers (group 2); the fostered children (group 3) did, however, have raised rates. Another well conducted longitudinal study in Christchurch, New Zealand, also found that by adolescence adoptees were doing well (Fergusson et al, 1995).

Taken together, these studies suggest that, while early adopted children have somewhat increased levels of problems in childhood, these will probably disappear by late adolescence and early adulthood. This is in stark contrast to late adopted children for whom the rates of difficulty and low achievement go up as the age at which the children were adopted rises. In a very large survey of over 4,000 adoptees in the USA, Sharma et al (1996) found that there were far more emotional and disruptive problems in later adopted children; these were especially serious in those placed after ten years of age, where drug and alcohol abuse and crime were much commoner, and were accompanied by a range of other serious difficulties. In the UK, Quinton and Rutter (1988) studied 61 newly placed 5–9-year-olds and found that 48 per cent had moderate or severe conduct problems, 49 per cent had emotional problems, 23 per cent significant hyperactivity (which was strongly associated with placement instability and risk of breakdown), 29 per cent were bedwetting or soiling and 43 per cent had substantial difficulties in their relationships with other children. For comparison, the level of these difficulties in a community sample would be under 5 per cent for each disorder, with an overall rate of any disorder occurring in 10 per cent of the population in England and Wales (Meltzer *et al*, 2000). Intellectual and school achievements were also very impaired in the late adopted children.

Three reasons are likely to account for these alarming figures. Firstly, the genetic background of late adopted children puts them at higher risk (see Figure 1). Many more of the parents suffer from disorders such as schizophrenia, severe drug and alcohol problems, and debilitating manic-depressive psychosis; often the general level of intellectual functioning is at the lower end of the normal range and only just adequate for independent living; frank generalised learning disability (mental retardation) is not uncommon. There is no automatic transmission of any of these traits for any one individual child, but as a group they are at high risk. Secondly, late adopted children have usually had a neglectful and abusive upbringing in the crucial early years. This early experience is especially damaging to children who are constitutionally more vulnerable (see far right hand column in Figure 1). Thirdly, even where the child is constitutionally at low risk and has been adequately parented up to the time of adoption, the turmoil of relinquishing or readjusting the fundamental attachments to the birth parents and making all the emotional, attachment, identity and practical adjustments to living in a new family are far greater in middle childhood than in infancy.

Implications of high rates of difficulties in late-adopted children for adopting parents and for service provision

Since the majority (but by no means all) of adoptions in the Western world are now late (Cohen, 2002), this has huge implications for the size of the task adoptive parents have to undertake, and for the formal and informal support services they need to help them. Providing adequate support requires a whole system perspective that includes the child, the adoptive and birth families, and the school. Unless all these are included in a coherent plan, the chances of failure are much higher. Psychotherapeutic treatments for emotional and behavioural difficulties are but one aspect of the interventions that will be therapeutic for a child. And if psychotherapeutic treatments are to work, they require the creation of a therapeutic and supportive context for the whole pre- and post-adoptive process.

Preparation that has addressed the couple's story of parenthood and childhood, including the treatment of infertility and experience of loss and abuse is crucial (see also tasks for parents in the adoptive family life cycle, Table 1). Failure to do this may create negative dynamics in relation to the placed child, who is also dealing with complex feelings of loss and often bewilderment. These issues frequently need to be re-visited in therapeutic sessions after the adoption.

Accurate information about the child's background and needs has to be presented in ways that enable the adopters to hear and understand the potential implications for the child's physical, emotional and cognitive development in the future. Omitting to do this, however difficult and irrespective of whether it might stop the placement, may result in a sense of grievance and disappointment, and lead to difficulties in meeting the child's needs. Giving such accurate information requires the social worker or agency concerned to have accurate information themselves, and to understand the likely risks and outcomes for the future. It also requires a straight exchange of information – this can be derailed by the agency either wanting to "sell" a child with complex needs to a family so that they underplay the difficulties, or by making the prospective adopters feel they should be "grateful" to be offered a child; they may then not fully voice any concerns in case they are perceived as choosy or difficult and are not offered this child, or any other child subsequently.

Contextual factors influencing the mental health and well being of adopted children and their families

While adopted children manifest the same types of disorders as other children – indeed as we saw above, they often have more – it is helpful to bear in mind the influence of the particular context they are in. Some of the stages that parents and children have to negotiate even in "simple" early adoption are set out in Table 1, which depicts aspects of the adoptive family life cycle.

Any of the considerations described in the table may come up during therapeutic interventions, and should be discussed openly at suitable times.

Table 1

Adoptive family life cycle

Stage	Adoptive parents' tasks	Adopted children's tasks
Pre-adoption	Coping with infertility and feelings of inadequacy as a man or woman, letting go dream of being a biological parent. Helping own parents and siblings, and children (if any), accept plan to adopt. Coping with prolonged evaluative assessments, and anxiety of not knowing when they may be offered a child. Preparing for social stigma of adopting. Planning for lifestyle change, e.g. giving up job, change in relationship with partner. Coping with feelings about accepting a child who may not be "ideal".	For older children, trying to cope with loss of birth parents, and uncertainty about future. Coping with difficulty of knowing they will lose current foster parents. Coping with anxiety about future adoptive parents.
Infancy	Taking on the identity of an adoptive parent and finding acceptable role models. Developing realistic expectations. Integrating the child into the family. Persisting with affection and establishing secure attachment even if faced by personal disappointment. Exploring thoughts and feelings about birth family.	

Stage	Adoptive parents' tasks	Adopted children's tasks
Preschool	Beginning the telling process. Creating an atmosphere conducive to openness about adoption and talking about birth family.	Learning elements of adoption story. Questioning parents about adoption.
Middle childhood	Helping child accept the meaning of adoption, including loss of birth parents, possible anger (especially directed to adoptive mother). Helping child develop a positive view of birth family. Managing any contact with or communication from birth family. Coping with the insecurity that telling may engender; worrying child may want to leave or not love adopters.	Coping with the adoption loss. Exploring feelings about being given up by birth parents, developing an acceptable story around this. Coping with stigma of being adopted. Validating dual connection to both families.
Adolescence	Helping young person develop own sense of identity including recognition of traits that may come from birth family; accepting difference from some of their values and style. Supporting search interest and plans, and helping to develop realistic expectations. Coping with adolescent rebelliousness with a sense of proportion, coping with feelings that young person may wish to leave home as soon as possible, thus rejecting the love they gave.	Integrating adoption into a secure sense of identity. Exploring feelings about search process, finding balance between idealisation and vilification of birth parents. Trying to understand extent to which feelings and behaviour are typical for adolescence and which may derive from being adopted.

Note: this table is adapted from the scheme proposed by Brodzinsky *et al* (1998).

In addition to the parenting tasks peculiar to adoption, all the stresses and strains that any parent experiences are likely to be felt by adoptive families. But these stresses may be more acute since adoptive parents generally have less time to adjust than parents who have a child from babyhood and who have more time to adapt as the child grows. Adoptive parents without children are often older and more used to living their own, relatively uninterrupted lives. It's hard enough for birth parents to cope with a new child when the children usually come one at a time. In contrast adoptive parents may get two children together, or more, of different ages and at different stages but sharing the same dysfunctional background. The adopters may have no previous experience of parenting, no prior long-term trusting relationship with the children, yet are suddenly expected to become their parents. This can be a hugely demanding task.

Understandably, agencies often wish for sibling groups to be placed together. But frequently sibling relationships from abused families are very poor, and most of the children are very hard to look after (and may have gone through a number of disrupted foster placements prior to adoption because they were so difficult). The needs and capacities of each child must be separately assessed and matched to the needs and capacities of potential adopters before they are placed. Each child needs the best chance of making long-term stable relationships. This may be better achieved by separate placement with frequent contact.

Mental health assessment: usefulness of psychiatric classification

When assessing children, mental health professionals are likely to consider whether or not the difficulties include a diagnosable disorder. Formal classificatory systems can offer considerable help to adopted children and their parents when the difficulties fit a recognised pattern. The World Health Organisation's International Classification of Disorders of Childhood and Adolescence (ICD 9 Multiaxial version, WHO 1993) is widely used in Europe. It has six axes. Only the first is concerned with the presence of a disorder. The second refers to specific learning disabilities, the third to intellectual level, and the fourth to medical conditions. The fifth characterises the environment in which the child is living

(including, for example, scapegoating or child abuse) and the sixth characterises the child's level of functioning. In the USA, the American Psychiatric Association's Diagnostic and Statistical Manual (DSM IV, APA,
1994) is fairly similar (Scott, 2002a). The advantage of employing such
systems is that, instead of a child's behaviour and beliefs being unique
and mysterious, a large body of knowledge can usually be applied about.

1) the typical pattern of manifestations of the difficulties;
2) associated other problems that are commonly present;
3) their cause;
4) the long-term outlook; and
5) what treatment or interventions have been found to work.

For example, if a child's lying and stealing are persistent and severe
enough to meet the criteria for a diagnosis of conduct disorder, a lot of
knowledge can be brought to bear.

1) In addition to the lying and stealing, the pattern of conduct disorder
   typically includes truancy, aggressiveness and destructiveness, along
   with less common behaviours such as fire-setting and cruelty to
   animals. It is important to ask about these behaviours, otherwise they
   may be missed.

2) Hyperactivity and depression are commonly associated, so should be
   looked for (easily overlooked with a difficult, aggressive child).
   Specific learning disorders such as dyslexia need to be assessed since
   a third of such children will have them; social skill deficits and few
   friendships are also common.

3) Ineffective discipline and lack of parental warmth are major
   contributors to the cause of conduct disorder, with the other factors
   above often playing a part.

4) The long-term outlook is poor if several of these factors are present –
   the young person will be unlikely to "grow out of it".

5) A lot is known about what works for conduct disorder and severe
   antisocial behaviour. For younger children (say up to eight or nine)
   systematic parenting programmes are very effective in about
   two-thirds of cases (Kazdin, 1997; Scott *et al*, 2001). In adolescence
   the task is harder, but there are relatively new therapeutic programmes for which there is solid evidence of effectiveness, such as
   Multi-Systemic Therapy (Henggeler *et al*, 1998) and Treatment Foster

Care (Chamberlain and Rosicky, 1995). These are not yet widely available in the UK. However, whereas there are currently over a thousand carefully conducted trials that attest to effectiveness of parenting programmes, there are few of individual therapies with the young person (Fonagy *et al*, 2002). This is not the same as evidence that they do not work ("lack of evidence is not evidence of lack").

Concerns about using psychiatric classification

There are several concerns about applying a diagnostic label. Firstly, that it may "label" the young person in a way that affects, for the worse, the way they feel about themselves, and the way parents, teachers, friends and classmates treat them. The counter argument is that many parents and indeed young people are actually relieved to know what is going on and to have an explanation for their feelings and behaviour, be it because they are depressed or currently have ADHD. Often the young person has been informally labelled ("miserable and joyless, no fun" in the case of depression, or "aggressive, impatient, a pain, horrible to be with" in the case of ADHD), and better understanding of the picture and reason for the behaviour usually leads to an improvement in the way other people treat the young person, with less hostility and scapegoating.

Secondly, there is concern that a diagnosis may stay with a person for a very long time. In fact, a diagnosis is based on no more than a particular description of how someone is behaving over a period (two weeks in the case of depression), so that as soon as the behaviour no longer fits the diagnostic description, the diagnosis is not applicable. It is therefore not necessarily an enduring trait or characteristic of a person.

Thirdly, there is concern that the diagnosis may obscure the person, and prevent recognition of their uniqueness. The counter argument is that this would be a misapplication of the diagnostic process. It may be relatively easy to decide whether a diagnosis is applicable (although often it is not) but this should only be a part of the assessment process that should include the young person's individual thoughts and meanings, their personal predicament and their strengths and aims. All this information should be incorporated into a *formulation* of how the young person got to be where they are, and what can be offered to help.

Fourthly, a diagnostic system may not capture the type of difficulties seen, especially in adopted children. Diagnostic systems are only as good as the knowledge that goes into them. Usually they look at the pattern of behaviour, and also the degree of impact or impairment. Thus a child may have a specific phobia (say of spiders) but it may not interfere with everyday life much at all, so that while the symptoms can be diagnosed, they do not indicate an impairment.

In contrast, surveys of children suggest that up to 10 per cent may be significantly impaired in their ability to get on with their lives (Angold *et al*, 1999), but yet do not have symptomatic behaviours that fit any diagnosis. In other words, something is interfering with their lives that is hard to define. Most of the difficulties are in the sphere of social relationships. Abused and maltreated children may exhibit a higher proportion of such "hard to diagnose" difficulties. The multiple and complex effects of such upbringing on basic abilities to relate and trust are still poorly characterised and understood.

Attachment theory has spawned a vigorous line of empirical research looking at the connection between parenting style and the relating pattern of the offspring. In future this may help to understand the behaviour of disturbed adopted young people who experienced abuse or neglect. While studies of adopted children are in progress, so far there has not been enough understanding for these to translate into diagnostic categories. The exception has been Reactive Attachment Disorder, seen as indiscriminate friendliness and failure to make selective attachments in children brought up in institutions by many, transient carers. Thankfully this is now getting rarer. An attachment category that is not at present a diagnostic one, but that may help to illuminate the behaviour of some adopted children, is the "disorganised" category. Here children who have had severely disjointed or abusive experiences at the hands of their parents display chaotic and disturbed (sometimes frankly bizarre) behaviour under emotionally stressful conditions (O'Connor, 2002).

Another pattern not infrequently seen in adopted children that also does not have diagnostic status is what Patterson *et al* (1992) described as "relational aggression". Here the child is highly aggressive towards one parent only – usually the mother. It is not hard to suppose it relates to difficulties in earlier attachment relationships. Even if and when such patterns are well worked out, the best way to repair the damage may not be clear.

In February, a nine-year-old boy who had recently been adopted got more and more aggressive towards his adoptive mother. He smashed her lipstick and poured her expensive perfume down the sink. His behaviour towards his adoptive father remained good. During a personal counselling session he revealed that he had been asked in school to make a mother's day card, as had the rest of the class. He was in huge conflict about which mother to send it to. Eventually we negotiated with him that it was fine to make two cards, as he had two mothers. He was happy with this solution.

The assessment process

Child and adolescent mental health teams are usually multidisciplinary, and may include psychiatrists, psychologists, social workers and nurses, as well as disciplines such as family (systemic) therapists, psychotherapists, and others. Prior to seeing the family, a clear statement in writing of what is being asked for is invaluable. Good background information on the child's life from before birth up to the present time is also vital if a thorough assessment is to be made. If at all possible, having the social worker for the child attend the assessment is important, as it will lead to better understanding of the child's difficulties, the intervention being offered, and how to co-ordinate this across different agencies that may include education and physical health such as paediatrics.

Usually it is necessary to see the child or young person alone as well as with their adoptive parents since there may be personal and private things to say and opinions to voice, while an assessment has to be made of their mental state for disorders such as depression and post traumatic stress disorder. Seeing siblings and other people living in the family alone often reveals unexpected information not disclosed by the adults or young person: 'Mummy smacks him with a slipper when he's naughty/tells him she wished she'd never adopted him/he likes to pull my pants down at night'.

There are a variety of projective tests that assess the quality of the child's emotional relationships and family relationships. One approach for younger children is to set up a doll's house and engage the child in a number of scenarios, which they are then invited to finish. For example, one doll will be given the child's name and then the clinician will enact a story where the child doll gets a bad tummy ache. The clinician then asks "what happens next" and judges the quality of the subsequent story. Broadly speaking, children who enact their carer looking after them in a responsive way may be judged to have a good relationship with their carer, and to be likely to be securely attached to them. In contrast, children who enact indifference to their carer, and depict them as offering no help, might be likely to have worse care and a dismissive attachment style. Some children enact scenarios with very painful or abusive endings.

A paediatric assessment may be requested, for example, to rule out the presence of organic factors in the child's problematic behaviour, such as epilepsy or a congenital syndrome.

The assessment is part of the therapeutic process. Serious unresolved issues from the birth family relationships may emerge, for example, in relation to contact, which may need addressing. Sometimes, the child's emotional difficulties are improved when arrangements for contact are altered:

> One adopted child's intense anxiety about contact, which affected her daily functioning, improved once her wish no longer to call her birth mother "Mummy" was conveyed and agreed to by the birth family.

> In another case, the arrangements for contact fitted the needs of the older child who wished to see her birth mother despite abusive experiences but her much younger and rejected brother's behaviour deteriorated so markedly with each visit, that an argument was made for cessation of contact for him.

Findings of assessment and subsequent action

The assessment should make sense of the child's life up to now. The formulation should include the child's strengths and difficulties, their understanding of their predicament and a view of their mental state: how happy and sad they are, their hopes and dreams for the future. Any significant problems and disorders should be clarified, and explained as far as possible; equally, it should be made clear if the symptoms do *not* fit any known pattern, or are excessive given what is known about causal factors. The predisposing, precipitating and perpetuating factors for any problems should be made clear. The assessment should also include an evaluation of the quality of parenting past and present: no child lives in a vacuum, and even if the current difficulties are not caused by the parenting context, they will influence it. It is very important that assessments include an explicit evaluation of current parenting.

The assessment should lead to change, at least in the understanding of the problem, and preferably in how the child is treated and should help all parties understand the child better. It should help the parents make sense of their child's behaviour, including not blaming themselves, especially where attachment difficulties are being played out by the child. The sort of considerations discussed in the earlier part of this chapter may well be relevant in formulating the situation. Hopefully after the assessment, the team may be able to offer the parents some specific strategies to manage and improve the child's difficulties. If the parents feel understood themselves, they are then more likely to engage constructively in the treatment process.

The assessment may begin a process of reducing adoptive parents' expectations of being rewarded soon with responsive love from a fairly damaged child. Sometimes helping parents let go of a "dream" child who is always fun and responsive is necessary before they can be expected to set aside their immediate emotional reactions of disappointment, and begin to construe the child in a way that lets them try out new strategies, be less critical and hostile, and respond sensitively to the child as he or she is, rather than as he or she was hoped to be. In sessions with parents, it often helps to rehearse in the here and now thoughts they might tell themselves next time their child, say, refuses a cuddle after falling down. One can help them find their own words such as 'he's distrustful because he's used to being hit when he cries' instead of perhaps 'he's so ungrateful, we've poured in so much love and this is all we get for a reward, it's not worth carrying on'.

The assessment should lead to a prescription for action. Many interventions may be recommended. Here, three main domains are covered: education, psychosocial interventions, and medication.

The importance of education as a crucial therapeutic element

Getting education right is crucial. This is the major experience the child has of the outside world of work and achievement and socialising with others beyond family and friends. Many children on whom thousands of pounds have been spent "therapeutically" have not had an educational assessment with psychometric testing. Such testing of adopted and looked after children reveals a high proportion with specific reading delay (severe dyslexia) and generalised learning difficulties (mental retardation). Often professionals involved with the child have been unaware of the low level of intellectual functioning. Sometimes, on the other hand, the psycho-metric assessment reveals that the child is much more intelligent than previously believed.

Getting the child's education right requires close liaison with schools and education authorities. A visit to the school to see the child in class is invaluable, followed by a talk to the teachers. Strategies for handling the child can be offered, and where necessary a request can be made for a full assessment for a Statement of Special Educational Needs. Other interventions at school that can make a substantial difference to the confidence and self-image of adopted children include reducing bullying, getting a teacher to encourage them and teach them at the right level, and promoting strengths, such as football or singing.

John, a 12-year-old boy had been difficult from an early age and was forever fighting with his siblings – initially his birth siblings, then foster brothers and sisters, and now his newly adopted sister of six. He had made the transition to secondary school poorly, and had already been excluded for being disruptive in class and not listening to his teachers. Now he was in danger of being excluded from the second secondary school too. A visit to the classroom revealed that he did indeed push, poke and disrupt the other pupils, and spent almost no time doing his schoolwork. His school attainments were very low, but his teacher explained that this was hardly surprising as he never got down to any work, and was forever needing to be told off for some misdemeanour or other – this was confirmed on observation, his teacher frequently criticised him and twice shouted at him during the observed lesson. His social worker felt that this behaviour was entirely understandable, given the abuse he had been subjected to by his birth parents in his first two years of life.

At interview, John was co-operative and spoke simply about his love of his Game Boy electronic game console and of watching Spiderman cartoons. On psychometric testing his verbal IQ was 62, performance IQ 57, full scale IQ 59. This put him clearly in the generalised learning disability range of intellectual functioning, in the bottom 1 per cent of the population. However well looked after he had been, he would not have been able to cope with mainstream schooling, and behaviour problems occur around five times more frequently in children of this level of ability, especially challenging, disruptive behaviour. Expecting him to perform like other children in school when he was unable to understand at all what was expected of him intellectually was in practice a form of abuse that had led him to have very low self-esteem and a view of himself as incompetent and unlovable. Once the fact that he was so impaired was explained (few children of his level grow up to live independently), his adoptive parents changed their expectations of him and his behaviour improved considerably with the help of some practical management strategies. He was moved to a school for children with moderate learning disability where his self-esteem and confidence increased a great deal and his challenging behaviour reduced since he was being taught at a pace at which he could learn, and he was receiving regular encouragement.

As the educational attainment of looked after children is particularly poor, assessment of abilities and attainments is especially necessary if potential is to be realised through appropriate remedial help.

Psychosocial interventions

Positive preventive work
Preventive and protective work to strengthen the child's positive attributes and relationships are as important as therapies to reduce problems. This work could include promoting good friendships, by planning how and when adoptive parents will, for example, invite classmates home to tea,

setting up training and club membership for sporting skills and hobbies, or arranging visits to encouraging relatives or friends. For adolescents, life skills work can make all the difference, for example, by learning how to shop, manage a weekly budget, go about finding a job and practising for an interview, and so on.

Parenting work

Parenting work covers a wide range, from formal programmes to talking issues through. Several researchers, for example Sinclair (2002) has shown that in the fostering and adoption context, three factors predict placement breakdown:

1) parental lack of confidence;
2) child behaviour problems; and
3) lack of "click", by which is meant the stated feeling of parents that they are getting on especially well with the child and understand them (further analysis of "click" showed it was strongly influenced by factor 2, child behaviour problems).

Parenting programmes are a logical intervention in that there is good evidence that (in biological families at least) they improve both parental feelings of competence and confidence, and reduce child behaviour problems (see multicentre trial of Scott *et al*, 2001).

Specific parenting programmes are beginning to be used in the adoption context. Parenting work with one family at a time at the Maudsley Hospital includes influencing live interaction between parent and child. The parent wears a small headphone in their ear, and is offered direct instruction in how to interact with the child. Adoptive parents are taken through several modules in a flexible way – play (to increase sensitive responding and child-centredness), praise (both for specific behaviours and to help them to see the positive aspects of the child's character), setting limits and boundaries, and strategies for discipline. The live coaching only lasts ten minutes, and is followed by 40 minutes or so working with the parent's notions of behavioural principles and, crucially, what the process brings up for them. Often the live interaction with the child elicits beliefs and fears that are not expressed when only talking about their predicament. The mother who says she plays with her child but when observed doesn't, and then reveals that nobody ever played with her; the father who says discipline is fine, but is observed *not* to be able to set limits and then reveals his own father was so authoritarian that he cannot imagine being firm because of the pain he associates with this manner of discipline.

Groups for foster carers cover much of the same ground, and the evaluation is encouraging (Pallett *et al*, 2002). However, Minnis *et al* (2001) reported a randomised controlled trial of short (6–8 sessions) groups for foster carers without close supervision of the workers, and failed to show any improvements in child outcomes. Possibly the sessions were too few, and there may not have been enough emphasis on helping the parents learn new practical skills so they could improve their relationships with the children. Research suggests also that at least 20 hours of parenting work are required to get a large, sustained improvement. Recently the Department of Health has commissioned a trial of parental support for adoptive parents (Rushton and Dance, 2002), a much needed boost to provide evidence as to what works in this field.

Research is needed to find out how parenting programmes work: is the crucial ingredient the altering of parental behaviour towards the child, or is changing parental beliefs and emotions sufficient? To date the evidence suggests (Scott, 2002b) that altering beliefs and emotions alone is not sufficient, and does not lead to better child outcomes. To help children, parenting programmes also need to offer skills for improving discipline and communication, and not just talk about them.

Behavioural treatments

Specific behavioural treatments can be very effective, when embedded within an overall package for the family. The sort of difficulties they are strongest for include:

1) tantrums, disobedience and defiance, aggression and destructiveness;
2) sleep problems;
3) eating difficulties;
4) wetting and soiling, for which they are often extremely effective;
5) mild to moderate hyperactivity;
6) specific fears and phobias;

7) behaviour problems arising in children and adolescents with generalised learning disabilities.

Treatment typically involves making a careful diary of precisely when the undesirable behaviour occurs, what is going on at the time, and how the parents are responding at present. A new regime of responses is then worked out, tried and revised. There is a strong evidence base supporting the effectiveness of these interventions, which can alleviate a great deal of suffering, and yet are underused. For further details, see the PACT series issued by the British Psychological Society (1996).

A 13-year-old late placed girl had been bedwetting since anyone could remember. The adoption agency had explained to the parents that this was an expression of her distress. She was ashamed of it, had begun menstruating, and felt everything to do with "down below" was horrid. After two weeks on a reward chart (a method of recording success on a daily basis – usually by sticking gold stars on a chart), she had stopped and never relapsed. Her self-esteem increased considerably.

Systemic family therapy

There are many different approaches to working with families systemically. What they all have in common is the idea that the focus of the intervention is on the relationships between people rather than on a problem located within the person, which tends to reduce the experience of blame and negative attributions. In work with adoptive families, it is often helpful to use the idea of narratives to explore the construction of alternative stories for the child and family to live by (White and Epston, 1990).

The level of mental health need in children to be adopted, implies a considerable challenge to the parenting abilities of new families, even when they have been parents before. The extent of this is not always recognised. In order to gain a full understanding of these complex situations, it is necessary to view the child in the context of their family of origin and the adoptive family. Their difficulties, which are affected by and affect those who care for them, may have their origins in past traumatic and abusive experiences and heredity. In particular, it is important not to fall into the trap of blaming the adoptive parents. This can be specially important when children have difficulties with making new attachments, often focused on the relationship with the adoptive mother. Offering parents explanations of the problems they are facing with their children, based on an understanding of the influence of early life experiences and of mental illness and other psychological difficulties in the birth family, may provide them with a way to manage and to continue with the task. Helping them to understand how long the process of really joining the new family may take, can also be therapeutic (Lindsey, 1997).

The first step in offering help to the families and their social workers, who are often still involved at the point of referral, is the systemic family consultation. This creates a map from everyone's perspective of how each sees the difficulties they are facing, what they want to change and what ideas they have about how to do so. Frequently, there is a wish for a therapist to "fix" the child with therapy. It is usually important to establish a therapeutic engagement with the family together, before considering individual interventions, because this carries the message that the significant relationships that need to be developed and consolidated are within the family.

It is sometimes helpful for the adoptive parents to work on the issues they are now having to reconsider, for example, their histories of infertility and the desire to adopt a child; how the placement was made, their expectations and how this contrasts with the reality; their own experience of being brought up and their beliefs about parenting; the impact on any birth children they may have and their extended families. Frequently, they are preoccupied about whether they will be able to meet the needs of the child over the long term. Fears of failure, and worries about attachment and behavioural difficulties may make them ambivalent about applying for the Adoption Order. However, this needs to be resolved for the sake of the child as soon as possible. Sometimes these understandable hesitations are seen by social workers as showing a lack of commitment to the child. The work then may need to extend to networking between the adopters, their social workers and the placing agency.

Using a systemic family therapy approach is one way to address the relationship difficulties, which arise in the process of trying to create a new family. It is important to remember that families who have never had children of their own are not always able to distinguish behaviours, which are regarded as part of growing up in birth families or at least, are not specific to the adoption context. Working with the family members on here and now issues of family life can help the resolution of behavioural problems, coupled with specific advice on how to manage the problems. In family therapy it is also possible for the children to tell the story of their previous life experiences in front of their adoptive parents, who can witness it and begin to weave a new story of family life, by which they can live in the future without denying the past. This avoids the unhelpful but understandable tendency to want to put the past behind them in a way which may create conflicts of loyalty for the children.

In one family, the daughter was adopted from a different religion and culture, as a very young child. At times, the family appeared to be flourishing but at others , the girl was plunged into the deepest suicidal despair, preventing her from concentrating on her studies, withdrawing from her parents and friends and destroying her possessions. It seemed as if it had never been possible for them to talk without fear of recrimination or regret about the lost birth family and the life that might have been. The parents were inhibited by anxieties that she might wish to return and she, by the fear of hurting them. The therapists enabled them to tell a new story, which incorporated both cultures and families.

Working with the family together also allows exploration of the attachment issues.

In one family, the five-year-old child's stealing in the home caused great distress to the parents, who felt she now lacked for nothing although they knew the extent of her earlier deprivation. It was possible to stop the stealing by offering a prescription that she was only allowed to steal from a special box of things put in a particular place. At the same time, work proceeded on strengthening the attachment to her adoptive mother, who found her indiscriminate manner of relating to strangers, family members and friends potentially dangerous. Talking and behaving differently in the sessions was complemented by helping the mother to find time for this child, separately from her siblings, which had not seemed possible for either of them before.

The evidence base for the usefulness of family therapy is growing (Cottrell and Boston, 2002). In most cases, the family therapy is one component of the treatment package which needs to be offered to the family and should take place within the context of a multidisciplinary assessment.

Individual psychodynamic therapy

Working with children individually using the relationship with the therapist as a therapeutic tool may allow children the opportunity to struggle with the experiences of a frightening and painful past and the need to let it go in order to be able to allow themselves to have new and more satisfying relationships in the future. Rather than waiting for children to be placed in the permanent family, psychotherapists have developed techniques for working with children in transition between home and a new family, which may make the success of the placement more likely. It is important to attend to the issues of loyalty and identity, which interfere with the capacity to accept membership of a new family. As with family therapy and indeed all other forms of therapeutic intervention, psychotherapy with the child is carried out in the context of ongoing work with the parents and attention to all the significant aspects of the child's life – school, in particular. Lively examples of what may happen during individual therapy with adopted children are given in her book by Margaret Hunter (2001).

> The brother of the child described earlier who was stealing, was tormented by his memories of his life with his birth parents. He had been a carer for them and his younger sister and worried about their safety now. He had vivid flashbacks of abusive experiences and so feared the return of the abuser that he kept his curtains drawn. In his treatment, he gradually found a way to articulate the many contradictory emotions that were inhibiting his capacity for friendships and adversely affecting his functioning in school.

Adoptive children of all ages can benefit from the chance to talk to or play with a therapist, who offers a safe space to explore and understand the intense experiences of earlier abusive relationships with parents who are both loved and hated, desired, rejected and rejecting. Sometimes, there is a need to work through the loss of previous foster carers. Timing of this work is crucial. On the one hand, it may threaten the new parents who do not yet feel established in their role, but on the other, may serve as a safety valve for the strong emotions, which may otherwise also threaten the newly forming family life.

Medication

Broadly speaking, medication is effective for three common types of problem. Firstly, moderate or severe depression: where the depressed young person is becoming withdrawn, sleeping poorly, losing their appetite, or seriously considering suicide or self-harm, antidepressants are usually of clear benefit. They need to be taken for at least three months, usually six, and it takes two to three weeks before any benefit is seen. Medication for depression is beneficial even where there are clear psychological reasons for the depression, such as the termination of a close relationship. This is because once depression has gone beyond a certain point, there is a biological closing down of coping systems beyond that normally seen. Prescribing of any psychotropic medication does *not* mean that psychological therapies should not be offered, indeed often lasting change will not occur unless they are, and medication can help put the young person in a state whereby psychological change is possible.

Secondly, medication is useful for marked or severe hyperactivity (ADHD). Usually the stimulant methylphenidate (Ritalin; Equasym) is prescribed, or Dexamfetamine. Once a reasonable dose is reached, the effect is striking, with a clear reduction in restlessness and moving around, an increase in concentration and application to work, and an increase in reflectiveness with less impulsiveness. These medications are stimulants, not tranquillisers and do not dull feelings or suppress passion or liveliness; they do not reduce aggression or defiant behaviour (though this may reduce if severe hyperactivity is present); they do not have any harmful long-term effects (unlike major tranquillisers used for psychoses), and wear off after four hours, when the original hyperactive behaviour re-emerges. As with antidepressants, stimulants should not be used in isolation but should be part of a package of treatment that includes psychological advice and addresses parenting and school issues.

Thirdly, medication is useful for psychoses such as schizophrenia. The newer antipsychotics have fewer side effects, but there are still concerns in some cases about substantial weight gain and the risk of movement disorders in the long term. Nonetheless, psychoses such as schizophrenia are so devastating that using antipsychotics is usually desirable since they generally have a powerful effect in improving delusions and social functioning.

Deciding which type of intervention should be chosen

Which type of intervention should be selected will depend on what the evidence supports as effective, and what is available. However, there is a great deal still to be learnt about effective help for adoped children and their families, particularly about how to foster good attachment relationships. Further research is urgently needed. In the meantime, it is arguably unethical not to use a proven intervention when it is available, since that would knowingly prolonging the child's suffering and damage their future chances of good functioning. Despite this, effective treatments are often not given to children. The average spend per child per year in the UK on Child and Adolescent Mental Health Services is £10. This has to cover everything from bedwetting to anorexia to psychosis to offenders to paediatric liaison. It is therefore hardly surprising that adopted children often do not get the service one would wish from this source. The increasing use of the private and voluntary sector is to be welcomed wherever standards are high, and recent UK government initiatives for adopted children may release more funds for the purpose. There is a need for good quality pre and post-adoption services, rather than the abrupt withdrawal of support that can sometimes occur once children are no longer in the care of local authorities.

Conclusion

In the world of new legislation for child care and adoption, it will undoubtedly be expected that all services, statutory and voluntary, that have a role to play with adoptive families will work together in multi-agency partnerships, since no one service can expect to meet all the needs. It has to be recognised that unless the serious mental health needs of the late placed children are addressed effectively, their outcomes may not be significantly better than if they had remained in the care system. The implication of this for the expansion of child mental health services and other therapeutic services are considerable. There are resource and training implications since it cannot be automatically assumed that all professionals have the necessary skills and knowledge relevant to adoption. Furthermore, the work is complex and long term in many cases, which also has funding implications.

Families who adopt need to be treated as families that are both similar and very different from other families in order to feel heard and understood. They need services that are dedicated to them. Adoption practice has become far more challenging in the last 25 years. The task now is to disseminate good practice widely so that the children get the best chance to flourish and maximise their potential.

References

American Psychiatric Association (1994) *Diagnostic and Statistical Manual of Mental Disorders – DSM IV*, Washington DC: American Psychiatric Association.

Angold, A, Costello, E, Farmer, E, Burners, B and Erkanli, A (1999) 'Impaired but undiagnosed', *Journal of the American Academy of Child and Adolescent Psychiatry*, 38:2, pp 129–37.

Bohman, M and Sigvardsson, S (1980) 'A prospective, longitudinal study of children registered for adoption: A 15-year follow-up,' *Acta Psychiatrica Scandinavica*, 61, pp 339–55.

The British Psychological Society (1996) *Parent, Adolescent and Child Training Skills series*, Leicester: The British Psychological Society.

Brodzinsky, D M, Smith, D W and Brodzinsky, A B (1998) *Children's Adjustment to Adoption: Developmental and clinical issues*, Thousand Oaks, CA, US: Sage Publications, Inc.

Chamberlain, P and Rosicky, J G (1995) 'The effectiveness of family therapy in the treatment of adolescents with conduct disorders and delinquency', *Journal of Marital and Family Therapy*, 21:4, pp 441–59.

Cicchetti, D and Toth, S L (1995) 'Child maltreatment and attachment organisation: implications for intervention', in Goldberg, S and Muir, R *et al* (eds), *Attachment Theory: Social, developmental, and clinical perspectives*, pp 279–308, Hillsdale, US: Analytic Press, Inc. xiii, 515 pp.

Cohen, N J (2002) 'Adoption', in Rutter M and Taylor E (eds), *Child and Adolescent Psychiatry*, 4th edn., Blackwells, pp 373–81.

Cottrell, D and Boston, P (2002) 'Practitioner review: the effectiveness of systemic family therapy for children and adolescents', *Journal of Child Psychology and Psychiatry and Allied Disciplines*, 43:5, pp 573–86.

Duyme, M, Dumaret, A-C and Tomkiewicz, S (1999) 'How can we boost IQs of "dull children"?: A late adoption study', *Proceedings of the National Academy of Sciences of the United States of America*, 96, pp 8790–94.

Fergusson, D M, Lynskey, M and Horwood, L J (1995) 'The adolescent outcomes of adoption: a 16-year longitudinal study', *Journal of Child Psychology and Psychiatry and Allied Disciplines*, 36:4, pp 597–615.

Fonagy, P, Target, M, Cottrell, D, Phillips, J and Kurtz, Z (2002) *What Works for Whom: A critical review of treatments for children and adolescents*, New York: The Guilford Press.

Henggeler, S W, Schoenwald, S K, Borduin, C M, Rowland, M D and Cunningham, P B (1998) *Multisystemic Treatment of Antisocial Behavior in Children and Adolescents*, New York: The Guilford Press.

Hunter, M (2001) *Psychotherapy with Young People in Care: Lost and found*, Philadelphia, PA, US: Brunner-Routledge, xiv, p 193.

Kazdin, A E (1997) 'Parent management training: evidence, outcomes, and issues', *Journal of American Academy of Child and Adolescent Psychiatry*, 36, pp 10–18.

Lindsey, C (1997) 'New stories for old? The creation of new families by adoption and fostering', in *Multiple Voices Narrative in Systemic Family Psychotherapy*, Papdopoulos, Renos, K and Byng-Hall, J (eds), Tavistock Clinic Series, London: Duckworth.

Maughan, B and Pickles, A (1990) 'Adopted and illegitimate children growing up', in Robins, L N and Rutter, M (eds), *Straight and Devious Pathways from Childhood to Adulthood*, pp 36–61. New York: Cambridge University Press, xix, p 389.

Meltzer H, Gatward R, Goodman R and Ford T (2000) *The Mental Health of Children and Adolescents in Great Britain*, London: Office of National Statistics.

Minnis, H, Pelosi, A J, Knapp, M and Dunn, J (2001) 'Mental health and foster carer training', *Archives of Disease in Childhood*, 84:4, pp 302–6.

O'Connor, T, Rutter, M, and the English and Romanian Adoptees Study Team (2000) 'Attachment disorder behaviour following early severe deprivation: extension and longitudinal follow-up', *Journal of the American Academy of Child and Adolescent Psychiatry*, 39, pp 703–12.

O'Connor, T G (2002) 'Attachment disorders of infancy and childhood', in Rutter, M and Taylor, E (eds), *Child and Adolescent Psychiatry*, 4th edn., pp. 776–792. Blackwells.

Pallett, C, Scott, S, Blackeby, K, Yule, W and Weissman, R (2002) 'Fostering changes: a cognitive-behavioural approach to help foster carers manage children', *Adoption & Fostering*, 26:1, pp 39–48.

Patterson, G R, Reid, J B and Dishion, T J (1992) *Antisocial Boys*, Eugene, Oregon: Castalia Publishing Company.

Quinton, D and Rutter, M (1988) *Parenting Breakdown: The making and breaking of inter-generational links*, Avebury: Aldershot.

Roy, P, Rutter, M and Pickles, A (2000) 'Institutional care: risk from family background or pattern of rearing?' *Journal of Child Psychology and Psychiatry and Allied Disciplines*, 41:2, pp 139–49.

Rushton, A and Dance, C (2002) 'Quality Protects: a commentary on the Government's agenda and the evidence base', *Child and Adolescent Mental Health*, 7:2, pp 60–5.

Rutter, M (2000) 'Resilience reconsidered: conceptual considerations, empirical findings, and policy implications', in Shonkoff, J, Meisels, P and Samuel J (eds), *Handbook of Early Childhood Intervention* (2nd edn.), pp 651–82, New York, Cambridge University Press. xxi, 734 pp.

Rutter, M, Giller, H and Hagell, A (1998) *Antisocial Behavior by Young People*, New York: Cambridge University Press.

Scott, S (1994) 'Mental retardation', in Rutter, M, Taylor, E and Hersov, L (eds), *Child and Adolescent Psychiatry: Modern approaches*, 3rd edn., Blackwells, pp 616–46.

Scott S, Spender Q, Doolan M, Jacobs B and Aspland H (2001) 'Multicentre controlled trial of parenting groups for child antisocial behaviour in clinical practice', *British Medical Journal*, 323, pp 194–97.

Scott, S (2002a) 'Classification of psychiatric disorders in childhood and adolescence: building castles in the sand?' *Advances in Psychiatric Treatment*, 8, pp 205–13.

Scott, S (2002b) 'Parent training programmes', in Rutter, M and Taylor, E (eds), *Child and Adolescent Psychiatry*, 4th edn., Blackwells, pp 949–67.

Sharma, A R, McGue, M K and Benson, P L (1996) 'The emotional and behavioral adjustment of United States adopted adolescents: Part 1: An overview. Part 2: Age at placement', *Children and Youth Services Review*, 18, pp 83–114.

Sinclair, I (2002) *Causes of Foster Care Breakdown*, Report on project commissioned for the parenting initiative, London: Department of Health.

Skuse, D, Bentovim, A, Hodges, J, Stevenson, J, Andreou, C, Lanyado, M, New, M, Williams, B and McMillan, D (1998) 'Risk factors for development of sexually abusive behaviour in sexually victimised adolescent boys: cross sectional study', BMJ, 317(7152), pp 175–79.

White, M and Epston, D (1990) *Narrative Means to Therapeutic Ends*, New York: W W Norton and Company.

World Health Organisation (1993) *The ICD-10 Classification of Mental and Behavioural Disorders – Diagnostic criteria for research*, Geneva: World Health Organisation.

15 A model of post-placement therapy and support for adoptive families

Alan Burnell and Jay Vaughan

Introduction – a brief history

Catherine Macaskill's (1986) study of the placements made by a specialist adoption agency showed that a successful outcome in the placement of what were then regarded as "hard-to-place" children was, to a great extent, dependent upon the provision of post-placement and post-adoption support. This awareness became one of the cornerstones for the setting up of the Post-Adoption Centre in London in 1986. One of the primary tasks of the Centre was to provide post-adoption support to adoptive families. During the first five years, the majority of the families that came forward were parents who had adopted babies and were experiencing some difficulties with their children in middle childhood and with identity issues in adolescence (Howe, 1990). Adaptive grieving, as defined by David Brodzinsky *et al* (1998), and explaining adoption to children became central themes of the work at the Centre. However, increasingly parents were presenting children whom they had adopted as older children, most of whom had experienced early trauma and for whom traditional ways of working seemed too little and too late.

In collaboration with Adoption UK (previously known as PPIAS) and a group of adoptive parents, the Centre hosted a day entitled "Make or Break" in 1994. As part of the programme, graphic and moving accounts of the struggles that parents were experiencing were given, and one parent described the process of going with her child to have intensive attachment therapy at the Evergreen Centre in Colorado, USA. This day was a turning point: it became apparent that a new specialist form of service provision needed to be developed that was dedicated to meeting the challenges of contemporary adoption for parents and children. As a result, in 1998, Family Futures Consortium was established.

It is our view that the innovative practice of permanency planning and older child placement, which developed in the 1980s, with the added complexity of contact, resulting from the Children Act 1989, were "bolted on" to an adoption service which remained, in essence, a baby placement service. Adoption services, both statutory and voluntary, have failed to embrace the radical changes needed to provide comprehensive and integrated adoption support for children who require permanent homes in the 21st century. Tragically, children requiring permanent homes today may have suffered prolonged trauma in their birth families and may have also experienced multiple placements and several failed rehabilitation attempts (Ivaldi, 1998). It is these children who, by the time they are placed in adoptive families, often exhibit severe attachment difficulties. It is these families, in particular, that Family Futures was set up to help.

The basic principles of Family Futures' work

Adoption is a solution not a problem
We realise that the problems that adoptive parents struggle with are the result of the impact of early trauma upon their children. Early trauma not only has a psychological impact on the development of children but also physiological, physical and neurological consequences. Damaged attachments are the result of early trauma and a change in the attachment pattern requires a developmental approach to re-parenting children by adoptive parents. Adoptive parents should be seen as the primary resource for their children. Professionals working with such families should see parents as co-workers and collaborators striving to help their children. The work of Dan Hughes (1997) and Alan Schore (1994) has been instrumental in deepening our understanding of the impact of trauma and how to help adoptive parents and their children.

Adoption has many facets
It is, in our view, an historical accident that social workers are primarily responsible for the provision of adoption services. If the needs of the contemporary adoptive family from recruitment through to placement are to be fully met, then adoption support needs to include the services of a range of professionals. In order to provide a complete assessment and

post-placement support service, Family Futures combines the expertise of:

- adoptive parents;
- social workers;
- teachers;
- therapists;
- a neuro-developmental therapist;
- an educational psychologist;
- a paediatrician;
- an adult psychiatrist;
- a child and adolescent psychiatrist.

Accumulated research shows that placement outcomes are not driven by one single risk factor but by an interaction of a range of factors and influences and require a multi-disciplinary response (Rushton *et al*, 2000).

Adoption is not an end but a beginning

Family Futures believes that from the moment the decision is made that a child will not return to their biological family, therapy and preparation should begin. Children need therapeutic support from foster carers and therapists during the highly uncertain period prior to permanent placement. Contrary to conventional "wisdom", children need therapeutic help in order to stabilise, not therapy once they have stabilised. Similarly, once a child is placed, the new parents and child need access to intensive therapeutic help immediately and continuously during the first few years in order for positive patterns of attachment to form. A systematic programme of therapeutic support, designed to meet the needs of the family throughout a child's life, is necessary. This programme should be family based, recognising that it is the child's disturbed patterns of attachment to adult figures that need to be addressed. This can only be done by changing the child's pattern of attachment to their adoptive parents and supporting these changes over long periods of time.

Family Futures attachment programme: a family perspective

Between 1998 and 2002, Family Futures has worked with 250 families. It is difficult, therefore, to cover the range of situations and describe every aspect of our service. However, the case scenario described below can be seen as an illustration of the experience of a "typical family". The families that come to Family Futures reflect the ethnic, cultural and structural diversity of the modern family and contemporary adoption. This diversity is also reflected in the staff group.

Nearly all the families are referred and funded by the statutory authorities. Although such long-term treatment is costly, this investment in a family is a cheap option in comparison to residential care that may otherwise be needed. Family Futures' Intensive Attachment Programme represents, in financial terms, two-thirds of the cost of an independent foster care placement and one-third of the cost of a children's residential home. The average age of the children we work with at Family Futures is eight. The national breakdown rate for children placed for adoption in this age group is estimated to be around 20–30 per cent. With breakdown rates this high, and the cost of alternative placement options being so significantly greater, intensive support for adoptive and foster families is not only a moral but a cost-effective option.

It is usual for a family to come for an assessment, followed by a week of work on the Intensive Attachment Programme, and a two-year follow-up programme. The therapy consists of a mixture of individual therapy, couples work, family therapy, parent mentoring and parenting strategies. The team for each family comprises two therapists, one social worker and one parent-support person. The team, in turn, has access to our psychiatric, paediatric, educational and neuro-developmental specialists. Our overall approach is to use a developmental model of attachment and recent research into the impact of trauma as our theoretical base, with a strong emphasis on using creative arts therapies. The follow-up programme consists of a combination of ongoing therapy for children, parents and the family, and parent mentoring and support. This includes fortnightly or monthly visits to the Family Futures Attachment Centre as well as home visits from the family support workers and 24-hour telephone support. What follows is a composite case example based not on a particular family or children but rather on a number of different, sadly familiar, scenarios.

Case example

The P family was only three months into placement and at the end of their tether: both parents were not certain whether they could go on caring for the children. They had two boys placed with them. The older boy, Peter, aged eight, was extremely aggressive and there were concerns as to whether or not the school would be able to continue containing him while the younger boy, Paul, aged seven, seemed to be in a world of his own. The parents had also recently become aware that he "wound up" his older brother to behave badly. Mr and Mrs P were desperate. Their family and friends were desperate for them and were urging them to give up. Their social worker was desperate. The school was desperate. A referral was made to Family Futures.

At the assessment, which takes a whole day and includes lunch, chaos reigned as the children littered the building with toys, broken biscuits and dirty finger marks. There were even smears of "poo" found on the toilet walls after they had left. Mr and Mrs P cried and explained their desperation to the therapy team. Their social worker also attended the assessment day and talked about her concerns for the placement's survival. She agreed that Family Futures could have access to the files in order to gain detailed knowledge of the children's history. Up until this point, the information that the parents had been given talked in general terms about neglect and physical abuse. It was suggested that it would be helpful to know what this meant for both children during the early years of their life when they lived in their birth family. Mr and Mrs P stated again and again that they had no idea "it" would be like this. They did not feel that anything could really have prepared them for the constant unrelenting and confusing experience of trying to parent two children who did not want to be parented. During the assessment, both children made it clear that they were, in their minds, still "up for adoption" by anyone from the therapists to the receptionist.

The assessment day reached a crescendo as Peter suddenly, with no warning, walked across the room and punched Mr P extremely hard in the stomach. Mr P doubled up in pain and Mrs P rushed to comfort him. One of the therapists took hold of Peter's hand as he was moving in for what looked like a second punch. During the family discussion that followed, Peter talked about the look on Mr P's face, which made him feel so angry that he 'wanted to wipe the smile off his face'. When one of the therapists said, 'I wonder who said that to you?', Peter went absolutely silent and gave her piercing eye contact.

Following the assessment, it was agreed that the P family would benefit from an intensive, focused six-month programme of work with Family Futures, at the end of which they would decide whether or not they could continue with either or both children. Part of this programme was going to focus on parenting strategies: establishing a way of managing life at home, and a structure that could hopefully make life more bearable. The other major part of the programme was to be disclosure work with both boys to try to help them, and their adoptive parents, understand the connection between their behaviour and their history in their birth family. This was to be the main content of a full week of work, Monday to Friday, 10am–3pm, followed up by six months of fortnightly sessions.

Another important input was a two-day parent preparation programme. This programme provides a space for parents to think about the impact of adopting on their relationship, their own history and how this connects with the children's history; it also inducts the parents into a partnership with the therapy team. These sessions would run in parallel with the six months of parenting strategies: a "hands-on help" pro-gramme, which consists of parent mentoring, telephone support and home visits. It was also agreed that the parent support worker would liaise with the children's school, in order to incorporate the teachers into the network of professionals supporting the P family and to suggest ideas about managing the children's difficult behaviour in school. At the end of the six months, there was to be a meeting with Mr and Mrs P and the social services departments involved to consider whether or not the placement could be saved.

Mrs P was exhausted on the first day of the intensive week of therapy with the two boys. Mr P seemed distant and preoccupied. The therapy team questioned whether it was all just too much and whether they would even survive the week, let alone six months. The boys on the other hand, were happy and lively and immediately settled into disrupting the building. The first day consisted of establishing "rules" for the week with the children. Mrs P said that they needed such rules up on the wall at home. Peter and Paul unanimously agreed that the rules were rubbish and that they did not have to keep to them, but they said so rather quietly. The four members of the therapy team in the room, along with the parents, seemed to drain some of the children's gusto.

On the first day the children worked individually with a therapist, reviewing what they knew and what they were prepared to say about their history in their birth family. They both found talking difficult and were easier to engage when using sand trays and small toys to depict their birth family and their adoptive family. Paul, when asked to do a task involving writing and drawing, became very agitated and the therapist made a mental note that perhaps some of his profound difficulties in school may be linked to difficulties with learning. She later recommended an educational assessment for Paul, which did indeed conclude that Paul had some learning difficulties that had not been picked up because of his behaviour. Individually, both children were relatively co-operative, when they were not able to distract each other, and more or less kept to the task in hand. Peter was particularly concerned about what Paul was doing in the other room. At the assessment it had been explained to the boys that their individual sessions would be shared with their parents later and this was restated at the beginning of these sessions. Sharing was much more difficult as the boys instantly worked at disrupting any adult conversation.

On the second and third day, the children's history, as learned by Family Futures from the social services files, was shared with the boys while the parents were present. This history had already been disclosed to Mr and Mrs P on the first day. Mr and Mrs P had been shocked by the extent of the physical abuse that both children had suffered. While they had known that the children had been physically abused, it was very different hearing the details of the abuse. What particularly struck them was how Peter had protected Paul and had taken most of the beatings. The chaos of the birth family world and the uncertainty of how the adults would behave helped Mr and Mrs P to understand both boys' behaviour better. Interestingly, one report recorded how Peter's birth father told a visiting social worker that he planned to 'wipe the smile off his face'. Family Futures pointed out to the parents the powerful impact that the sustained neglect would have had on the boys as they fought for food to survive. It was decided, during this discussion, that Peter's eating problems, small stature and low weight indicated that the family would benefit from a consultation with the Family Futures paediatrician. This was arranged to take place as part of the follow-up programme. It was hard for the parents to believe how long the children had remained in an environment of acute neglect and how many attempts had been made to keep the children in their birth family.

Paul seemed to know instinctively what was going to happen on the second day. For the first time, his parents saw him being subdued and still. He listened quietly as a member of the therapy team read out chunks from the file. In order to illustrate the extent of the injuries being described and to help explain to the children what it actually meant, a plastic doll was used to mark the bruises. Peter, on the other hand, became glazed and fiddled with his fingers, which he dangled over his face, just like a baby does in a pram when it first discovers its fingers. Mr P, who was sitting beside him, instinctively put his hand on Peter's shoulder. Everyone seemed shocked by what they heard, but Paul most of all. It was as if the "unsayable" had been said and there were now no words that could make it unsaid. Paul looked terrified as he heard about what had happened and clearly was back there reliving it all over again. Mrs P was asked to go over to Paul and comfort him. Paul accepted the arms she put round him and for once did not push her away. Mrs P glanced at Mr P, registering her surprise. Mrs P rocked Paul gently to and fro, humming to him. She cried quiet tears of her own as she rocked him and he reached up and touched them, uncertain what they were. Paul seemed so little, so scared and confused, a child lost and alone. He did not understand her tears but his touch and silent question moved her. She broke down and sobbed saying over and over, 'Oh my little one, oh my little one, how could they?' Much later on, while they still held the children, the parents were asked to show, using the doll, how they would have washed away the marks if only they had been there. Paul and Peter were both gripped by this discussion and watched captivated while Mrs P gently soothed, washed and rocked the baby doll. This washing took over half an hour and no one spoke a word during it, but all the family were deeply engaged in the ritual.

The family was again exhausted but it was a different kind of exhaustion. There was no miracle but a pause in the process. Paul quickly tried to reinstate his old position of power, but that one moment of connection had helped the parents feel that there was hope. It was this hope that sustained them all. On the fourth day, Paul made a life-sized model of his birth mother and father and told them he would 'wipe the smile off their faces' if he ever saw them again. He also said in a letter that he dictated to one of the therapy team (it was made clear to Paul that this letter was not to be sent) that he missed them and could he come home soon. All feelings merged together for Paul as he struggled to work out how he felt about anyone. By the final day of the week, Mr and Mrs P felt that they were closer to the children and were clearer about the different ways in which both boys needed to be parented. Paul was driven by his fear and rage, wishing to control the world in order to keep himself safe. Peter was trapped alone in a world inside, needing to be treated like a baby much of the time and gently encouraged to connect with those around him. Huge tasks, but ones the parents now felt they understood.

The next six months of sessions and "hands-on help", which included parent mentoring by another adoptive parent, continued to focus on these themes and, by the end, Mr and Mrs P said that they could not give up on the boys. They felt that somehow they had to make this work and that the children were now theirs, scared and scary but theirs. Paul's behaviour had calmed down a bit and both parents said that most of the time they could contain him. In the last month there had been no incidents of violence towards either parent from Paul, although there was still a great deal of sibling so-called "play fighting". Peter was back in a nappy at night and relishing having a bottle at bedtimes. He was also able to manage eye contact for short periods and, on one occasion, ran in for a cuddle after falling over. It was a start. The P family struggled on, dreading the prospect of adolescence, but were determined that, with help, they would survive.

At the end of the six months of sessions, a network and review meeting was held, whereupon the parents and the professionals agreed that the placement would continue with a further year's support from Family Futures.

To summarise our approach to the treatment process, it is essential for the child's early trauma to be addressed in the first instance as children cannot move on to resolve the loss issues if they are still frozen by trauma. The meaning of contact and the significance of continuity have to be looked at in the context of how they help or hinder the resolution of firstly, trauma and secondly, loss. The development of positive attachments is an integral part of the trauma and loss resolution process. By putting adoptive parents "centre-stage", it is with their new parents that children work through trauma and loss and, in so doing, they repair and re-model their attachments to them.

Conclusions

Twenty years ago, our understanding of adoption revolved around identity issues in adolescence for the adopted child who would, typically, have been adopted as a baby. For adoptive parents, the key was acknowledging differences and the dual inheritance that adoption confers on the family. Today we believe that the key to supporting adopted children and meeting their needs is to understand the impact that early trauma has on children throughout their life. The task for contemporary adoptive parents has become infinitely more complex and demanding, as they have to learn to re-parent their children. With skilled help, parents need to be able to provide not only a family, but also a therapeutic environment where a child can grow and develop. Family Futures is working to find an effective way in which parents and children can join together in the drama of adoption. John Byng-Hall's work of re-scripting family experiences is a helpful way of considering the use of drama in therapy (Hills, 2002). This drama, for the child, begins even before birth and dominates their earliest years, forming a template for their expectations of the world. This template cannot be reshaped by logic and words alone, but only by going back to the very essence of our beings, to what is felt through touch, smell, taste, sound and sight. The importance of what the body says is fundamental to the creative arts, as described by Lorna Marshall (2001) and to understanding trauma (Van der Kolk, 1994). Trauma impacts on all our senses and it is for this reason that we have looked to the creative arts. The creative arts, with emphasis on symbolism, metaphor and the non-verbal interactions between people, have shown us a helpful way to rewrite the distorted scripts that children and their families bring.

Children find it so hard to put their feelings into words but can use the arts to say the unsayable. One teenage girl in a therapy session wrote a furious letter to her abusing birth father – her hand shaking. Trembling with feelings she stabbed the paper. When asked how to end the letter she wrote her name and then without thinking added a kiss. Horrified she stared at the paper and was frozen in terror. She was finally able to explain that she wanted the kiss removed. The therapist suggested another pen could scribble it out. Only after this was she able to explain, very quietly, what she had been unable to say earlier – that he had forced her to kiss him, he had forced her to do "things". The letter and her unconscious kiss had freed her to speak of it. Actions speak a thousand words as children come and express their hopes and fears through the arts. The lift of a dolls skirt, the scream of a puppet and the smear of brown paint can say so much that cannot be said any other way.

The primal nature of attachment and re-attachment transcends class and culture. They are universal themes. With the help of the creative arts, it is possible to enhance the understanding and the therapeutic healing that individual work and family work can bring about. If adoption is to remain an effective way of creating a family, then the focus of all our efforts has to be on helping children and parents to form new and positive attachments. We hope that Family Futures is developing a creative, dynamic way that will meet the needs of adoptive families in the 21st century.

References

Brodzinsky, D, Smith, D and Brodzinsky, A (1998) *Children's Adjustment to Adoption – Developmental and clinical issues*, New York: Sage Publications.

Hills, J (2002) *Rescripting Family Experiences: The therapeutic influence of John Byng-Hall*, London: Whurr Publishers.

Howe, D (1990) 'The Post Adoption Centre: the first three years', *Adoption & Fostering*, 14:1, pp 27–31.

Hughes, D (1997) *Facilitating Developmental Attachment: The road to emotional recovery and behavioural change in foster and adopted children*, Northvale, New Jersey: Jason Aronson Inc.

Ivaldi, G (1998) *Children Adopted from Care*, London: BAAF.

Macaskill, C (1986) 'Finding families for "hard-to-place" children: evidence from research', in Wedge, P and Thoburn, J (eds) *Post-adoption Support*, London: BAAF.

Marshall, L (2001) *The Body Speaks: Performance and expression*, London: Methuen.

Rushton, A, Dance, C and Quinton, D (2000) 'Findings from a UK-based study of late permanent placements', *Adoption Quarterly*, 3:3, pp 51–71.

Schore, A (1994) *Affect Regulation and the Origin of Self*, New Jersey: Lawrence Earlbaum Ass.

Van der Kolk, B (1994) 'The body keeps the score: memory and the evolving psychobiology of post traumatic stress', *Harvard Review of Psychiatry*, Jan–Feb, pp 253–65.

16 Health and adoption support

Mary Mather

From Moses to the internet twins

One of the earliest recorded adoptions in the Western tradition is that of Moses. The daughter of Pharaoh, a rich and possibly single parent, rescued him as a baby from the River Nile. Breast-fed by his birth mother, brought in as a wet nurse, he grew up in a transracial, transcultural and transreligious adoptive placement, which ran into difficulties when he discovered his true family and the religion of his birth. Over 3,000 years later, the public and the media on two continents were spellbound for weeks by the story of twins bought on the internet. Adoption always generates strong feelings, is always influenced by social change, and has always had a medical component.

Healthy babies for the perfect couple

Adoption became legal in England and Wales in 1926 in response to the orphans of the First World War and the 1918 influenza epidemic. Adoption, however, only became practical with the development of safe artificial infant feeding, which made it feasible to move newly-born babies from their birth mothers to foster mothers.

For the next 50 years, adoption practice was primarily about finding babies for childless couples. The "perfect" baby was new-born, white, healthy and developmentally normal. As the number of potential applicants was always greater than the number of babies, age, health, material wealth, and marital and professional status could be used to refine the definition of "the perfect adopter". The medical input to adoption in the early days was minimal. Essentially healthy babies were given a brief physical examination to exclude major health problems or congenital malformations. Children unlucky enough to have any medical problems were likely to be labelled as unadoptable. The medical needs of children requiring other types of permanent care, most of whom would be placed in local authority nurseries or foster homes, were largely forgotten until the pioneering work of Jane Rowe, published as *Children Who Wait* (Rowe and Lambert, 1975).

Adoption practice focused on three primary principles: secrecy, anonymity and the sealing of records. Systems were specifically designed to prevent birth and adoptive parents from meeting and sharing identifying information. A child's family medical history was likely to be lost as the adopted baby was always given a completely new blank medical record. Genetics, currently the fastest growing area of medical practice, was in its infancy. The fact that a child might need to know about conditions of genetic significance in the birth family was not even considered as an issue. The emotional needs of adopted children and their families were not recognised. Even today, elements of this early practice remain as each child is still given a new NHS number at the time of legal adoption.

For many years there was a reluctance to spotlight medical concerns too precisely for fear of delaying or stopping a potential placement. It is fascinating therefore to read about a very robust medical discussion which took place over 30 years ago at ABAFA (now the British Association for Adoption and Fostering) Medical Advisory Group (in Mather, 2000). The minutes of the meeting record a vigorous debate about when exactly an adoption medical should be done. Some medicals were obviously being completed after placement and, if doctors found a problem, the children were being returned! The Medical Group, very much in advance of its time, was emphatic that this was not only bad for the child and family but totally unethical practice. They were adamant that medicals and reports came *before* placements and strongly advised their members to have no part in this practice.

Mental health issues have a similar history. There is currently a much-needed focus on the mental health needs of children in general and looked after and adopted children in particular. For many years, however, there was a reluctance to engage in discussion with substitute carers about mental illness. Thankfully we have moved on, but the stigma can remain. Even today there can be an unwillingness on the part of some professionals to recognise the life-long nature of difficulties with emotional development and attachment experienced by adopted children. There is sometimes an even greater unwillingness to accept that these difficulties can begin in very young babies, if they are subjected to an unacceptable number of placement moves, and that the difficulties are preventable with good social work practice. (Howe *et al*, 1999)

Where did all the babies go?

By 1970, effective contraception, the legalisation of abortion, increasing acceptance of the single parent and better state welfare benefits led to a dramatic drop in the number of babies available for adoption. Adoption began to be seen as a solution to the care problems of children whose parents were unwilling, unable or judged by the legal system as unfit to care for them. The children for whom adoptive parents are now sought are likely to have complex physical, emotional, developmental and educational needs and are often damaged by inadequate parenting, abuse and neglect (Mather, 1999). They are children from a variety of ethnic and cultural backgrounds. Few are babies. Most are older children who often require placement with siblings. Many will have had multiple placements in the care system. There is an acceptance that many children will remain in contact with birth families and siblings. Social work practice and the medical skill and experience needed to support the substitute care of children have changed dramatically during the course of this century.

To know is to understand

The information we received at matching was very comprehensive: even though we had our problems we always felt that we understood the reasons why she behaved as she did.

(Adopters of a seven-year-old girl)

Try to imagine what it would be like if suddenly your children went to live with another family. For several months you had absolutely no contact with them, before they returned to live at home again. Most parents would find this blank in their knowledge of the child's life intolerable and would naturally be desperate for information. This desire for information would encompass every area of the child's life while they were away. Where did you sleep? What did you eat? Where did you go to school? Did you make any new friends? Were you happy? If the child had been ill or in hospital during this period, then the search for information would be even more frantic. We all need comprehensive and detailed knowledge about our children in order to parent them sensitively and no one should ever be asked to parent a child in the absence of this information.

'I don't know, I'm adopted'

Introductions can be a tense and fraught time for all concerned. The potential adopters, who have undergone a long assessment process and endured a long wait, will have felt that their lives have been on hold for months, if not years. The social worker, who may have been involved in tortuous legal care proceedings, may be equally anxious for a vulnerable child to move into a permanent placement. The process can become rushed and events can move at breakneck speed. In addition to the emotional excitement and tension generated by the possibility of a long awaited child, adopters are often organising or renovating family homes, tying up loose ends at work in preparation for adoption leave, and undertaking tiring journeys to the child's foster family. In this heady atmosphere, many of the questions that have been formulated during assessments may be left unasked. Medical information, particularly on a superficially healthy child, may not seem a very important issue.

Between 1926 and the 1989 Children Act, 876,601 adoptions took place in England and Wales. For many of these adopted adults faced with a doctor taking a basic medical history, the answer can only be 'I don't know, I'm adopted.' This humiliating scenario is then repeated at every health consultation. It is important that this does not happen to children in the future. Adopters must seek every opportunity to obtain as much health information as possible about a prospective child. Adopters need to ask questions, and they must, if necessary, make a nuisance of themselves in order to get the answers.

Post-adoption support in health starts with a comprehensive adoption medical

Comprehensive identification and appraisal of problems are likely to facilitate a placement rather than threaten it. Substitute carers require a very honest assessment of the difficulties they could face in meeting a child's needs.

Children requiring placement with adoptive families frequently come from backgrounds of abuse and neglect. The trauma of their early years will have long-lasting effects, not only on their physical health but also on their development, their education and their emotional and social growth. Examinations of these often damaged children must be done by doctors experienced in child and adolescent health, who are able to complete a holistic assessment of the child or young person. It may be advisable for children with particularly complex or subtle problems to be examined by a community consultant paediatrician or by the agency medical adviser.

The adoption medical is more than a basic physical examination. The pre-adoptive assessment of children needs to be an accurate and realistic review of the child's physical health and development as well as their social and emotional growth. It must include a comprehensive family medical history as well as the personal medical history of the child. Health is not just the absence of illness, preventative health is also important. Vision, hearing, dental checks and previous immunisations matter.

They never told us that her mother was short-sighted and it was two years before we realised that she needed glasses . . .

(Adopters of a six-year-old girl)

The medical report is a very important document to which the child will have access in the future. It must therefore be legible and avoid medical jargon and emotive judgements. For many children this information will be the only glimpse of their medical history that they will ever have.

If a child is brought up within his or her birth family, there is little need to depend on accurate medical records. Most birth parents have an intimate knowledge of their own child's health and development. For children separated from their families, however, the story is all too often one of loss or delay in the transfer of medical records, disrupted medical histories and inadequate record-keeping. Social workers who are not trained health professionals may be the only people who have contact with birth families. Whereas the social history of the family is often well documented in the BAAF Form E (which gives details about a child needing a permanent family), medical information is often sketchy, inaccurately recorded or even worse, omitted on the spurious grounds of confidentiality.

A child's medical history starts before conception when the genetic material of both parents is combined to form a new and a unique individual. This individual will, however, carry a tendency to develop the same genetic conditions that affected both his or her parents. Genes to a large extent determine our physical characteristics, intellect, behaviour and pre-disposition to illness and disease (Turnpenny, 1995). However, they are not the only influence and the "nature v nurture" debate is likely to continue. Genetics in the adoption process is far from straightforward because huge information gaps often exist. The family tree may be complicated and tortuous. The mother may be unwilling to divulge the father's identity or may disappear during the legal proceedings. Some of these difficulties can be overcome by inviting birth parents to adoption medicals. Parents alienated from social services are often more than willing to talk to doctors or nurses about their family history when they know the information is being recorded for their child in the future.

A child's medical history continues on through pregnancy, delivery and the early neonatal period. Pre-birth traumas can include the exposure to violence (including attempted abortion), feelings of ambivalence, rejection or grief in the mother, maternal illness or poor nutrition and, increasingly, the abuse of tobacco, alcohol and drugs.

It is important that adopters have full information about the child's birth. This should not only include information such as the hospital where the child was born and the child's birth weight, but any possible areas of distress to the infant that could have occurred around the time of delivery. This distress can include instrumental deliveries, caesarean section, long labours, time spent in the special care baby unit, prolonged separation from the mother after delivery because of drug withdrawal, serious neonatal complications and painful medical procedures.

Some children may have had repeated or extended early separations from their birth mother. Postnatal depression can make mothers emotionally unavailable to their babies. Many children are subjected to inappropriate attempts at rehabilitation, or may have spent periods of time in a drug withdrawal unit. Early childhood experiences, the arrival of siblings, common childhood illnesses, admissions to hospital, accidents, exposure to the effects of poverty, deprivation and abuse all contribute important factors to a child's medical history.

Adopters need to see a full record of both the child's and the parents' medical history. They must be given the opportunity to discuss them with medical specialists involved or the panel medical adviser. If the child has ever received a psychological or a psychiatric assessment, the prospective parents should have a copy of the report.

Health is always more than physical health. Children are growing and maturing, and reports from nursery or classroom teachers offer essential observations about a child's developmental skills, particularly in a social setting. When appropriate, therefore, adopters should ask to speak with a health visitor, teacher or other key figure who knows the child in a context outside the social work field. They should request medical and developmental information about siblings if children are not to be placed together and they should know the reasons for separation.

A very important and frequently forgotten point is that a child's family history does not stop with adoption. It must be kept up to date; family members die or develop serious illnesses that may be of genetic significance and siblings can develop a number of health or learning problems. Adopters and children need to know about these conditions, although concerns about medical confidentiality may place obstacles in the way of information exchange. There is still a conflict in the minds of doctors between a child's right to know about her/his birth family and the parents' right to medical confidentiality. Doctors urgently need updated guidance in the whole area of medical confidentiality in adoption to reflect modern adoption practice.

'It's all right, our doctor has done a medical'

Despite the change in adoption practice, there is considerable research evidence to suggest that adopters are still not being adequately prepared for the experience which could face them with their adopted child.

Lowe and Murch *et al* (1999) looked at the quality of information that had been given to 168 adopters. Only 61 (36 per cent) thought that the information they had received had been clear and realistic. One-third (33 per cent) did not. The remaining 30 per cent had mixed feelings.

The placements that had proved most problematic or which had disrupted understandably prompted the most comment. Broadly, there were four kinds of unfulfilled parental expectation: firstly, adopters who had experienced problems different from those that were anticipated; secondly, adopters who had anticipated difficulties but despite receiving good support did not anticipate their severity; thirdly, adopters who felt problems had been understated or simply not recognised; and finally, adopters who considered they had been deliberately misled.

In the same study, ten per cent of parents had received no information at all about the child's medical background, five per cent no information about the child's past history in the birth family, and 20 per cent had received no information about the child's behaviour. Fifty-seven per cent of adopters had received both written and oral medical information, 11 per cent written information only and 22 per cent oral information only. Serious questions need to be asked about whether oral information alone is worth giving during the emotional maelstrom of introductions.

The social worker did not have time to collect a medical history, and then the mother disappeared. We found out after his first fit that there was a family history of epilepsy.

They apparently had no time to tell us he was dyslexic. We felt so guilty, we wasted all those years of school.

(Quoted in Lowe and Murch *et al*, 1999)

There is a suggestion in this same study that disruptions could be minimised or even prevented by giving adopters sufficient information. Some adopters said that, although they had been promised sight of the child's case history, they had never seen it. In some cases, adoptive parents felt that had they been given sufficient information about the child, they might have considered saying no to the match. Others thought information might well have enabled them to better understand and cope with the child and the problems that arose in placement. Depressingly, many of the parents in the study told researchers that it was only at disruption meetings that they discovered the most detailed information about the child's background.

The authors make strong recommendation that all adoptive parents should be given full background information about children in a written form to include the reasons why they were looked after, their history in the birth family and in the care system, the reasons for any disrupted foster or adoption placements and a full medical history.

Difficult beginnings with happy endings

The evidence is that children who suffer severe physical, nutritional, and material deprivation during early childhood enjoy more or less complete physical recovery once placed in a safe and nourishing environment. Good health is restored, height and weight potentials are reached and normal physical milestones are achieved (Howe, 1997). Several large-scale studies involving intercountry adoptions also report a good physical recovery of children who arrive in their new country with a variety of health problems, including malnutrition, skin disease, poisoning by toxins and physical disability (Rutter *et al*, 2000).

All children adopted after infancy will have been damaged by the past to some degree. They will have developed a blueprint for survival, which becomes more entrenched with age. All adopted children are capable of testing their adopters to the limit and beyond. But it must not be forgotten that all children have some degree of resilience. Having survived the traumas of early life, many make a successful transition to a substitute family. However, in the vast majority of cases, adopted children and their families will require health and educational support for life.

What does the NHS offer to adopted children and their families?

In the United Kingdom, the National Health Service provides comprehensive health care for children and their families to cover all issues related to physical health. A comprehensive programme of child health surveillance ensures that all children have the opportunity to be seen regularly by a health professional. Immunisations are free and widely available. Routine checks of vision and hearing are easy to obtain. Dental care is free for children under 16. Therapeutic support is available for children with speech and language difficulties, and occupational therapy support for children with motor co-ordination difficulties. There is easy access to hospital care for the acutely ill child. National quality standards ensure that most hospital wards are child-friendly environments, where parents are welcome to stay with their children. Most adopters will, therefore, have little difficulty in ensuring that their child is and remains in robust physical health.

The sympathy and understanding with which adopters are treated within the NHS is, however, very variable. General practitioners and most general paediatricians have little or no training in adoption. Unlike social work journals, there is little published work in medical journals to show how specialised the area of adoption practice has become. Medical expertise has to change to support this new population of children and their adopters.

Our general practitioner is a lovely man whom we had known for many years. We were so shocked when he told us that we had tried hard enough with our daughter and should consider sending her back . . .

(Adopters of a 12-year-old girl)

The health visitor was very angry with us because we did not know how many immunisations the baby had been given. She told us we were lucky to be allowed to stay on the practice list because the doctors did not like unimmunised children.

(Adopters of a 14-month-old baby)

Our general practitioner was a real friend. She supported us through our infertility treatment and was very understanding of our anxieties about our adopted child.

(Intercountry adopters)

The situation may be more difficult for the adopter whose child is disabled or who has special needs. The quality of NHS services for these children is patchy. A child may have a comprehensive assessment of special needs before linking, only for adopters to find that, after the child is placed, the local health or education services are unable to meet those needs and the child's name goes to the bottom of a long local waiting list. The added dimension which being an adoptive parent brings to caring for a disabled child is often not appreciated by health or social care professionals. Adopters may find it difficult to access short breaks or a suitable educational placement. They can suffer intense feelings of guilt if the only suitable educational placement is a boarding school (Argent, 1998). The provision for the young disabled adolescent or teenager is disappointing. The educational expectations for disabled children remain generally low and consequently many children find adult employment difficult to secure. Sadly, some healthcare professionals are even suspicious of the motives of parents who adopt disabled children.

Are we going mad?

It is in the area of psychological adjustment, personality and relationships that early life experiences appear to have the most impact on later development. Living with traumatised children is probably the longest, most challenging, most stressful task that any adult ever undertakes. For everyone involved, making sense of the way a child behaves and of the psychological and treatment support available to adopted children and their families, can be a therapeutic nightmare.

There is no doubt that early childhood trauma affects both attachment and development, but parents and paediatricians frequently become lost in a confusing diagnostic maze. The range of emotional and behavioural difficulties in adopted children is vast and the picture varies over time. There are a large number of clinical diagnoses that attempt to describe discrete groups of clinical symptoms which may appear to fit a child more or less accurately at one stage. It is not uncommon for children to receive several such diagnoses as they pass through childhood into adulthood. Adoptive families and general practitioners are often passed from pillar to post and offered conflicting explanations and advice depending on the skill and interest of the diagnostician.

Some of the common clinical diagnoses given to adoptees during childhood include borderline personality disorder, anti-social personality disorder, post-traumatic stress disorder, obsessive/compulsive disorder, anxiety and panic disorder, conduct disorder, learning difficulty, and most commonly, attention deficit disorder or reactive attachment disorder. Each of these diagnoses will call for different therapeutic interventions, different management strategies and will be promulgated enthusiastically by the practitioners as the solution to the problem.

It is virtually impossible for a family to make sense of this confusion and general paediatricians or general practitioners experience similar problems! To find the right therapy for a child is often a decision that is left to increasingly desperate parents or social workers. The explosion of therapies for children with attachment disorders is undoubtedly market driven. Parents desperate for help and social workers desperate to prevent a placement disrupting frequently pay large amounts of money for "therapy". Although many therapists are skilled, genuine and well qualified, the whole process of psychotherapeutic intervention is nationally unregulated to an unsatisfactory degree.

Clarity is urgently needed in this situation. There are few outcome studies for the many therapeutic interventions on offer. A substantive evidence base for efficacy is often missing. Results are judged on individual case histories rather than controlled trials. Whereas evidence-based medicine is becoming the norm in most areas of conventional practice, in this area it is very much lacking.

What adoptive parents, general practitioners, paediatricians and social workers need to know is which of the many therapies on offer will suit the needs of a particular child. Should only specialists carry out these interventions? Can non-specialists use simpler, less expensive programmes effectively for the benefit of all adopted children? What then are the implications for social work practice? When substantial local authority resources are involved, can there be any process that will enable the right resources to be directed to the right child? The present situation can leave adoptive parents dissatisfied and placements at risk.

Health support for life

Adoption is an important but neglected issue within the medical profession. A doctor can write "adopted" on a patient's record without realising the significance for the patient or his or her family. Separation from a birth family can underline a whole range of chronic psychosomatic illnesses in adult life. Doctors who counsel infertile couples need to appreciate that few will succeed in adopting the baby they desperately want, and they need to be more aware of the magnitude of the task involved in the adoption of older children. Medical examinations of potential adopters are often done outside the NHS and paid for by adopters themselves. This practice should be reviewed. Society urgently needs substitute parents from all classes and cultures.

Ideally, medical practitioners involved in adoption work should have knowledge of the long-term consequences of childhood trauma, child abuse and neglect. Regulation 6(4) of the Adoption Agencies Regulations (1983) requires the appointment of a named medical adviser to work with each adoption panel. This is normally a senior consultant community paediatrician or a senior clinical medical officer. General practitioners also carry out the role. There is very little peer group support within the local paediatric community for the medical adviser who tends to work alone. Training in adoption for doctors has largely been confined to the voluntary sector and is rare within mainstream paediatrics. It is only recently that adoption as a topic has been added to the core syllabus for higher specialist training in paediatrics. It does not appear as a core subject in the recommended training for general practice registrars.

The role of the medical adviser in post-adoption support is currently limited. Increasingly however, medical advisers are meeting with adoptive families as part of the linking process. This sharing of medical information by a doctor who has collated all the child's medical history and often performed a comprehensive examination of the child is very much appreciated by adopters.

Dear Doctor,

I am writing to thank you for seeing us last week. We found the information you shared with us very helpful. We had a lot of concerns about going ahead with this placement and the likely impact of drug and alcohol abuse on the future development of Chloe. We were very appreciative of your advice and your openness and honesty. We realise that the future is an unknown for any child but now feel very positive about what we can do to help and support our new daughter. We are very grateful for your time. Thank you for giving us the opportunity to meet you.

(Letter to adoption agency medical adviser)

Many medical advisers are now routinely preparing written medical summaries, which are given to adoptive parents and the child's new general practitioner. However, a wider role for agency medical advisers in the long-term follow-up of adopted children is unlikely without significant additional resources and service development. Disappointingly, a recent Government consultation (Department of Health, 2002) on providing effective post-adoption support does not envisage an increased role for medical advisers. The same document also omits the general practitioner and the family health visitor as important sources of family health support. The main health agency mentioned in supporting adoptive placements is the Child and Adolescent Mental Health Services (CAMHS). While some adoptive children will need these specialist services, it is important to emphasise that the vast majority of adoptive placements are successful and that adopted children and their families must not be seen or treated in isolation. Most placements should be adequately supported by good mainstream services.

The resources and medical support given to adoption and fostering within the NHS are very small. If adoption is to become a real option for a group of very damaged children, appropriately trained medical advisers with experience and knowledge in paediatrics and child health must be available to support the service. The doctors involved must be able to function as part of a multi-disciplinary team working closely with local social services, foster carers and adopters. The paediatric contribution to adoption represents a speciality that needs to be located within mainstream paediatric services. The health service must match increased social resources with appropriately trained, knowledgeable and sensitive general practitioners, as well as paediatricians and child psychiatrists, to provide post-adoption support to children and their families. It is becoming very apparent that adopters require not only personal reserves of tolerance and understanding but also the unflagging interest and support of a variety of adoption support services. Health and educational provision for these vulnerable children may make or break an adoption placement.

Thousands of children have benefited from the generosity and commitment of their adoptive parents. The ability to give a child a second chance, which is cost effective, is rare within medicine. It is vital to assure the quality and continued resourcing of this small but important service within the NHS.

References

Argent, H (1998) *Whatever Happened to Adam?* London: BAAF.

Department of Health (2002) *Providing Effective Adoption Support*, Issued for Consultation August 2002, London: Department of Health.

Howe, D (1997) *Patterns of Adoption*, London: Blackwell Science.

Howe, D, Brandon, M, Hinings, D and Schofield, G (1999) *Attachment Theory, Child Maltreatment and Family Support*, Basingstoke: Palgrave.

Lowe, N and Murch, M *et al* (1998) *Supporting Adoption: Reframing the Approach*, London: BAAF.

Mather, M (1999) 'Adoption: a forgotten paediatric speciality', *Archives of Disease in Childhood*, 81, pp 492–95.

Mather, M and Batty, D (2000) *Doctors for Children in Public Care*, London: BAAF.

Rowe, J and Lambert, L (1975) *Children Who Wait*, London: ABAA.

Rutter, M and the English and Romanian Adoptees Study Team (2000) 'Recovery and deficit following profound early deprivation', in Selman, P (ed.) *Intercountry Adoption: Developments, trends and perspectives*, London: BAAF.

Turnpenny, P (1995) *Secrets in the Genes*, London: BAAF.

17 Adoption support from an education adviser

Michael Prior

Catholic Children's Society, Nottingham, is a voluntary adoption agency, working mainly within the East Midlands. Since the late 1970s the agency has focused increasingly on the family placement needs of children from public care. These children, who may originate from anywhere in the country, are placed through inter-agency arrangements with adoptive families who have been recruited and assessed by the Society. Their placements are supervised by the child's local authority and supported by Catholic Children's Society until an Adoption Order is made.

After adoption the children and families have access to continuing support through the Society's long-established post-adoption service. The Society is firmly of the view that the quality of a child's experience in their adoptive family, and indeed the stability of the placement, are in many cases inextricably linked with a satisfactory experience of education. For this reason the Society has created the post of Education Adviser and is committed to making his expertise known and available to families in the course of their child's growing up.

In the autumn of 1999, when I retired after 30 years as a Headteacher in Leicestershire, I was invited to become the first Education Adviser to the Catholic Children's Society. At the same time, I was asked to work on a consultancy basis for Leicestershire Local Education Authority (LEA) helping to place pupils who are in public care in schools and securing adequate support for the school to cope with any problems the children may have. The work with the LEA has given me insights into the difficulties which may well face adopters and children in their dealings with the education system. Prospective adopters are therefore introduced to the role of the adviser in the early stages of their training and preparation for adoption so that they, as well as social work staff and adoption panels, benefit from my involvement with the agency.

When asked to contribute to this book, I asked myself: 'What is my function and why do I think it is important?' I have a job description, which acts as a clear guideline. It is the implementation of this job description which is important to all parties: the Society, the adopters and the adopted children. It also presents a challenge to me to help to improve the lives of children who have previously had a variety of bad experiences. I firmly believe that education for these young people has to be promoted and needs to be valued by them, their families and the schools they attend.

Pupils in public care are currently a priority for the Department for Education and Skills (DfES). Extra resourcing is available for work with this group of pupils who are often seen to be a failing group in school. In extreme cases, this failure leads to poor exam results, low self-esteem, poor prospects, disaffection with school and, in some cases, exclusion from school. Each LEA has to appoint an officer to look after the needs of this group, while each school has to appoint a designated teacher to support and monitor the welfare and progress of any looked after children in the school.

Local authorities have to ensure that all looked after pupils have a Personal Education Plan (PEP), which is initiated by social services and has to include comprehensive health and education records. This plan follows pupils from foster placement to foster placement and from school to school and is meant to improve continuity in the welfare and education of such pupils. Once children leave public care, the responsibility of the designated officer and teacher ceases, as does the need to maintain a PEP.

I am convinced through my knowledge of how children learn and my experience of looked after children that any pupil moving from public care into adoption will still have many special educational needs. I believe that if adoptive parents wish, their adopted child should have access to the same level of educational input and monitoring as was available when the child was in care. This view is shared by some LEAs. For example, Nottinghamshire's designated officer for children in public care also has responsibility for monitoring and advising on the education of children who have been adopted. I sincerely hope that all agencies, whether statutory or voluntary, are in a position to ensure that all newly adopted children have their educational needs addressed thus also providing further support to adopters.

Special needs and statement of needs

Education has always been seen as a way forward. Movements and legislation such as "Education for All" in Victorian times and the 1944 Education Act have been milestones in our history. Yet, despite major advances, any educational system has its difficulties and sometimes failures. Today we see that many children who are adopted have been unable to make the most of opportunities provided to the population as a whole. When in care, children are likely to move from one placement to another. Each time this happens it almost invariably means a change of school. The change from one school to another can take weeks rather than days (the official DfES guidelines say that 20 school days should be the maximum time to arrange a school place). Missing school means that regression and omission rather than progression and action take place. A succession of such moves means that, by the time a child is adopted, there are usually serious or very serious educational losses. For example, I have seen adopted children who should have a Statement of Special Educational Needs, who do not have one due to the lack of continuity in that child's education. Such a statement is essential for the development of children with special learning, emotional or behavioural needs as it usually carries with it extra funding for support to address the identified problem(s). It is not unknown for the issuing of a Statement to take several months or even years!

A Statement of Special Educational needs is normally given after a school has produced sufficient evidence to the LEA that a child requires a Statement to ensure that his /her needs will be met. If parents feel that the school has not done enough to meet the needs of their child, they are entitled to ask the LEA to arrange for a full educational assessment of their child. The results of this exercise could lead to the granting of a Statement of Special Educational Needs or an Individual Education Plan (IEP) that the school should use to support the needs of the child.

During my time with the Society, I have been asked to advise on educational issues for children with behaviour and learning difficulties.

One eight-year-old boy on placement presented both the adopters and the school with disturbing behaviour. This included disrupting the whole class on a regular basis and refusing to carry out reasonable requests from the class teacher. The adopters became very concerned and the Catholic Children's Society asked me to try to help both the family and the school. John had been receiving some classroom support funded by the LEA. On moving to his current school and changing LEAs, the support he had in the previous school ceased. He did not have a Statement, yet clearly needed one, and the lengthy process had to be started from the beginning. The Headteacher was concerned about the lack of support and the impact of John on both the class teacher and the rest of the class. She was very sympathetic towards the boy but was unable to find funding from her own school budget to provide the necessary support. Along with the Headteacher, I approached the LEA. The result of our discussions and negotiation led to some extra learning support time and a promise to speed up the statementing process. The LEA understood that the adoption placement was very fragile and that it could break down if extra support were not forthcoming. The LEA officers involved saw that if a breakdown did occur, John would go back into the care system, and having experienced further rejection, would probably prove even more challenging and stand a very good chance of being excluded from school.

Understanding the system

Many parents need professional advice when dealing with education issues, especially if they have no previous experience of the system and their adopted child goes into a school after the normal starting age. Often the pressure of being "approved" parents can weigh heavily and they may become over-anxious about approaching the school if there are any difficulties with their child. They may feel that they should be able to cope or that they will "upset" the school and make matters worse. I have helped parents like this by suggesting questions to ask and points that might be discussed to help lead to a resolution of their problem. It is not, however, only when starting school that problems arise.

One family with an adopted teenage daughter was very concerned about her relationships in school and potential for self-harm, which resulted in her work suffering and a reluctance to attend school. When the parents went to the school, they never managed to talk to anyone beyond the Head of Year. They felt that the Head of Year did not really comprehend their concerns and were becoming quite desperate and frustrated. They spoke to me and asked what else I thought they could do. I suggested that they arrange an interview with the Headteacher, which they had not done previously as they thought he would be too busy or did not deal with such cases. The Headteacher agreed to see them. He was both encouraging and helpful, eventually agreeing to the girl being educated at home.

Parents need to realise that good headteachers do care about their pupils and if the system has not worked lower down the management structure, they are able to make informed decisions based on their wider knowledge of available provision and resources.

Another family adopted a seven-year-old boy and secured a place for him in their local school. They became very anxious after their initial interview with the Headteacher, feeling that perhaps he did not really want to take their boy. In a conversation about school discipline, the word "exclusion" was used. They took this out of context and thought it was being used in relation to their son. I spoke to the Headteacher, who was horrified at the misinterpretation of the conversation and immediately reassured the parents, as did the social worker involved with the family.

Teachers have to be helped to understand that new adopters may be more apprehensive and less confident than other parents in dealing with schools because they are often only beginning to get to know their child.

Training adopters

At the Society we accept that if education, and particularly education post adoption, is to be successful, it is crucial that it is wholly supported by parents. To this end, the Society has embarked on a series of training days to enable parents to understand and use the education system to the best advantage for their children. The first day of the programme was well attended, with a crèche facility organised in partnership with the East Midlands Children Society Resource Team[1] for those who would

---

[1] An adoption agency which also works in the East Midlands.

otherwise not have been able to attend. The day consisted of short talks and tasks to explore the language of education such as "Foundation Stage", "Key Stages", "National Curriculum", "Literacy and Numeracy Hours", "Levels of Attainment", "Code of Practice". We also looked at some acronyms used such as SEN (Special Educational Needs), SENCO (Special Educational Needs Co-ordinator), SATs (Standard Assessment Tasks). Input from professionals and the experiences shared by adoptive parents informed and empowered the participants.

When discussing admissions to schools, both first time or transfer, there was evidence of much uncertainty, and of some bad experiences. The parents formed small groups to discuss key issues in choosing the right school for their child. This may not necessarily be the local school or a school in the state system, although adopters have to be aware of the implications of distance, of their child's interaction with their neigh-bourhood peer group, funding and, possibly, the child feeling even more "different". Adopters, like other parents, might not be granted a place for their children in the school of their preference. How to appeal against a decision was explained during the training day.

Appeals

All parents have the right to appeal against the decision of the school's admitting authority, e.g. Governors in faith schools, LEA in community schools. Parents appeal in writing to the admitting authority. Their appeal is considered by an independent appeals panel, which usually consists of five people but can be as few as three. The panel reads the appeal and, if the parent wishes to have a personal hearing, will listen to their case. The representative of the LEA or governing body explains to the panel why they have refused the family the place in the school of their preference. The consequent decision of the panel is binding on the admitting authority. Although adoption is not seen as a "special" case, if there are serious social and domestic issues involved, there is a possibility that the panel will uphold the appeal.

Long-term foster carers who were hoping to adopt their foster child were having a hard time with the birth parents of the child. Rather than send the child to the local school, where members of the birth family were pupils and unwelcome contact would be even more likely, they applied for a place in a school in a neighbouring authority. Their application was turned down because the school was full. They appealed against the decision on the grounds that the welfare of the child could be at risk. The appeal was upheld and the child was able to attend the school of the foster carers' choice, a school that could provide a very good quality of education as well as a safe environment.

Transfers

The recently established Adoption Register could mean that children will be more likely to move a long way to their adoptive family. This will almost certainly lead to difficulties in understanding the differences between LEAs, differences which may include school organisation, funding and statementing. These difficulties are already well known to the parents who have adopted through inter-agency arrangements. Before children are placed for adoption, it is essential that the agency involved initiates school transfer, making sure that the child has a PEP, which will be invaluable for the school the child will attend. This is particularly true of a pupil with a Statement of Special Educational Needs.

Training given to adoptive parents also includes guidance on how to find out about the practices of individual schools by looking in the school prospectus, the school website (if available), requesting OFSTED (Office for Standards in Education) reports, talking to other parents and, most importantly, by paying a visit to the school. Some parents find negotiating with schools quite daunting. I wonder if this could be due to bad memories of school when they themselves were pupils. During one of the training sessions, the group compiled questions that should be asked of a headteacher. In my experience, headteachers like parents who come with questions as it gives a focus to the meeting and does not leave the headteacher wondering whether he or she has answered all the queries the parents may have. Many parents want to know how a school deals with behavioural, emotional and learning difficulties and how the school sets about building up self-esteem and self-worth in pupils.

Adopters are also guided to consider aspects of the school to look at when visiting classrooms: the relationships between pupils and between pupils and teachers, the degree of purpose evident in the work observed in the classroom, displays of work, positive strategies for multi-cultural and multi-faith education, safety and evidence that the fabric of the building is well maintained.

The feedback from the participants in the workshop has been extremely positive and reaffirms the need for further, regular training opportunities for adopters. The Society envisages offering more training days on education in the future.

Advising the professionals

As Education Adviser, I see that there is also a role to play in liaising with social workers and school staff as well as adoptive families. Schools are under enormous pressure to raise standards. This can lead to a narrowing of the curriculum, especially in Key Stages 1 and 2 where league tables are only concerned with English, Maths and Science. Teachers may find that the time they can give to those with emotional, behavioural or learning difficulties is not always as much as they would wish. Children in the public care system often have at least one of these difficulties, so it is essential that schools have as much appropriate information as possible about the child to help in both planning and in the day-to-day understanding of the child, especially in the area of relationships. When the child comes out of public care, he/she will have a PEP, which should tell the school a great deal as social services, health and education will have provided ongoing reports. There may, however, still be confidential information about the child that the school does not know. Parents have to be sensitive to their child's feelings and wishes when they judge what to disclose, even on a "need to know" basis. This is certainly an area where the adviser could be extremely helpful in determining what is relevant and, if the parents prefer, talking to the school about the information and its sensitivity. Once a child is adopted, the PEP will revert to an Individual Education Plan if the child has special needs but is not subject of a Statement.

Some schools and individual teachers are unaware of the issues surrounding adoption. I heard a teacher who was about to receive an adopted child into her class say that it would not prove to be a problem as adoption was just like divorce. She obviously failed to understand either. Where schools have adopted children on the register, it would be very appropriate for an education adviser to talk to the staff group about possible feelings and behaviour of adopted pupils, such as a sense of failure, low self-esteem, wanting to be in control and relationship problems. It would also be important to convey that the adopters will probably have to deal with challenging behaviour and that the school can give support by not making demands on the child which could lead to a confrontation at home. Equally, the school needs to know that it should not over-compensate for the pupil's background and that adopted children usually like school as it is a place where they can fit into a routine, learn more about themselves and grow in confidence if they are praised for even small achievements.

Staff also need to know that some aspects of the curriculum like sex education, genetics or family trees can cause pain to adopted pupils. These subjects will need careful planning and delivery to classes where there are adopted pupils or pupils in care. Adoption UK has produced a very useful booklet for schools: *What Does Adoption Mean for Today's Children? A Guide for Teachers*. This should be available in all staffrooms and adopters should read it so that they know what they might reasonably expect from teachers.

This educational aspect of the work of the adviser with professionals will take a while to establish and grow. Initially, it might happen through contacts with individual social workers and teachers, where support can be given over educational matters which concern them. It can also be developed through networks in LEAs and agencies. LEAs will know, through their designated officer for children in public care, which children have been placed for adoption. A system could be established to inform schools that there is still advice and support available for these children through adoption agencies. Parents need to know that their adoption agency has an education adviser so they can use him/her in a positive way when dealing with school-related issues.

Conclusion

The under-achievement of children who have moved through the public care system is widely recognised as an area for research and development. It is imperative that those who are responsible in local authorities for children in care also look sympathetically at those who have been adopted, whether they were previously the responsibility of their department or have moved in to the area through inter-agency adoption arrangements or with their adoptive parents.

I do not think that I can stress enough the need for an education adviser in an adoption agency to support the post-placement needs of pupils. Who should do such work? Firstly, the person must have a very comprehensive knowledge and experience of the education system, both public and independent. He/she should be a good communicator and negotiator. It will help if the adviser has an extensive network of key workers within at least one LEA through whom key personnel in other LEAs can be identified. He or she needs to have a particular empathy with the problems likely to affect those who have been adopted, and so needs to have a good knowledge of the *Code of Practice for Special Educational Needs* and an understanding of the whole adoption process in order to be able to advise the adoption panels, placement workers and families.

For most voluntary adoption agencies, certainly the smaller ones, it may only be possible to employ a part-time adviser who would be able to work on an as-needs basis. Adjoining local authorities could well consider sharing an education adviser to work with adopted children and their families.

The education adviser needs to be seen as an integral part of the agency team, as is the medical adviser. It seems, therefore, that an ideal person would be somebody who has retired but still wishes to remain active within the system, someone who was a senior manager within a school or the LEA. Anyone interested in this work would be well advised to begin by reading *Adopted Children Speaking* (Thomas *et al*, 1999) and *Nobody Ever Told Us School Mattered* (Jackson, 2001) to develop an understanding of the exciting potential offered by this role.

References

Adoption UK, *What Does Adoption Mean for Today's Children? A Guide for Teachers*.

Jackson, S. (ed.) (2001) *Nobody Ever Told us School Mattered*, London: BAAF.

Thomas, C and Bedford, V with Lowe, N and Murch, M (1999) *Adopted Children Speaking*, London: BAAF.

18 'Where next?' A perspective on post-adoption services in Scotland

Barbara J Hudson

If we buy a car, we have presumably arranged a budget to allow us to run it. So it should be for planning for children. Post-adoption services are not an additional extra or a luxury. They are an essential part of the provision, ensuring that the placement has as good a chance of succeeding as it possibly can.

These were the words of Phillida Sawbridge in her introduction to *After Adoption*, a collection of papers on working with families, published in 1996.

So, how are we doing in Scotland with our car? In an attempt to answer the question, this paper presents illustrations of some services and interventions, which are currently available in Scotland within the present policy and legislative framework. It concludes with reflections on future developments.

Adoption support is taken as meaning those services that are provided to adoptees, adoptive families, birth parents and other relatives. We need to recognise the life-long impact of adoption on all concerned. Within a context of increased openness, the interaction, be it direct or indirect, between the birth family and the family formed through adoption, is crucial. Birth parents and other birth relatives cannot be expected to provide information and explanations about the child's history if they themselves have not been helped and supported in their grief and enabled to deal with the loss of the child from their family. Adoptive parents cannot cope with the complex feelings that arise when caring for a child not born to them, and who still has contact with members of their original family, if they themselves do not have the opportunity to explore their conflicting feelings and their dilemmas. Adoptees themselves need support in different ways and at different stages in their life cycle to enable them to deal with the issues arising from being born into one family but growing up in another. Adoption support, therefore, is not just a service for adoptive families but a service for *all* those involved in adoption.

In the course of writing this paper, and following discussions held with adoptive parents and with staff from a range of agencies across Scotland, a number of themes have emerged. A wide range of services and interventions is being provided by the voluntary and statutory sectors and self-help groups. The variety and creativity of the services available reflect the wealth of experience and expertise that exists in Scotland in this area of work. The services and initiatives have been researched and recorded; service users and service providers have attested to the benefits (Phillips and McWilliam 1966; Watson with McGhee, 1995). To return to the metaphor used by Phillida Sawbridge, there is no lack of understanding and willingness to ensure that the car runs. The question is: in which direction?

In 2001 an Adoption Policy Review convened by Scottish Ministers had, as part of its remit, to consider 'the provision of post-adoption support for families'. The review group's report, published in June 2002 outlines some key principles for the delivery of such services, but the mechanism for developing them and the structure to take them forward is as yet not decided. It is important, therefore, to consider the strengths of current service provision, what has impeded its development, and what the options are for the future.

Current context

The Children (Scotland) Act 1995 introduced a number of amendments to the Adoption (Scotland) Act 1978 which remains the primary legislation concerning adoption, but with new subordinate legislation, Adoption Agencies (Scotland) Regulations 1996. *Scotland's Children*, Volume 3, was published in 1997 and provides guidance on both the 1978 Act and the new Regulations, and also includes directions on the payment of adoption allowances.

In the introduction to the guidance, specific reference is made to the fact that

Adoption services which were predominantly designed to find adoptive parents for healthy babies have changed and developed into family

finding services for some of the most disadvantaged children in Scotland. At the same time, and partly as a consequence, greater need for post-adoption services for adopted children and adults, adoptive parents and birth parents has been recognised.

The Guidance goes on to highlight that there is a "duty" on adoption agencies to provide these services 'in ways which are supportive to those involved and can easily be accessed without undue delay'. Partnership between statutory and voluntary agencies is seen as beneficial and details of post-adoption services are required to be included in Children's Services Plans. It should be noted, however, that although responsibility for providing post-adoption services was placed on local authorities, there was no procedure for monitoring whether, in fact, these services were being provided.

From 2002, when the Regulation of Care legislation came into force, the adoption services provided by local authorities were subject to scrutiny for the first time. Hitherto, only the voluntary adoption agencies had been inspected by the Social Work Services Group of the Scottish Executive. Since April 2002, those services provided by local authorities acting as adoption agencies have also been inspected against the Care Standards published in January 2002. These Standards, developed through consultation with key stakeholders, make a number of statements about post-adoption support:

You can be confident that the agency will identify any extra help you or your adoptive family might need so that you can realise your potential. If you have difficulties arising from your adoption, the agency will advise you where you can get help. (Standard 9)

You have access to a full range of support services after your child has been adopted. (Standard 30)

What services are available?

Statutory provision
The 32 Scottish local authorities all act as adoption agencies, planning adoptions for children, assessing prospective adopters and placing children with adoptive families. They also provide services to birth parents

and relatives. Several have negotiated service contracts with the voluntary agencies in order to ensure that a more specialist service is provided in relation to some aspects of adoption work. Fourteen local authorities have service agreements with Barnardo's Scottish Adoption Advice Service and four local authorities have service agreements with the Scottish Adoption Association and St Andrew's Children's Society for the provision of information, advice and counselling, and also for the recruitment of a certain number of families for children needing placement. Nonetheless, in spite of these specific contracts, the local authorities still retain responsibility for a number of areas.

- Funding, particularly in relation to adoption allowances and payment for specialist services. The introduction of an adoption allowance scheme in 1996 made it possible for agencies across Scotland to pay adoption allowances. However, there continues to be considerable variation in the way in which this legislation is interpreted and in the level of payments. There is also the added difficulty that some children with complex needs are being cared for by foster carers who receive a professional fee, but that if they decide to adopt the professional fee will be discontinued.

- Initial work with birth families and children, i.e. assessment and planning. The assessment of family functioning, relationships and children's needs is crucial in making effective plans for children and for the provision of good quality information to prospective carers. There has to be concern that there is no Scotland-wide assessment framework and that there is considerable variation in practice between agencies. There is also concern that child development and attachment are not well understood by workers and that therefore the assessments may be flawed.

- Maintaining contact between birth families and children in placement, where arrangements have been made either for direct face-to-face contact, or for the exchange of information through a letterbox. Such arrangements have only been developed over the last few years, and the impact of contact and information exchanges on birth families, adopters and children is not always fully understood. All involved are likely to need support before and after meetings and when they send and receive information.

- Local authorities make a number of arrangements to provide support to adoptive families by organising meetings, social events, training courses and, in some areas, by publishing a newsletter. Such arrangements are usually the responsibility of the family placement teams, and may be over and above their other duties. One local authority has recruited a specialist adoption support worker, a development specified in the local Childrens' Service Plans. One or two of the larger agencies have either purchased or are contemplating purchase of *It's a piece of cake*, the parenting training package for adopters produced by Adoption UK.

The support needs of birth parents are not an area of service development within local authorities; indeed it is arguable whether birth families who have been involved in protracted disputes with the local authority would be able to accept help from that source. It would be interesting, however, to see whether a Family Group Conference approach might facilitate a less adversarial position, and thus lead to support being made available to birth relatives.

Voluntary sector services

Voluntary sector provision in Scotland consists of services provided by Scottish-based UK agencies and some agencies specific to Scotland.

Three of the Scottish agencies – The Scottish Adoption Association, St Margaret's Children & Family Care Society and St Andrew's Children's Society – are the only "placing" agencies working with birth parents who relinquish their children for adoption.

- *Barnardo's* provides the following services:
  Scottish Adoption Advice Service, based in Glasgow, provides a wide range of after adoption support to birth parents, adoptees and adopters, offering both individual sessions and group activities. Support is available for adopted people who are attempting to trace their birth families and also for contact negotiations and reunions. Originally a telephone support service for families who were awaiting placements, the agency now has service agreements with 14 local authorities. It provides training for counsellors and social work departments.

Barnardo's Family Placement Service recruits, assesses and approves prospective adoptive parents and provides ongoing support to adoptive families. The organisation finds it is able to offer consistency to families because the same workers who assess and prepare them continue to support them once they have children in placement. This strengthens the working relationship, making it easier to provide support when families encounter difficulties after adoption.

The Khandan Project for Asian families is a related but separate part of the Barnardo's Family Placement Service. The Project recruits, assesses, approves and supports Asian adopters. Working with these families has raised a number of practice issues including the use of interpreters. Interpreters were used in the assessment of families, but it was recognised that once there was a child in placement and the family was encountering difficulties, having to talk through problems and concerns with yet another person could be perceived as intrusive. It required a great deal of skill on the part of the interpreter to express not just the content of people's conversations but also the meaning behind it. Consequently, interpreters have been included in training organised by the Project so that they would be in touch with some of the issues. As well as individual support for the families, the Project has helped to form a social group, which includes both adopters and adopted children. It is seen as supportive to the families and as a source of strength for the children, as they grow up, to be in touch with other youngsters who are in the same position as themselves.

- *Birthlink Family Care*, based in Edinburgh, holds the Adoption Contact Register for Scotland. The organisation counsels and helps those individuals who are undertaking a search for their birth families, as well as providing advice and information about adoption.
- *BAAF Scotland*, based in Edinburgh, provides general advice, information, training and consultancy to all involved in adoption.
- *Step-Family Scotland*, also based in Edinburgh, offers advice and information and has a telephone helpline. It also provides training for professionals writing assessment and court reports in step-family applications.
- *St Margaret's Children & Family Care Society* undertakes the full range

of adoption placement services and will make an initial assessment if anyone comes back to the organisation asking for advice, information or support after adoption. If they are unable to meet a request, they will refer to another agency. St Margaret's offers post-placement and post-adoption groups for adoptive families and has created opportunities for people who have adopted children of similar ages to come together, acknowledging that the problems facing people who have adopted very young children are not always the same as those facing people who have adopted older children with more complex needs. The organisation also offers a group for birth mothers and for adult adoptees.

- *St Andrew's Children's Society* operates the full range of adoption services and once placements are made, establishes an agreement with all families about the specific post-adoption services which they think they might need. St Andrew's find it helpful to have a written agreement even if the family, at the stage of making the agreement, feels that they are not going to need any ongoing support. The act of setting up an agreement places support on the agenda and that makes it easier sometimes for families to come back for help. The agency also provides respite care for children in adoptive placements using families, which they themselves have recruited, as well as services to birth relatives.

- *The Scottish Adoption Association* provides a comprehensive adoption service, which has, for some years, included a range of post-placement and post-adoption support services. These have ranged from individual counselling to groups for children (one of which led to the production of a video), adoptive families and birth parents. Recognising that sometimes words are not the most effective way of helping people, the agency recently ran a painting class for birth mothers. This provided an opportunity for a creative activity to build self-esteem and perhaps a way of moving on.

Adopters' groups

As well as the services provided by the statutory and voluntary adoption agencies, Scotland has seen the development of several adopter-led groups.

- *The Lothian Adopters Group* has been in existence for some 17 years.

It was initially established by Lothian Regional Council as part of its strategy for the placement of older children in recognition that extra support was needed for families taking on children with complex needs and that experienced adopters could be helpful when recruiting new families. At one stage, funding by Lothian Regional Council paid for the services of two counsellors to be made available to adoptive families through the group itself rather than through referral to the social work department. This direct access to support was seen by many people to be extremely helpful. With some financial support from a local adoption agency, the group continues to organise events for adoptive families and children, publish a regular newsletter and keep members informed about relevant training opportunities.

- *PACS (Post-Adoption Central Support)* has been running for over ten years. The group publishes a newsletter and organises a range of events, and was recently able to fund a worker for ten hours per month. This enabled the group to produce a leaflet for teachers, giving some information about the impact of attachment difficulties on children's ability to learn and on their behaviour in school. Teachers do not routinely receive, as part of their training, information about the circumstances of children who are placed for adoption and the impact of poor attachments on their general functioning and behaviour. The group was also able to provide a training event for teachers, giving them an opportunity to look at these issues in more depth. This attracted a considerable amount of interest among local teachers and further afield.

- *Adoption UK* has grown into a UK-wide organisation with regional and country branches. It was formed in 1978 by adopters who became concerned about the needs of older and disabled children in the care system. The Scottish group, active since the late 1990s, organises monthly evening meetings and drop-in sessions as well as circulating information through a newsletter and the internet.

- *OASIS group for families* are parents who have adopted children from overseas. The group exists to provide information and support to one another, as well as activities for their children to help promote their sense of identity.

Working together

The tradition of collaborative working between the voluntary and statutory sector is an important one in Scotland. In adoption, as in other areas of children and family work, agencies co-operate to enhance each other's efforts rather than duplicate or compete.

The Voluntary Agencies Forum is particularly concerned with post-adoption work, sharing skills and dilemmas and updated information on current activities. A recent initiative of the Forum has been the development of a user-friendly leaflet to be available in as many places as possible, providing basic information about adoption and support and where it can be obtained.

Another example of collaboration was when Scottish agencies came together to provide an open forum at the end of a drama event presented at the Edinburgh Festival Fringe, which dealt with the whole area of adoption.

BAAF Scotland hosts a Practice Development Forum at which workers from voluntary and statutory services can meet to look at wider practice issues. Agencies have collaborated on a number of training events, workshops and conferences; representatives from both the statutory and voluntary sector came together for a series of workshops to look at attachment issues in relation to children in adoptive and permanent placements.

Related services

A number of individuals and organisations offer therapeutic treatment for children and also for children and their adoptive families. These include the Scottish Institute of Human Relations and the Notre Dame Services, as well as independent psychologists, counsellors and therapists.

There is also the service provided by CAMHS (Children and Adolescent Mental Health Services), although this is heavily oversubscribed, not only by adopted children but also by children who are looked after and accommodated.

What lies ahead?

For adoptees

The profile of children being placed for adoption has changed considerably in the last 15–20 years. Nearly all the children who need alternative families today are older and have complex needs. Many are being placed against the wishes of their parents and with quite distressing histories. Some children are being placed with their siblings while others are separated. The increased openness of adoption, in terms of sharing information, means that it will be necessary for children to be helped to have an understanding of all the circumstances surrounding their admission to care, the plan for adoption and, if applicable, the decision to separate them from their siblings.

For adopters

The issues confronting adopters in the future are going to be similar to those they face at the present time, namely, how best to provide good parenting for children whose behaviour and attachment patterns make it very hard for them to respond to what parents have to offer. Recent developments in our understanding about the neurological development of children may help to give adoptive parents a better appreciation of what is happening to their children, but also create a greater demand for access to more specialised services which can attempt to redress and repair some of the early damage their children have suffered. There will continue to be a need to support adoptive parents managing direct contact or the exchange of information between birth families and children. An issue that will probably become more acute is how adopted children fare within the education system. As the whole philosophy of education moves towards allowing the child to take the initiative, children who have difficulty in developing a positive view of themselves and in being able to seek out information, may find it even harder to get the best out of the education system.

For birth parents

Hitherto, much of the work has been with birth parents who have made the decision to place their child for adoption, but increasingly, it is parents who have battled, sometimes for several years, against the plans of the local authority to place their children permanently away from them, who have need of adoption support. It is not clear at this stage who would be best able to provide this support and what would be the most effective form, and how birth parents and other relatives could access this support in Scotland.

Points for further consideration

- The Scottish Ministerial Review has made a number of suggestions about how services might be delivered to all parties to adoption. Key recommendations relate to developing standards, post-adoption support agreements, service agreements and an Adoption Support Network for Scotland. The latter recommendation is vital if services are to be delivered equally across Scotland and if skills and expertise are to be shared. The structure of such a network is the subject of further debate and consultation, but it is unlikely to succeed without adequate resourcing.
- When social work departments have to prepare budgets in the face of competing demands, adoption support struggles, often unsuccessfully, to be seen as a priority. This became evident when adoption received little or no attention in the first round of Childrens' Services Plans, after the introduction of the Children (Scotland) Act 1995.
- Voluntary organisations suffer from fragile funding, since service agreements may only run from year to year and project funding, which is short term, would seem to be incompatible with developing services that are for life.
- Funding apart, there is the issue of who would adoptees, adopters and birth parents want to approach for help. Local authorities can be viewed as stigmatising and unreliable because of frequent changes of staff; voluntary agencies are seen as more "neutral" and stable and better able to develop specialist services. But should there be a division or should the approach be more pragmatic, to map what is available and where, and then establish services in areas where they are needed? Or would it be in the interests of children and their birth and adoptive families for all adoption support work to pass from statutory agencies to the voluntary sector?

- If post-adoption support is separated from family placement, workers undertaking the initial intervention and assessment of children and their families could be cut off from the experience and knowledge which goes with working with children in adoptive placements. This can mean that frontline staff are either over-optimistic about the outcomes of children separated from their families or overly despondent about the implications of taking children away from their birth families. It is vital that there is feedback between all the workers and managers involved in planning for children at different stages.
- At a more strategic level, adoption work is only one part of the range of services to children and families provided by local authorities. Education, health, employment and housing are also the responsibility of the local authority acting as a corporate parent and the adoption dimension needs to be brought into these mainline services.

Conclusion

In the course of writing this paper, it became clear that there is a wealth of experience and skills in Scotland about how to provide effective adoption support. But time and time again, individuals and agencies expressed anxiety about how such services could continue to be provided unless funding was both increased and secured. This then is perhaps the major issue which faces us in Scotland.

To return to the car . . . although it may not be completely out of petrol, the warning light is certainly starting to flash. Several hundred children a year will continue to be placed in new permanent families in Scotland. All the information that we have to hand tells us that these children and their new families and their birth families will continue to need support of varying kinds throughout their lives. Not to have a co-ordinated, clear and consistent framework in place to deliver those services across Scotland is to short-change these children. Adoption support services cannot be an optional extra; they must be an integral part of providing services for children and families. Support should not be dependent on funding from the Lottery, Children in Need or other charitable foundations, but should be a core part of the forward planning made by all statutory agencies about their budget requirements for the foreseeable future. The health and education needs of adopted children and their families should also be recognised and included in the planning of those departments. What is required in Scotland is agreement on a framework for the delivery of post-adoption support services, backed by adequate funding and the passion and determination to drive it forward.

References

Phillips, R and McWilliam, E (1996) *After Adoption: Working with adoptive families*, London: BAAF.

Watson, J with McGhee, J (1995) *Developing Post-Placement Support: A project in Scotland*, London: BAAF.

Edinburgh: Adoption Policy Review, Report Phase 1 (2002): Scottish Executive.

Scotland's Children (1997) *The Children (Scotland) Act 1995, Regulations and Guidance, Volume 3, Adoption and Parental Responsibilities Orders*, Edinburgh: Scottish Office.

National Care Standards – Adoption Agencies 2001, Edinburgh: Scottish Executive.

19 Adoption support services for adults

Julia Feast

Introduction

Since 12 November 1975, adopted adults in England and Wales have had the right to apply for information held on their birth certificate, thus effectively giving them the identifying facts they need to begin a search for birth relatives (section 26 of the Children Act 1975, subsequently section 51 of the Adoption Act 1976). Much has been learned about adoption since the opening up of adoption records. We understand that for adopted people there are beneficial effects from gaining information about family background or medical history. Having the opportunity to find answers to questions such as, 'Who am I?' 'Where do I come from?' 'Whom do I look like?' can really help adopted people gain a fuller sense of identity and enhance their self-esteem.

I suppose I did think about my birth family from time to time as I was growing up but it wasn't until I was expecting my first child that it really became an issue. I suddenly became acutely aware of the gaps I had about family medical history, personality and talents. It just became really important to find out. (Anne-Marie, adopted person)

Section 1 of the Adoption Act 1976 placed a duty on each local authority to provide a comprehensive service to all those involved in adoption including:
a) children who have been or may be adopted;
b) parents or guardians of such children; and
c) persons who have adopted or may adopt a child.

The Act acknowledged that people who have a personal connection to adoption should have a right to a service if they have unresolved issues and counselling needs. Adoption is now accepted as being a life-long process, which may impact on adopted people and their birth and adoptive relatives in different ways across the life span. But while this is acknowledged, the service provisions and resources available in local authorities and adoption agencies can be patchy or limited, and may therefore not meet the needs of the adults affected by adoption. Post-adoption work, particularly birth records counselling and intermediary services, is sometimes seen as "a luxury piece of work" and therefore often ends up being a low priority when there are competing demands such as child protection and mental health issues. People having to wait 12 months for an appointment to be seen is not unheard of. Yet the knowledge gained from working with adults affected by adoption can do much to enhance adoption practice today. It is an opportunity for practitioners and policy makers to experience circular learning, to inform their practice and ensure that service provision really does aim to meet the needs of all those affected by adoption.

Adoption is currently high on the Government's agenda. The recently published Adoption and Children Act (2002) and Adoption Standards (2001) do much to provide for the needs of children who may languish in care without such stringent guidelines.

The National Adoption Standards, including the draft National Standards for Adopted Adults and Siblings, currently fail to address the service needs of *all* people affected by adoption. They do not, for example, take into account the need to provide intermediary services for all birth relatives, but only for siblings of the adopted person. However, the Adoption and Children Act has acknowledged the importance of providing services that meet the life-long issues of adoption. There is now a legislative framework for providing intermediary services for birth relatives of past, present and future adoptions. Adoption standards that recognise the needs of all adults affected by adoption are to be issued.

This chapter raises some of the issues that adopted adults and their birth and adoptive relatives may encounter and the services that need to be in place in the 21st century to help them through the adoption journey. It describes the needs of the key parties involved and sets out the framework that should be in place to ensure that these are met.

Adopted adults

Since 1975, local authorities and adoption agencies in England and Wales have had a duty to provide birth records counselling services for adopted people over the age of 18 years, who wish to access information so that they may apply for a copy of their original birth certificate. This applies to people who were adopted before 12 November 1975 and who do not know their original name. If adopted people have enough information (birth family name and date of birth) to obtain a copy of their original birth certificate, then they do not have to attend a counselling interview. People who were adopted after 12 November 1975 also do not need to attend a counselling interview before obtaining a copy of their original birth certificate. It is a matter of choice.

However, if an adopted person wishes to receive information from the records held by the adoption agency that placed them for adoption, then it is most unlikely, as well as undesirable, that access to this information would be given without the adopted person first having met with the adoption counsellor/ worker. It is recognised that, whilst it is crucial to be able to access background information, it is equally important for the adopted person to have an opportunity to discuss the implications of receiving such information.

Howe and Feast's study (2000) reported that, for the vast majority, receiving information from the agency records had been helpful. Seventy-nine per cent of people reported that they had received a substantial amount of new information. Many had gained an increased understanding of the reason for their adoption, a more compassionate view of their birth mother's situation and an improved sense of personal identity.

On the other hand, 13 per cent were upset by the information, which underlines how essential it is that all adopted people have the opportunity to consider what they may encounter when accessing information from the record. For instance, there may be racist remarks or derogatory comments about the birth mother and information may not always be correct.

Case examples

Liz contacted the adoption agency requesting access to the files for background information. She was very religious and an active member of the Church of England. Her adoption records revealed that her birth mother and father were Jewish.

Andrew, at the age of 30, learned that he was in fact of mixed heritage. His father was Asian. His adoptive parents had known this, but as

Andrew looked white they had decided not to pass on the information. Andrew had been brought up in a family which preferred to deny his ethnic background and which was part of a racist community. Over the years Andrew himself had made derogatory and racist remarks about Asian people.

The information that Liz received about being Jewish and the information Andrew received that he was half-Asian was totally unexpected and came as a complete shock to them both.

Inevitably, not all the possible outcomes of receiving information can be covered in an "implications counselling" interview prior to the sharing of records. But the mere fact that it is an expected part of the procedure underlines the need for adopted people to have an opportunity to talk through some of their hopes and fears, and for the adoption counsellor to assess how best to assist the adopted person to manage information that may be unsettling or upsetting.

The majority of adopted people who begin a search for more information are often not satisfied to leave it there; they begin a search for birth relatives. The Howe and Feast study (2000) reported that, of the 88 per cent of people who had made a decision to search, 65 per cent had made contact with a birth relative within six months. It is essential, therefore, that adoption counsellors are equipped to give accurate information about the whole process and possible outcomes.

Agencies vary in what services they can offer, so it is important that the adopted person is fully aware of the range and limitations. For example, some agencies will offer an intermediary service to facilitate contact and reunion, while other agencies lack the resources to do so. In these situations, information about voluntary organisations which provide such services should be given to the adopted person. Some agencies also run support groups and workshops for adopted people and their birth and adoptive relatives.

There is no doubt that working with people who are keen to have a service and are appreciative can be a welcome change from working with people who do not have a choice about the involvement of social workers in their lives. But working with adults who have been adopted raises many complex issues and demands a high level of skill and understanding.

Counselling the adopted adult

During the counselling interview it is important to have a discussion about the adopted person's motivation and expectations, an understanding of their present circumstances, experience of adoption, and knowledge of the information they already have. The adoption counsellor needs to ensure that the range of feelings that may surface, and outcomes an adopted person may encounter, are considered at the outset of the search and reunion process.

Case example

Simon was 28 years old when he decided to trace his birth mother. The adoption agency records showed that his birth mother had been deeply distressed at parting with him. She had looked after him for six weeks and given him a special gift as a token of her never-ending love. Simon's adoptive parents had always told him how much he was loved by his birth mother. It therefore came as a bolt out of the blue when his birth mother refused to have any contact with him. She would not even send him a letter explaining why or a photograph of herself. She told the social worker that she had been married for 27 years and her husband and her children were unaware that she had placed a baby for adoption. Simon felt distraught by her response, but took some comfort in what the adoption counsellor had told him before the approach. She had explained that, even though a record might indicate that a birth mother has not willingly relinquished her child for adoption, circumstances may prevent her from having contact. He recalled his adoption counsellor's words: 'remember it is not you she will be rejecting, as she does not know you. It will be the situation.'

Birth relatives

Research studies about the experiences of birth mothers have indicated that parting with a child for adoption has life-long implications. (Winkler and Kepple, 1984; Bouchier, Lambert and Triseliotis, 1991; Howe *et al*, 1992; Wells, 1993; Hughes and Logan 1994).

Offering services for birth relatives is a growing area of work. During the past decade there has certainly been acknowledgement of the continuing needs of birth relatives, as seen by the development of inter-mediary services specifically for them. In 2000 the Department of Health issued practice guidance to help promote uniformity in the provision of intermediary services for birth relatives by their local authority or adoption agencies. The recently published Adoption and Children Act has indeed acknowledged the life-long issues of adoption. The legislation makes a provision so that birth relatives now have the right to ask for an intermediary service to let the adopted adult know of their interest in contact. It is retrospective and has therefore recognised the particular needs of those birth mothers who felt they had no choice but to place their baby for adoption in the era when having an illegitimate child was frowned upon. The challenge now is to ensure that the new legislation is implemented in a way that takes account of the needs of all those involved.

Howe and Feast's study (2000) of adopted people included 72 non-searchers. These were adopted people who had not initiated a search for information or birth relatives but had been approached by an adoption agency to let them know of a birth relative's enquiry. Over 90 per cent of non-searchers agreed to have some form of contact with the enquiring birth relative (which was usually the birth mother), and five years on, 55 per cent non-searchers compared to 63 per cent searchers were still in contact with the birth relative. Over 80 per cent of non-searchers reported that the contact with the birth relative had enabled them to answer important questions about their background. However, providing intermediary services can present emotional and practical challenges not only for the key players – adopted people, adoptive parents and birth parents – but also for practitioners and adoption agencies. It is important that birth relatives have been given the opportunity to think about how their enquiry and desire for contact may impact on the adopted person and the adoptive family. It is important that their own families are aware of their wish to have contact with the adopted person and can support them, otherwise complications can arise, as in the case of Jim.

Case example

Anna made an approach to her now adult birth son – who had been adopted – through an intermediary service. She was delighted to hear that Jim wanted contact. She had always thought that her children would accept Jim, but to her surprise they were not at all welcoming and instead ostracised him. The atmosphere was so cutting when her children were in his presence that she felt very uncomfortable. She felt torn between them. In the end she decided to limit her contact with Jim. He was left feeling upset and rejected.

Learning about a birth relative's enquiry is likely to be unexpected and can trigger a range of feelings, thoughts and questions for the adopted person. Equally, adoptive parents may feel total shock and be unprepared to deal with the challenges this situation brings.

Although we had told Fiona that she was adopted, it was never really a subject that was talked about. She just felt like our child, so to some extent I think we subconsciously buried the fact that she was adopted. So you can just imagine how shocked we felt hearing from the adoption agency that the birth mother wanted contact. Suddenly our world fell apart. We were scared and so anxious that the loving relationship we had with Fiona for 40 years was now under threat. (Margaret, adoptive parent)

Adoption counsellors have to be knowledgeable and skilled to negotiate the different scenarios they may face. They need their own support, consultation and expert advice. No two cases are exactly the same; each one will present new issues, which need to be addressed on a case-by-case basis.

Case example

Norma was a birth mother who had access to an intermediary service. She discovered that her son Alex, whom she had placed for adoption 35 years ago, had committed suicide. He had been a drug addict for several years. His adoptive parents felt unable to engage with the adoption agency and did not want to give any further information that would be passed on to the birth mother. They could not face returning to the emotional minefield they crossed following his suicide and were afraid that his suicide and drug addiction could be interpreted as Alex being unhappy in his adoptive family. It was decided that the issues involved were too complex for one worker. The adoptive parents and birth mother were each allocated their own worker. This meant that they were able to express their feelings, knowing that the worker was not being placed in a compromising position and would not have divided loyalties. They did not feel that the worker was taking sides or that they were being pressurised into doing something they were not ready for. Eventually the adoptive parents were reassured that Alex's death would not be seen as a reflection on them. A year after the first contact, the adoptive parents and birth mother met and formed an ongoing friendship. Alex's parents eventually felt able to take Norma, the birth mother, to visit the grave.

It is not always possible to meet everyone's needs. Where contact is not established, birth relatives may require a lot of support to help them cope with the disappointment.

Adoptive relatives

In contemporary adoptions, post-adoption support for adoptive parents and relatives is very much part of the adoption service. During assessment and preparation, adoptive parents are, or should be, well informed about their entitlement to services that can support them in the parenting of an adopted child. It is recognised today that the love and security of an adoptive family may not be sufficient to prevent difficulties occurring in the ensuing years. Each adoption panel should discuss and consider which services and future help the adoptive parents may need, including support if their children have contact with, search for, or are reunited with their birth family.

In the past, when adoption of babies was the norm, adoptive parents were often told that provided the child was loved and cared for, there were unlikely to be problems. Prior to 1975, adoptive parents were given to understand that their adopted son or daughter was now legally theirs and that all links with the birth family were severed. Generally, adoptive parents were left to get on with it, as adoption was not often acknowledged as a life-long process. The issuing of an adoption order was the start of a new beginning. There was no thought that adopted adults would be enabled to search for their birth parents. Not surprisingly, therefore, parents who adopted prior to 1975 feel that their needs and dilemmas have been overlooked.

Studies such as Howe's (1996) have extensively quoted adoptive parents on adoption, but there have been no studies of the experience and feelings of adoptive parents about the search and reunion process. How do they feel about their son or daughter's reunion? Do they feel it has lessened the bond between them? A forthcoming study will give some insight into these questions (Feast *et al*, forthcoming, 2004), but meanwhile we have to rely on anecdotal evidence. Although there are no official statistics available, adoption agencies report that few enquiries are received from adoptive parents of children who were adopted before 1975. But perhaps this is because they are not aware that they are also entitled to a service should an issue about the adoption affect them.

Case example

Ben, at the age of 40, had recently made contact with his birth mother. They had met several times since, enjoyed each other's company and were keen to maintain the close relationship they had developed. Mabel, Ben's adoptive mother, was 75 years old. She had always been understanding about the fact that Ben might need to trace his birth mother and told him that she would support him wholeheartedly. However, now that it had happened she felt anxious, resentful and depressed. She could not understand the powerful feelings of jealousy. She was a woman of great compassion and had always had kind thoughts towards the birth mother. Ben felt concerned about his adoptive mother and so contacted his adoption counsellor who agreed to see her. Mabel saw the adoption counsellor just once but that meeting did much to validate her feelings and to look at strategies for managing them. Mabel felt a lot better and was, with this help, able to welcome the reunion of her son with his birth mother, confident that the bond they had forged for 40 years would not be undermined.

This example highlights how important it is for adoptive parents to know what services are available to them, even after the adopted person has become an adult.

A framework for adoption support services

It can be a challenge to work within a framework that includes the underlying principles that underpin the work, but is also not too rigid to meet individual needs. People's adoption journeys and experiences will be different, therefore services and case decisions need to be flexible. The following is not an exhaustive list of what might be in a framework for offering adoption support services for adults, but it is proffered as a beginning to build upon.

Policy and procedures

Adoption has life-long implications and this therefore needs to be reflected in the adoption agency's policy and procedures. It is essential that adoption counsellors have a clear understanding about the principles behind providing adoption support services for adults, and the benefits they can bring. The needs of children are paramount, but if adults who have been affected by adoption are living with unresolved issues to do with the adoption, this could have a profound and negative impact on their lives. It may affect their parenting skills and relationships with their own children. It can therefore be argued that helping adults who have concerns about their adoption and background will, in turn, directly help their children and enhance the quality of family life.

Case example

Tom had been told that he was abandoned as a baby and always had the impression that he was unloved. He always felt rejected and believed that this had a profound effect on his personal relationships. He never felt he was worthy of love even from his own children. He shied away from their expressions of affection. He felt that this made him emotionally distant from them.

When Tom was 35 years old he contacted the adoption agency to obtain background information about his adoption. He learned that he had not been abandoned but had, in fact, lived with his birth mother for nine months. She had tried desperately hard to keep him, but because of her financial situation she had not been able to provide him with the care he needed. Tom was sad to hear this but felt better within himself knowing that she had loved and cared for him. He couldn't help wondering whether, had he been brought up knowing this, it would have given him the emotional freedom and safety to demonstrate his love for his own children.

Tools for the job

Adoption counsellors have to be equipped to do the job. They must have access to evidenced-based practice, research, other professional bodies, good supervision and peer support. It is important that adoption counsellors have the opportunity to reflect on their practice so that learning and change can be identified and achieved.

Ethical advisory forum

Working with adults affected by adoption means that adoption practitioners, managers and policy makers will be faced with some difficult issues. Each case will be unique in what may be presented, but it is essential that there is a framework of references so that the best possible decisions and practice are achieved. One way of achieving this is to have an agency Ethical Advisory Forum where dilemmas can be discussed and managed in the context of the particular case and the agency's policy and procedures.

Case example

John contacted the adoption agency where his wife, Joan, had placed her daughter Sandra for adoption 32 years ago. Joan was in the later stages of Huntington's chorea. They had an 18-year-old daughter from their marriage who had decided not to be tested for Huntington's chorea until she had finished university and would be more able to deal with the outcome of the test if it proved positive. John wanted to make sure that Sandra knew she had a risk of developing the disease.

The adoption records showed no indication that Huntington's chorea was part of the family medical history, although the records described the maternal grandmother as being grumpy, with a personality disorder. John told the adoption agency that she had died from Huntington's chorea.

The Ethical Advisory Forum's dilemma was whether or not to inform Sandra, and if so, how this should be done. It was agreed to go via the adoptive parents. When Sandra was told, she felt angry that this information had not been made available to her before, as she already had a five-year-old son. After counselling, Sandra decided to have the test for Huntington's chorea which proved positive.

Record-keeping

The necessity to maintain accurate and clear records cannot and should not be underestimated. It is a way of accounting for the service that is, and has been, provided and the decisions that have been made in any particular case. However, it is also a way of recording the events that will show how the case has unfolded. Guidance or pro-formas should be given about how best to record relevant actions. This way people can work to expected standards and create data for measuring whether the standards are consistent and maintained. For example, a pro-forma when recording a section 51 piece of work could look like:

- *Reason for referral* Why have they contacted? Has any particular event spurred them on at this time?
- *Current circumstances* What information about the adoption do they have? What is their employment and marital status? Do they have children? What is their network for support?
- *Experience of adoption* When were they told? Was it a subject openly discussed with parents, friend and relatives, including the positives and difficulties of being adopted? Have they told their parents about their request for information?
- *Hopes and fears* How did they feel about receiving information, searching for birth relatives, the effect on the adoptive family?
- *Action taken* What information was given from the records? Were documents signed for? What was discussed, was information given about other support agencies? Have they had information leaflets, useful reading lists, advice about tracing?
- *Future plans* What other work needs to be done and what was agreed with the adopted person?

Over the years we have learned how important it is to record in a non-judgemental, concise and accurate way. Adoption workers will develop their own style, but this has to fit into the system for recording that has been established by the agency. We need to reflect on the quality of recording and think about how it can achieve what it is meant to do. For example, if someone else had to pick up on a case which was first referred and worked with ten years ago, would the reasons for previous involvement be clear? Equally, we need to account for the professional decisions we make, particularly when there are controversial issues involved.

Case example

Christopher was 17 years old and wanted to contact his half-sister, Rita, who was placed for adoption 25 years ago. His and Rita's birth mother had died ten years previously. The adoptive parents refused to pass on information about the enquiry to Rita because she never spoke about her adoption or birth family to them. After discussion at the Ethical Advisory Forum a decision was made to inform the adoptive parents that a direct approach would be made to Rita.

The adoption worker recorded the decision-making process, the professional reasons for making a direct approach, and that a duty of care exercise had been undertaken in relation to all parties concerned.

Service users

Just as adoption workers should be aware of policy and procedures, adopted people and their birth and adoptive relatives need to have information about the services they can access either through the adoption agency or another support agency. A range of information leaflets ought to be available which describe the services on offer and answer some of the questions that are commonly asked. For instance, if the agency provides intermediary services for birth relatives, it is important that an information leaflet covers some of the feelings and experiences that are frequently expressed. It is vital for adoptive parents to know and be reassured that the bonds formed in childhood are usually robust enough to withstand the search and reunion process. Also, it is important for adopted people to know that it is not uncommon to feel disloyal and elated at the same time, and for birth relatives to understand that not every adopted person has a burning desire to have contact with their birth relatives.

Written information can assist people to normalise feelings and experiences. Knowing that others have encountered similar situations can help them feel less isolated

Signposting to other services

Sometimes the adoption agency which placed the child is not able to meet all the needs of adults who return for help with a query relating to their adoption. It is helpful to have a resource pack available in the agency which lists local and national support services for adults affected by adoption. For instance, whilst an adoption agency can provide a birth records counselling service, it may not be in a position to offer ongoing counselling about questions which may be raised for all parties by the search and reunion process. Also, adults affected by adoption should be informed about self-help organisations they may wish to contact. These could be listed in the information leaflets provided by the adoption agency in a resource pack, or details can be given during the initial counselling interview. Posters could be displayed in adoption agencies, libraries and GP surgeries.

Summary

The face of adoption has changed significantly during the past few decades and adoption support services need to adapt accordingly to take account of both historical and current practice.

Offering and providing support after adoption is often one of the best ways of learning what resources need to be in place to ensure that contemporary adoptions have been given the right ingredients for success. We know, for example, from adopted adults that whilst they thought about their birth parents and wondered why they were adopted, such thoughts were not easily shared with their adoptive parents. Knowing this means that we can refine the preparation and training for prospective adopters so that they can develop more skills to encourage their child to feel comfortable to talk about their adoption and background.

It is likely that the nature of birth records counselling, access to information and search and reunion may be significantly different in the future. Many children today will have retained some links with the birth family. They may therefore not have the same needs to seek out their birth relatives in the way that adopted people have done before them. However, there will certainly be new and different issues and dilemmas that are just as likely to require the same amount, or even more, adoption support services for adults.

References

Bouchier, P, Lambert, L and Triseliotis, J (1991) *Parting with a Child for Adoption: The mother's perspective*. London: BAAF.

Feast, J, Triseliotis, J and Kyle, F (forthcoming, 2004) London: BAAF.

Howe, D and Feast, J (2000) *Adoption, Search and Reunion – The long term experience of adopted adults*, London: The Children's Society

Howe, D (1996) *Adopters on Adoption*, London: BAAF.

Howe, D, Sawbridge, P and Hinings, D (1992) *Half a Million Women: Mothers who lose their children by adoption*, London: Penguin Books (now available and published by the Post Adoption Centre)

Hughes, B and Logan, J (1994) *The Hidden Dimension*, London: Mental Health Foundation.

Well, S (1993) 'Post traumatic stress disorders in birth mothers', *Adoption & Fostering*, 17;2, pp 30–2.

Winkler, R C and Van Kepple, M (1984) *Relinquishing Mothers in Adoption: Their long-term adjustment*, Monograph No. 3, Melbourne: Institute of Family Studies.

20 Online adoption support and advice

Lois Williams

Log on to www.postadoptiononline.com – the first ever inter-active adoption support service freely available on the internet! At a time when new adoption legislation, regulations and guidance are being welcomed and assimilated, how can a website fit into the new framework for adoption support?

History

www.postadoptiononline.com has been developed by PACT (Parents and Children Together), a voluntary adoption agency based in Reading, in partnership with web developers, Idamus, based in Loughborough. The website is seen as a complementary service to the more traditional post-adoption support provided by PACT and other agencies regionally and nationally.

A bid was made to the Department of Health Section 64 Project Scheme, which gives funding to voluntary organisations, to provide a local web service. The proposal was based on ten hours a week for a project co-ordinator and twenty hours of adviser time. The bid was successful and funding runs over three years. The project started in the May of 2001 and is currently a little ahead of schedule.

Although adoption support must begin even before the time a child is placed with a family, it was decided, after careful consideration, that the website would address *post*-order issues. Anything else could create a situation where advice is given to people who are still actively involved with other agencies, and who have an allocated social worker. It would be inappropriate for PACT to offer advice in such circumstances.

Need for online services

Adoption agencies and other organisation connected with adoption have long been aware of the need to provide good long-term adoption support.

In the past, post-adoption services may have primarily focused on the needs of adopted adults who seek information from their files or need counselling and assistance when searching for birth relatives.

The National Adoption Standards (2001) state that adoptive families have the right to be assessed for post-adoption support, that birth families should have the opportunity for independent support and that children's voices should be heard. Extra finance has now been made available to turn policy into practice.

Local authorities and voluntary agencies need to ensure that their services provide value for money, as well as being focused, expert, responsive and quantifiable (Adoption Standards E1 & 6). How such services can be delivered in the future needs to be carefully considered, because of the increasing scarcity of experienced social workers in this field. This is due to the high vacancy rate in substantive posts throughout all social services departments and specifically within Children and Families Teams. Such teams provide the necessary experience for social workers to move into family placement and adoption work. The post-adoption website can go some way to provide specialist help in a pleasing and welcoming format.

Services for families and individuals connected to adoption need to be easily accessible, non-stigmatising, relevant and locally available, as well as available over time. Experience has shown that people often need to 'dip in and out' of support services, and that they may not always want to return to the agencies originally involved nor to social services departments. Families or individuals neither want to go through a difficult referral process, nor do they want to be stigmatised by being referred only to highly specialised and perhaps pathologising services. People can't predict when they will need support or what kind of support they will need. In keeping with the adage 'adoption is a life-long condition', chosen services should be available at chosen times. The internet offers just that.

Objectives of the service

Provision of online post adoption advice, support and information for all parties involved with adoption.

- information available 24 hours a day;
- advice and support available some evenings and part of weekends for individual service users;

- easy-to-use and access website, with information for service users and professionals;
- confidentiality and security built into to the system;
- links with local industry, business and communities to help recruit volunteers with IT (information technology) skills to assist in the technical development of the service;
- involvement of service users in the formulation and development of the service;
- consultation and development process to reflect local ethnic and religious diversity;
- evaluation of developed service;
- sharing of information about the development of the website with other agencies to assist set up of similar services.

Steering and focus groups

In line with the objectives, our steering group includes the whole range of potential service users and reflects the ethnic and cultural diversity of our locality.

In keeping with the IT technology, we use emails, and "virtual meetings" as a basis for communications, with an added quarterly "face-to-face" meeting.

For the first months we hosted a focus group of adopters and children, who were used to working with the medium, to give speedy reaction to the initial technical developments.

Idamus

We are fortunate in having the expertise of web developers Idamus. They have been generous in offering their support free of charge to PACT, which is a charity. Working together has enabled us to have a technologically sophisticated site with a range of facilities that meets the requirements of the service. This pioneering development has a wider application to other areas of child welfare and support. In future, the web-based service will need to be self-financing through subscriptions. PACT works currently in the region of Berkshire, Buckinghamshire and Oxfordshire. Subscribers from other agencies will be able to have their own "front page" and information, as well as the interactive, online advice and support which will be available to people in their locality.

For all connected with adoption

The website provides information for all of the three traditional sections of the adoption circle; this is a concrete acknowledgement of the importance of each party individually and in relation to each other. Whilst some information and advice are specific, say to birth parents or adopters, the ability to check out other areas of the site is likely to widen the perspectives of every user.

IT is a chosen medium for many young people and is likely to become more so. The website invites their interest without putting pressure on them to see more than they are ready for.

Information for adopted children, and how it is presented, differs from what young people who are heading towards independence and maturity want to know. The needs of an adoptive adult will be different yet again. Grandparents, siblings or aunts and uncles are another targeted group of users. Birth relatives' concerns are different from those of birth parents, and from those of adoptive relatives. The site aims to provide areas that are specifically designed for such varying needs.

Lastly, the site provides information for a range of professionals. This is not just aimed at specialist adoption workers, but also others working with children and families in health and education, such as therapists, psychologists, psychiatrists, health visitors, GPs, community workers, teachers and education welfare workers. Information about the site is being distributed to a range of workers in the community as we think it is very important that adoption issues are understood by all who may come into contact with adoptive or birth families and adopted adults.

This website encourages people to seek information from different perspectives and gives an unusual opportunity to gain a rounded view of adoption. The increasingly wide access to the web means that there are no social barriers to accessing information.

Information on the website

- News items – a mixture of adoption and parenting topics are put on the front news page, and this is updated regularly.
- 24 hour availability – this means that the post-adoption information is there for people when they want it. There are three main advantages to this:
  1. availability outside of usual office hours;
  2. the information can be obtained from a variety of locations – either work or home, via mobile machines or those based in public places like schools, libraries, Citizens Advice Bureaux and other community provisions;
  3. users have privacy afforded by direct access to information. For some people this is likely to be welcome because of the social/emotional aspects of adoption, such as loss, litigation, child protection, contact, searching and reunion.
- "Signposting" local resources, services, workshops and training are an important part of the adoption support. Details can be changed and updated easily, providing up-to-date information to a large number of people very quickly.

Online advice

This is an entirely innovative service that provides "one-to-one", post-adoption advice and support from experienced social workers directly to individuals. Currently sessions are available four times a week, outside of office hours, and this will extend according to demand.

Confidentiality

Confidentiality is essential in adoption matters. We provide a service that has been built on the need for security and safety; this is particularly important because children and young people use it. Safety has been secured by a number of features:

- The adviser controls the opening and closing of each advice session.
- Each session is only between the adviser and the person wanting the service.
- The sessions are via web pages, so there are no emails, and the insecurity associated with them.

- Records of the advice "text" are stored securely in an encrypted form.
- There are clear child protection procedures and advisers are experienced in this area.

Sharing and feedback

The person wanting advice is in control of what information is shared. The service is reactive and responsive to the person's specific circumstances and needs. The user feels "heard" and can give direct or indirect feedback about the service. A young person wrote '...I think it is really good what you are doing here, and the way u have people ready to listen to other people's problems'. Indeed people are encouraged to "take part" in the site, by using the bulletin board or submitting their own stories. The opportunity to hear about the experiences of others is an important aspect of feeling empowered. There is a creative opportunity to develop a "community" of users.

Visits to the website are thoroughly monitored, and all direct feedback logged and considered. The bulletin boards are monitored, for safety reasons.

Advisers

We have three advisers who work on a sessional basis from home. They are all qualified social workers with long-term experience of work with children and families, family placements and the court process. During the development stage they have been active in working on the information for the website and testing procedures and practice. Telephone support and consultation is available after every advice sessions, and the advisers are accountable to the online co-ordinator.

All articles and other items for the website are submitted to the co-ordinator, who has editorial control. Technical development has been rapid, and we now have the facility to put articles/copy directly on the site ourselves.

Challenges

Different language

Local authorities and other agencies which subscribe to the internet service will have the opportunity to translate their own front page information into languages used in their area. Further work would be needed to assess the feasibility of using some of the web translation programmes to provide the advice session in other languages.

Different perspectives

At the very beginning there was a need for the staff at PACT and the technicians at Idamus to find a common language. Each profession has its "jargon", but with a conscious effort on both sides we have found a clear way forward: the problem-solving techniques have proved to have more in common with the task-centred work of social workers than we may at first have thought, and we have all gained from a greater understanding of the limitations of both forms of very different work. In many ways this has been good preparation for us, as social workers, embarking on a very new way of service delivery. We have felt deskilled at times but this has made us sensitive to the pressures that may be there for new users contacting us "out of hours".

The medium

The medium itself has undoubtedly been the main challenge. We not only had to learn how to become "good enough" at working with a computer, but we also had to manage the very different way that this medium requires one to work. The qualities of the medium are many. It is fast, immediate, direct, visual, concise and current.

As with so many things, the qualities can also become the problems! The very immediacy of communicating in "real time" with someone you don't know, can't see or hear can seem initially like trying to thread a needle in the dark, against the clock and with gloves on! All the usual clues that social workers are adept at interpreting and using – tone of voice, body language, speech patterns, etc. – are not there. Instead one needs to deal with the rather stark form of text, in a way that is friendly, yet concise and informative. Training and practice have proved helpful in developing our skills, and some initial disadvantages have been outweighed by the sense that the 'user' has of feeling in control and clearly having someone "to listen" (to wait and to read) to their contribution.

The website is being well used with over 16,000 "hits" a month from all over the world. But there has been a slow start to the take-up of the interactive online advice and support service. This may be due to several reasons. Firstly, local publicity takes a long time to become effective and has to be ongoing. Secondly, we are aware of a tension between trying to publicise a regional advice service on a website that, by definition, has national if not worldwide availability. Thirdly, the targeted users, those people connected to adoption in some way, are a small minority of the population. Only a fraction of them live in our region and of those only some will be experiencing problems, and then even a smaller number would choose to use the web advice service for support. One person, heard about the website on the local radio playing in her workplace. Not having a computer, she got her partner to phone the radio station to get PACT's telephone number!

There are lesson for us to learn. We are expanding the online advice and support service to other local authorities for people living in their areas, and we look forward to the results of working with a potentially larger user base.

Conclusion

We have all been clear about the need to "embrace" the technology, and use the qualities it has. It has usefully made us focus on what, and how, we want to present on the site, and has encouraged clarity in our thinking about post-adoption advice. Keeping the balance has been important to ensure the "message" is not secondary to the medium. The site now looks very different from our first tentative attempt – undoubtedly there will be other changes and developments as we learn from user feedback in the future.

This project is innovative, and at the cutting edge of a new way of providing adoption support. We have found no other agency/website offering "one-to-one" online advice, either here, in the USA or Australia. There is a little research beginning to be done in the USA about individual therapists providing counselling "online", which is essentially a fee-paying transaction between two individuals – very different from this service. Such newness has meant that there are risks involved, but by remaining flexible and open to options we have learned a great deal as we have gone along. The remaining risks are ones that have been carefully considered, and not ones that will jeopardise our duty of care and our wish to provide useful post-adoption support.

At an early presentation about the new website, we used the image of a person balanced on the crest of a wave to illustrate that particular stage of the project development. Peaks and troughs have definitely been a feature of the months that followed, but we remain enthusiastic about using the web as a medium to make post-adoption support available from 'shore to shore' and beyond.

21 **Ending in disruption**

Hedi Argent

Disruption is never the result of what one party has done or left undone. It is usually a combination of:
* *unidentified circumstances;*
* *misinterpreted circumstances;*
* *unpredictable circumstances.*

(Kay Donley, 1981)

Managing disruption has to be regarded as belonging to adoption support services. It is not something to be wheeled in at the last moment, at crisis point when child, adopters and social workers are at their wits' end and there is no alternative. Families and children have to know from the beginning of the adoption adventure that, in spite of the most careful preparation, training, assessments, shared information, experience and knowledge, it is not possible to anticipate exactly what will happen when this child is placed with this family because nothing in the child's previous life or in the family's will have been exactly like that. Often we stand by and watch in respectful admiration as children and parents, with incalculable effort and patience, make the most improbable placements for adoption last. But we also have to stand by while seemingly promising placements crumble.

> *There is no way in which anyone could get used to this part of adoption work and the disruption of a placement must be considered as part of the work. The agony of those involved is different every time but no less agonising one time than another. We know, and we assure the family and reassure the child, that the failure is rarely anybody's fault; everyone has tried hard to make it work; and wanted it to work, it just cannot work every time. 'But why not this time?' is the angry or the mute reproach from the wounded child and family to the distressed workers.* (Argent, 1984)

Adopters and children should believe that the support and trust they have been given to make the placement work will continue even if the placement does not. Danger signals should never be ignored: if problems are mounting, an open discussion at every stage should pave the way for both progress and retreat. That is not to say that a family's commitment should ever be undermined, but they should feel confident that there is a safety net and that the impossible is not being expected even if they achieve it, as they so often do.

As the profiles of children placed for adoption become more complex and many older children need alternative families and there is pressure on agencies to place more children, it is inevitable that the number of disruptions will rise. The most common causes of disruption, as presented at disruption meetings, are incomplete information about the child and birth family history, inaccurate assessments of the child's attachment patterns and continuity needs, the child's experience of "too many moves" in the care system, and lack of appropriate education and therapeutic services. Precise statistics of disruptions are not available but there is a generally accepted figure of around ten per cent of placements. If one-in-ten placements are going to disrupt, supporting families through and after disruption had better be an established element of adoption services.

How disruptions are managed needs to be enshrined in policy. Will there be a placement meeting with all concerned, either to save the placement or plan for the disruption? Will there be an intensive period of preparation for disruption? Will every effort be made to hold the child until she or he can return to previous carers? Is the agency able to make priority arrangements for school transfers and any health or therapeutic treatments? How will the birth family be involved? If two agencies are concerned, who will do what? How will support, contact and continuity be maintained for the child and family after disruption? How soon after disruption will there be a disruption meeting? Who will convene it, chair it, be invited to attend and receive a disruption report?

Convening disruption meetings is a daunting task. It can be very hard for families to attend while still struggling with their own feelings for the child. Professionals may be reluctant to share their opinions and to have their practice scrutinised. Former carers and birth family members may feel angry and under-valued. Teachers and therapists may consider themselves to be outside the adoption process. And the child, even if old enough, may choose to stay away. It is vital for everyone to understand how important their contributions will be in order to assess the current needs of all parties and to learn from what has happened.

Case examples

The disruption meeting for Arleen, aged 12, was attended by her adopters, her previous and present foster carers, her birth mother, her teacher and social workers with their managers from both the child's and the adopters' agencies. There had been contact with birth parents and foster carers throughout the six-month placement. The meeting was planned before Arleen left the prospective adopters but after she had set their house on fire; it took place a month later to give everyone time to begin to recover and look towards the future. Arleen joined the meeting when she came home from school. She listened to a summary of what had been said and added her version of the story.

Arleen remained with her present foster carers. She had moved 27 times and it seemed she could not make an investment in permanence away from her birth family, but she could manage in a safe and stable foster home where she was not expected to make a total commitment.

The prospective adopters had another child placed with them and went on to adopt two more children.

*   *   *   *

Brad's disruption meeting was very different. The prospective adopters had been hailed as a perfect match and their cries for help remained unrecognised until it was too late.

This was an inter-agency placement where both agencies blamed each other for the problems leading up to disruption. Information had not been freely exchanged and some vital facts had been unintentionally withheld from the adopters. Brad, aged five, had said a "final goodbye" to his mother two weeks before placement and there were no other contact arrangements. Adoption support was limited to responding to specific requests, which became irritatingly frequent for the social workers. The family had been promised therapeutic help but after five months they were still waiting. By this time, Brad had completely rejected the adoptive mother and was making sexual overtures to strangers. No one discussed the possibility of disruption with this seemingly perfect couple. They abandoned Brad abruptly in their local social services offices when they could bear no more.

Six months after disruption, the child's agency called a disruption meeting because the new social worker did not know how to deal with Brad, who was not settling in his foster home. The adopters refused to come to the meeting or to send any comments – they would not speak to the social workers on the telephone. Presumably they had closed the door on adoption forever. The adopters' agency did not send any of their workers because they were some distance away and could not spare the time. The birth mother had moved and her address was unknown. The child's new social worker turned up, but she did not know the history, and her line manager, who did, was called away in the middle of the meeting. The family placement worker had not been involved in the adoption placement but was ready to step in if asked to find another family. The foster care support worker came with the current foster carers. This turned into a departmental planning meeting with an independent chair but without enough information to make informed decisions.

We have to become sensitive about hearing demands for material aid, which are hidden cries for help. We also have to be able to tell when threats of sending the child back are no more than a cry for help. And we have to be aware when a placement is beyond help so that we can enable adopters to give up for the child's sake and their own.

A useful agenda for a disruption meeting might look something like this:

- *The child's progress from birth to adoption placement*
  Attachment pattern, quality of parental and foster care, physical, emotional and intellectual development, changes and moves, losses and continuity, nurseries and schools, listening to the child.

- *The adoptive family's progress from application to matching*
  General preparation, preparation to meet specific child's needs, training in attachment, separation and continuity issues, information and communication, apprehensions and expectations.
- *Agency practice*
  Decision to place for adoption, recruitment, decision to match, panel recommendations, plans for continuity after adoption, inter-agency liaison and exchange of information, post-placement and post-adoption services.
- *Birth family's involvement*
  Attitude to local authority intervention, ability to work together and with social workers, understanding of child's needs, view of foster care and adoption, contribution to arrangements for continuity.
- *The introductions*
  How was plan negotiated? Who was involved, was there a child appreciation day? Did adopters meet birth relatives, carers, teachers and medical adviser? Timing, liaison, monitoring and feedback, hopes and doubts, the child's voice.
- *The placement*
  Family systems and lifestyles; ethnicity, culture and religion; progress and regression; rewards and challenges; sibling relationships; attachment patterns; contact and continuity; supports and services; adjustments and sticking points.
- *Disruption*
  Process leading to disruption, decision to end placement, preparation for disruption, child's perception of disruption, management of disruption, plans for continuity, support after disruption.
- *The present and the future*
  The child's current placement; implications for stability and perm-anence; further assessments, treatments and preparation if adoption is still the first option, contact arrangements with previous carers and birth relatives; education and health; the child's wishes.
  The adopters' situation, future plans and support needs.
  The birth family's circumstances, involvement in future plans, changes in the family.

The agency's position, learning from disruption, implications for practice.

• *Summing up*
Themes, vulnerabilities, tensions, practice issues, recommendations.

Disruption meetings should be held in light, comfortable rooms with informal seating arrangements and a steady supply of juice, biscuits, tea, coffee and sandwiches brought in for lunch. Most meetings take six to seven hours and it is best to eat and drink and stretch along the way, without breaking up the group.

With careful planning, good support and management, disruption, when it cannot be avoided, may be the first step towards a new placement, with better understanding of the child's needs and the preparation and information prospective adopters will require. There is also evidence that people who cannot parent one child, can go on to parent other children successfully. However painful the process of disruption inevitably is, it can be viewed as a stage on the path to stability for the child and no one need lose everything.

References

Argent, H (1984) *Find Me a Family*, London: Souvenir Press.

Donley, K (1981) *Adoption Disruption*, US Department of Health and Human Services.

Further reading

Fitzgerald, J (1982) *Understanding Disruption*, London: BAAF.

Smith, S (1994) *Learning from Disruption*, London: BAAF.

List of contributors

Hedi Argent is an independent adoption consultant, trainer and freelance writer. She is the author of *Find Me a Family* (Souvenir Press, 1984) and *Whatever Happened to Adam?* (BAAF, 1998), the co-author of *Taking Extra Care* (BAAF, 1997) and the editor of *Keeping the Doors Open* (BAAF, 1988), *See You Soon* (BAAF, 1995) and *Staying Connected* (BAAF, 2002).

Alan Burnell is a qualified social worker who began his career in a local authority social services child care team. He was a counsellor at the Post-Adoption Centre in London for 13 years and helped pioneer the development of post-adoption services to all parties in adoption. For the past four years he has been a Co-director of Family Futures Consortium, an innovative service dedicated to developing therapeutic support to families who have adopted or are fostering traumatised children. The project offers a collaborative, family-based approach using a variety of techniques.

Kay Chamberlain is an adoptive parent and qualified counsellor. She has an MA in Counselling Studies and has researched the views of young people who were adopted as older children and who are now in their 20s. Kay worked for a number of years for Barnardo's New Families in Colchester, as part of the Network Post Adoption Team. She is currently working for LINK as a co-ordinator of the counselling service and takes a lead on support meetings for adoptive parents. She is also an independent counsellor and trainer.

Jeffrey Coleman qualified as a social worker in 1977. He has considerable experience as a social work manager in West London and has been Director of the BAAF Southern Region since 1999. He is the Chair of several adoption panels and is currently involved in developing the *Parenting the sexually abused child* training pack for BAAF.

Maureen Crank is the Chief Executive and founder member of After Adoption, the largest independent provider of adoption support in the UK. She is a member of the Adoption and Permanence Taskforce and was on the Expert Working Party for the Adoption Standards. She is currently on the Department of Health working party which is developing a Framework for Adoption Support. Maureen is co-author of *Still Screaming* (After Adoption Manchester) but says she would rather "do" than write.

Monica Duck is the Director of the Post-Adoption Centre in London, which provides a comprehensive range of services to London and the south-east regions. She is a qualified social worker with an advanced post-qualifying award in social work management. She has worked with children and families within the statutory and voluntary sector for over 20 years, and has considerable experience of adoption and post-adoption work. Monica has served on adoption panels and acted as a consultant to both voluntary and statutory agencies.

Stephen Eccles completed a Diploma in Community, Play and Youth Work and gained a B Phil. in Community Play and Youth Work studies at West Hill College, Birmingham, following work overseas with the Church Missionary Society. He was appointed to the newly created Adopted Children's Worker post at the West Midlands Post-Adoption Service in September 2001.

Julia Feast is the Development, Research and Policy Consultant at BAAF. In the past she has managed The Children's Society Post Adoption and Care Counselling Research Project, worked as a local authority social worker and team leader, and as a guardian ad litem and reporting officer. She has research and writing interests in adoption and the information needs of children born as a result of donor-assisted conception.

Jacky Gordon has worked in fostering and adoption in both local authority and voluntary agencies since she qualified as a social worker in 1971. She gained a Post-Graduate Diploma in Management Studies from the University of Westminster in 1997. Her current role is Manager of the Family Placement Service of Norwood, which includes adoption, fostering and respite services. Jacky has been responsible for processing inter-country adoption applications on behalf of local authorities and she was instrumental in Norwood's application to the Department of Health to become an intercountry adoption agency in 2000.

Jane Horne has been Project Leader at Barnardo's New Families Project for 12 years. She has a BA in Social Administration and gained her C.Q.S.W in 1980. She worked for the London Borough of Brent in fieldwork and adoption and fostering teams before her move to Suffolk in 1989. Jane holds management responsibility for Post-Adoption LINK and takes a lead on support meetings for adopted adults and events for adopted children.

Barbara Hudson has been Director of BAAF Scotland since 1998. Previously a fostering and adoption worker in Leeds City Council, she worked for 11 years in Bradford managing a range of services for children and families including the fostering and adoption services. Barbara is a member of a number of Adoption and Permanency Panels in Scotland and provides training and consultancy to agencies in Scotland and Northern Ireland.

Marion Hundleby has been a qualified social worker for over 25 years. Her research experience includes two national projects funded by the Department of Health (Fostering and the Children Act 1978–82 and the Placement Outcome Survey 1984–88). Marion has provided consultancy to agencies in both the statutory and voluntary sectors, and has a particular interest in service design and delivery. For the past nine years she has worked for Catholic Children's Society, Nottingham, specialising in post-placement work and providing consultancy for two government-funded projects. Her most recent publication is *Adoption: Theory, policy and practice* written in partnership with John Triseliotis and Joan Shireman (Cassell, 1997). This has become a standard text.

Jenny Jackson has been employed in a variety of local authority social work settings since 1977. She is presently employed by Nottingham City Council and Nottinghamshire County Council as a social worker in the Support After Adoption Team.

Alan Johnstone is Independent Adoption Panel Chair for four agencies in Essex and North East London. He undertakes training and review work for adoption agencies.

Caroline Lindsey is a Consultant Child and Adolescent Psychiatrist and Systemic Family Psychotherapist in the Child and Family Department at the Tavistock Clinic, London. Her longstanding interest in the field of fostering and adoption began when she worked for Camden Social Services in the Observation and Assessment Centre in the 1970s and 80s. Caroline works in an adoption and fostering team with a group of multidisciplinary colleagues, providing consultation, assessment and treatment for children, young people and their families. She also undertakes medico-legal work, training and conferences.

Dr Mary Mather FRCP, FRCPCH has been a Consultant Community Paediatrician in Greenwich since 1993. She is the Chair of the Medical Advisory Group of BAAF, the Medical Adviser to the Greenwich Adoption and Fostering Panel and also acts as a medical consultant for Parents for Children. She is a member of the Department of Health Reference Group reviewing the implementation of "Quality Protects". Dr Mather is a member of the Editorial Board of *Archives of Disease in Childhood* and the author of *Doctors for Children in Public Care* (BAAF, 2000), a textbook for medical advisers working in the fields of adoption and fostering. She has been involved in both local and national training of medical advisors to adoption and fostering panels.

Cas O'Neill is a special needs adoptive parent and support foster carer. She has a PhD in Social Work, is a Research Fellow at the University of Melbourne (Australia), works at Melbourne's Royal Children's Hospital (on projects in the areas of child welfare, health and consumer participation) and is involved in setting up a Centre for Post-Placement Support.

Michael Prior has worked in primary education for 40 years, 30 as a headteacher. Currently he is a part-time Education Adviser to the Nottingham Catholic Children's Society and consultant to Leicestershire LEA working to place pupils, who are in public care, in appropriate schools. Michael is a member of the Management Committee of Gorse Hill Farm in Leicester, which provides educational opportunities to disaffected pupils and those close to exclusion. He is also a school inspector and a member of the Leicestershire Scrutiny Committee for Education.

Stephen Scott is Reader in Child Health and Behaviour at the Institute of Psychiatry, Kings College London, and Consultant Child and Adolescent Psychiatrist at the Maudsley Hospital, where he heads the National Specialist Adoption and Fostering clinic and the National Specialist Antisocial Behaviour clinic. His interests include devising and evaluating parenting programmes to support foster, adoptive, and birth parents, and uncovering the mechanisms through which interventions work. He is senior editor of the journal, *Child and Adolescent Mental Health*, and co-author with Professor Robert Goodman of the textbook, *Child Psychiatry*.

Jay Vaughan is a state registered drama therapist and co-director of Family Futures. She has been working with traumatised children for over ten years. Jay has worked at St Bartholomew's Hospital with children who were terminally ill, in a children's home with children who had been abused and neglected, and with young people in psychiatric hospitals. For the last seven years she has specialised in working solely with fostered and adopted children, first at the Post-Adoption Centre and now at Family Futures.

Lois Williams is Senior Adoption Social Worker and Co-ordinator of the online post-adoption website at Parents and Children Together (PACT). She has specialised in adoption and fostering over the past decade and worked for voluntary agencies and local authorities.

Helen Wilkins Oakwater is a Consultant Trainer for Adoption UK, the UK charity, which supports adoptive families before, during and after adoption. As one of Adoption UK's 120+ local co-ordinators, she has heard stories which have inspired, horrified and enlightened her. Helen's three adopted children have taught her many unexpected things for which she is deeply grateful. She sits on a local authority adoption panel and is a member of the Adoption and Permanence Task Force. Prior to becoming a parent, Helen taught in secondary schools.

Index

abuse
  alcohol 210, 214, 215, 266
  drug 214, 215
  emotional 142, 209
  physical 142, 182, 245, 247–8
  sexual 52, 101, 110, 142, 143,
    157, 183, 206, 209, 214, 240,
    322
adopted adults 4, 43, 74, 80, 91, 94,
  112, 126, 129, 131–3, 135–8,
  140–6, 204, 256, 285, 292–306,
  308, 310, 324
adoption panels 4, 62, 189–200,
  202, 207, 265, 268, 277, 299,
  322–3, 325, 327
aids and adaptations 187
allowances 3, 35, 55, 60, 64, 69, 77,
  181, 187, 189, 194, 199, 280,
  282
assessments 51, 54, 66, 99, 155,
  182, 187, 194, 209, 226, 256,
  282, 316–7, 320
attachment 5, 10, 15, 23, 31, 43, 45,
  47, 63, 88, 90, 95, 97, 99, 112,
  117–8, 121, 127, 150, 155, 159,
  176, 180, 194, 216, 223, 225–6,
  232–3, 236–7, 239, 241–4,
  251–2, 254, 263–4, 267, 282,
  286, 287–8, 317, 319, 320
attachment disorders 31, 43, 117,
  121, 223, 239, 264

benefits 8, 20, 64, 83, 98, 100, 108,
  181, 185, 187, 196, 255, 280, 301
birth parents 3, 4, 7, 10, 12–4,
  16–9, 24, 26–34, 36–9, 44, 45,
  47, 69, 74, 80–2, 86, 95,
  100–3, 104–7, 109, 111, 127,
  129, 141, 143–4, 148, 154, 165,
  167–8, 171–2, 177–80, 185, 197,
  202, 204–5, 207, 209–10, 212–4,
  216, 220, 225, 228, 234, 248–9,
  251, 253, 257–9, 273, 279, 281,
  283, 285, 288–9, 294, 296–7,
  299–301, 304–5, 310, 318–9,
  326
birth relatives 4, 5, 42, 45–6, 59,
  81, 88, 96, 112, 116, 118, 129,
  131–2, 139, 156, 165, 168,
  172–3, 178–9, 187, 193, 203–4,
  208–9, 225, 232–3, 245–8, 254,
  257, 259–61, 265, 273, 279, 283,
  285, 292, 294, 299, 304, 306,
  317–8, 320

communications 309
community 14, 22, 45, 60, 63, 97,
  98, 113, 124, 129, 131, 138, 139,
  140, 160, 162, 166, 168, 195,
  215, 257, 265, 273, 295, 310,
  311, 312, 323, 325
connections 13, 20, 53, 141
consultancy 3, 73, 76, 78, 79, 83,
  84, 85, 268, 284, 324

contact 4, 5, 17, 36–8, 46, 54, 59,
69, 82, 88, 90, 95–6, 103, 107,
118–9, 122, 127, 132, 134, 137,
148, 172, 176, 178–80, 186,
187–8, 194–5, 197, 203, 205–7,
209, 213, 220, 225, 242, 246,
250, 255, 258, 274, 279, 282–4,
288, 295–300, 304–5, 310–11,
317–8, 320

continuity 46, 96, 179, 187, 250,
269, 270, 317, 319, 320

contracting out 3–4, 76–9

counselling 4, 44–5, 89–90, 102,
112, 121, 123, 132, 134, 145,
148, 150–1, 153, 156, 172, 175,
177, 199, 202, 206, 224, 282,
285, 292–6, 300, 303, 305, 308,
315, 322–3

culture 45, 61–2, 74, 129, 132, 136,
140–1, 148, 156, 160, 163,
166–8, 177, 187, 233, 251, 320

disability 3, 4, 18, 55, 83, 96, 100,
102, 105, 133, 171–88, 204, 213,
216, 228, 261, 263, 286

disruption 14, 17, 22, 24, 55, 62,
98, 118, 151, 172, 176, 199, 261,
316–21

education
education advisers 183, 268–77
individual education plans 270,
275
LEAs 268–71, 273–4, 276–7, 326
teachers 7, 12, 16–7, 19, 23,
31, 38, 41, 46, 61–2, 123,

142, 174, 179, 183, 222, 227,
243, 246, 259, 269–70, 272,
274–6, 278, 286, 310, 317,
320

ethnicity 45, 74, 123, 142, 146,
148–50, 152, 158, 163, 170, 177,
187, 320
black children 91, 103, 129–30,
145, 147–59, 177
black families 147, 153, 155,
157, 159
dual heritage 4, 103, 123
Judaism 4, 160–9, 294–5
minority ethnic groups 4, 147,
177
transracial issues 129–44

experts 23, 172, 174, 183–4, 187

family systems 45, 320

finance 185, 308

foster care 17, 22–3, 32, 37, 44, 64,
133, 137, 221, 240, 244, 319–20

funding 2, 41, 56–7, 69–70, 78,
115, 133, 237, 270–1, 273–4,
282, 286, 289–90, 307

grandparents 7, 12, 16, 161, 197,
199, 302, 310

group work 79, 100–1, 120–2, 125
adopters' groups 192, 205
children's groups 92–3
birth parents' groups 100–3, 106,
111

health 2, 4, 17, 23, 39, 44, 47–8,
50–2, 54–5, 57–9, 62–3, 66,

68–71, 73–4, 78, 83, 86, 100,
102, 104, 108, 116–7, 127, 130,
133, 137–8, 145–7, 160, 163,
170, 172–4, 182, 187–8, 190–4,
200, 202, 204–5, 208–10, 214,
217, 220, 224, 230–1, 236,
238–40, 253–67, 269, 275, 287,
290–1, 293, 297, 306–7, 310,
317, 320–1, 323–6
medical advisers 182, 265, 266,
  325
medicals 254, 258
medical records 173, 257
medical reports 257
medication 105, 226, 235
NHS 43, 49, 254, 262–3, 265–7
hyperactivity 3, 212, 215, 221, 230,
  235
ADHD 43, 212, 222, 235

identity 24, 45, 54, 88, 99, 115–7,
  121, 127, 136–7, 139–40, 147,
  151, 156, 159, 163, 166, 177,
  210, 216, 234, 241, 250, 258,
  286, 292, 294
infertility 3, 26, 98, 157, 158, 217,
  232, 262, 265
information 10, 14, 18, 20, 27, 31,
  42–3, 55, 58, 61, 64, 66, 69, 75,
  77, 79, 82, 84, 87–8, 92–6, 104,
  106–7, 120, 127, 132, 134, 137,
  148–9, 151, 157, 163, 165, 168,
  172–4, 178–9, 184–5, 187, 189,
  191–2, 194–8, 202–3, 205–7,
  212, 217, 222, 224–5, 254–61,
  265, 275, 279, 282, 284–8, 290,

292, 294–8, 301, 303–5, 308,
  309–13, 316–21, 323
inter-agency 85, 198, 205, 268, 274,
  277, 318, 320
inter-country 164, 323

languages 1, 51, 53, 75, 102, 105,
  129, 132, 143, 167, 168, 207,
  262, 273, 313
learning difficulties 104, 175–6,
  188, 204, 227, 247, 270, 274–5
legislation 2, 52, 73, 144, 209, 236,
  270, 280–2, 297, 307
  Acts 2, 49–52, 55, 58–9, 68–9,
    189, 191, 242, 256, 270, 280,
    289, 292–3, 297
  regulations 2, 49–50, 53, 66–71,
    163, 170, 191, 265, 280, 291,
    307
letterbox 77, 80–1, 102–3, 180, 203,
  207, 282
lifecycles 23, 106, 217, 279
lifestories 38, 41, 156, 167, 176
loss 26, 45, 103, 106, 115, 118,
  121, 125, 127, 129, 131, 138–40,
  149, 159, 178, 202, 217, 234,
  250, 258, 279, 311

mental retardation 213, 216, 227,
  239
mutual support 4, 98, 100, 172, 185

neglect 26, 32, 34, 46, 133, 154,
  177, 194, 204, 209, 223, 245,
  248, 255, 257, 265, 326

paediatricians 44, 174, 243, 248, 257, 262–6, 325

peer groups 2, 6, 87, 98, 164, 169, 265, 273

policy 1–3, 24, 52–4, 56–7, 61, 67, 71, 82, 131, 172, 188, 190–3, 198, 203, 239, 279–80, 291, 293, 301–2, 304, 308, 317, 323–4

practice 1, 3, 24, 46, 49, 54, 61, 71, 77, 80, 82, 84, 101–2, 107, 124, 130, 163, 182–3, 186, 188, 190–3, 203, 208, 212–4, 228, 237, 239, 241, 253–5, 259–60, 262, 264–5, 273, 277, 282, 284, 287, 293, 297, 302, 305, 308, 312–3, 317, 320–1, 324

preparation 1, 60, 69, 71, 96–7, 157, 162–3, 166, 172, 175, 180, 195–7, 217, 243, 246, 256, 268, 299, 305, 313, 316–7, 320–1

racism 52, 91, 123–4, 131, 135, 139–41, 142, 143, 150, 154, 156, 177, 294, 295

religion 5, 74, 160, 162–7, 187, 233, 253, 320

resources 5, 10–12, 27, 40, 51, 54, 63, 84, 111, 113, 122, 127, 151, 191–2, 264, 266, 272, 293, 295, 305, 311

Scotland 1, 5, 63, 279–91, 324

search and reunion 4, 131, 132, 133, 143, 145, 296, 300, 304, 305, 306

self-esteem 8, 109, 115–6, 122, 140–1, 156, 169, 228, 231, 269, 274, 276, 285, 292

self-help 14, 22–4, 100, 280, 305

service users 2, 15, 58, 74, 81, 83, 85, 100–1, 110–1, 121, 132–3, 187, 192, 280, 304, 308–9

special needs 5, 55–6, 65, 172–3, 177, 181, 194, 263, 270, 275, 325

therapeutic intervention 209–37, 264

behaviour modification 45

family therapy 15, 24, 231–4, 237–8, 244

mental health assessments 220

parenting work 229–30

psychiatric classification 220, 222

psychotherapy 15, 24, 234, 238

tracing 4, 303

training 5, 24, 45–6, 52, 61, 67, 75, 78, 83, 97, 109, 113, 134, 172, 175, 186, 192–3, 196, 229, 237–8, 240, 262, 265, 268, 272–5, 283–4, 286–7, 305, 311, 313, 316, 320, 322, 324–5

trauma 5, 26, 46, 56, 72, 105, 115, 121, 131, 145, 148–9, 162, 177, 224, 231, 241–2, 244, 250, 252, 257, 263–5, 306, 322, 326

youth work 112–27, 323